Advertising Realities

A PRACTICAL GUIDE TO AGENCY MANAGEMENT

WES PERRIN

Mayfield Publishing Company
Mountain View, California
London ◆ Toronto

To Joanne, Doug, and Jack

Copyright © 1992 by Mayfield Publishing Company

All rights reserved. No portion of this book may be reproduced in any form or by any means without written permission of the publisher.

Library of Congress Cataloging-in-Publication Data
Perrin, Wes.
  Advertising realities: a practical guide to agency management / Wes Perrin.
    p.   cm.
  Includes bibliographical references and index.
  ISBN 0-87484-999-3
  1. Advertising—Management. 2. Advertising—Vocational guidance.
I. title.
HF5823. P39 1991   91-16167
659.1'125'068—dc20   CIP

Manufactured in the United States of America
10 9 8 7 6 5 4 3 2 1

Mayfield Publishing Company
1240 Villa Street
Mountain View, California 94041

Sponsoring editor, C. Lansing Hays; managing editor, Linda Toy; production editor, Sondra Glider; manuscript editor, Margaret Moore; text and cover designer/production artist, Jean Mailander; illustrator, Robin Mouat. The text was set in 11.5/13 Berkeley Book and printed on 50# Glatfelter Spring Forge by Thomson-Shore.

Cover art: Frank Ansley

Text credits appear on page 184.

"Men wanted for Hazardous Journey. Small wages, bitter cold, long months of complete darkness, constant danger, safe return doubtful. Honour and recognition in case of success."

Advertisement for Polar explorers by Ernest Shackleton, London *Times, 1900*

"Can you stand up under pressures that would have most ordinary mortals climbing the walls? . . .Are you willing to work *hard*? . . . Do you have a good energy reserve? . . . Do you have a good strong backbone?"

Advertisement for account managers by Ogilvy & Mather, Adweek, *1975*

CONTENTS

Preface **vii**
Introduction 1

CHAPTER ONE

Understanding How Ad Agencies Live and Breathe 8

Sizing Up the Critical Differences: Right Brain Versus Left Brain 8
Examining the Structure of an Ad Agency 11
Assessing the Accounts 40
Sorting Out the Bosses 42
Previewing the Career Paths 44
Evaluating Job (In)security 46
Probing the Pay and the Perks 48
Looking Toward Ownership 52
Observing the Stepsister, the Public Relations Agency 54

CHAPTER TWO

Coping with Clients 59

Scoping the Basic Types of Clients 59
On Selling When They're Not Buying 66
Explaining Agency Compensation 74
Collecting Bills 81
Handling the Way-Over-Budget Project 84
Entertaining Your Clients 88

CHAPTER THREE

About Surviving and Thriving in an Ad Agency 91

Dealing with Collateral Projects 91
Making Small Budgets Look Huge 97

Seeking Out and Winning New Business   103
Handling Those Myriad Details   115
Clipping and Ripping: A Nothing-Fancy-But-It-Works Tip   118

CHAPTER FOUR

What's Wrong with Today's Account Managers   119

Identifying "Empty" Account Managers   119
Strategic Thinking and Big Ideas: The Cornerstones of Effective Advertising   121
Judging the Results of Advertising Strategies   123
Dissecting the Crucial Components: Interruption, Emotion, Information   132

CHAPTER FIVE

The Nitty Gritty of Landing the Job   136

Why MBA Doesn't Automatically Equal VIP   136
Confronting Bias and Prejudice   139
Examining Optional Routes to the Agency Goal Line   141
Accepting Geographic Bias   144
Learning More About the Business   145
Lobbying for Literacy   146
Creating the Convincing Résumé   149
Gaining and Grappling with the Interview   151

CHAPTER SIX

Improving the Breed   156

The Need for Tough Professional Standards   156
A Plan for Establishing Advertising Bar Exams   157

Additional Reading   161
Glossary   164
Index   175

PREFACE

This is written for men and women who want to work for advertising agencies committed to doing extraordinary creative work.

It is aimed primarily, but not exclusively, at those still in the classroom and at pilgrims just starting in the business. Not because there is special magic always connected with younger minds, but because people who have already set their opinions in cement are generally beyond hope of rehabilitation. They either know everything already or couldn't care less.

Does this handbook have a palpable bias? Clearly. I believe an advertising agency has only one real justification for its existence: to manufacture outstanding advertising, advertising that breaks through the mass media mire and is honest, human, memorable, intelligent, evocative, informative and, yes, powerfully persuasive.

While this book provides insights on all aspects of the advertising agency world, it uses account management as the lens through which key subjects are focused. Is that because I want every reader to become an account manager? Not so. It's because I think every agency staffer can profit from understanding the critical interplay this function demands. This is the one place in the business where individuals must manage challenges daily both *inside* the agency—with all departments—and *outside*—with all types of clients.

Now, there are those who would prefer that my focus had more of a creative perspective. They would have you believe that the difference between good and bad advertising can be measured *solely* by the brainweight of an ad agency's Creative Department; that all other departments are incidental, at best mere plumbing. I beg to differ. To me, a minimum of two proficient midwives always attend the birth of remarkable advertising: Yes, the credit for conception must go to the copywriters and art directors. But without the delivery assistance of Account Management—teamed with the right mix of Research, Media, and Production—the greatest ads would never leave the maternity ward.

And my background? Twenty years in ad agency work and another five on the client side. During those halcyon days I worked for agencies varying in size from six people to 150, on accounts ranging from banking to dog food to furniture to port authorities to fast food. I wrote plans, bought media, set up trade show booths, typed news releases, pitched new accounts, collected past due bills, hired and fired, and retired early—to cite just a few specifics. In 1977, I helped found a regional advertising agency that grew into one of the largest in the Pacific Northwest, thanks to some terrific creative partners. Through the years I have developed an enormous respect for the power of the proper creative product. But I am not, and never have been, a member of any Creative Department.

Moreover, I do not subscribe to the notion that good work is its own reward. I do, however, strongly believe *it is good business*. Original, stand-alone advertising not only wins awards; it woos and wins customers, and it drives sales and profits. The correlation between mind share and market share is undeniable.

As you read through these pages you may note a partiality for examples pertaining to smaller agencies and smaller accounts—not because they are implicitly more worthy but because most of the mainstream advertising textbooks dote on the big guys. I, too, enjoy the case histories of Ford, Xerox, General Foods, *et al.*, but the January 1990 edition of the *Standard Directory of Advertising Agencies* listed 5,000 U.S. agencies! It's safe to say the vast majority are dealing with accounts far removed from *The Fortune 500,* or even *The Fortune 5000,* if there were such a thing. So while the basics of this handbook apply to New York, New Orleans, or Newberg, Oregon, I must confess that the often-ignored smaller agencies are close to my heart. And I suggest beginners nurture some affection for them, too, as they may offer the best chances for securing a job.

Should readers need more evidence that big is not always better, they need only check out the agencies winning the top creative awards. They'll quickly find that a passel of pulse-quickening work is coming from modest-sized agencies these days—in places like Minneapolis, Providence, Seattle, Portland, Richmond, and the Carolinas.

Finally, about the advertising industry's prospects for the future: In my opinion, they are pretty good, *if* we can attract the bright new talent needed to upgrade American advertising everywhere. As far back as 1963, in *Confessions of an Advertising Man,* David Ogilvy said, "Our business needs a massive transfusion of *talent."* It was true then, and it's true right now. Or, to paraphrase the Marine Corps slogan, America's advertising agencies are constantly looking for a few more good men and women.

I hope some readers of this book will be among them.

Acknowledgments

I would like to thank the reviewers of the manuscript for their helpful comments: Lee Bartlett, Brigham Young University; Marian Friestad, University of Oregon; Hugh Heinricks, Ohio State University; Ann Keding, University of Oregon; Deborah Morrison, University of Texas at Austin; Barbara Mueller, San Diego State University; Joseph R. Pisani, University of Florida; Martha Rogers, Bowling Green State University; Esther Thorson, University of Wisconsin; Willis Winter, University of Oregon; Fred Zandpour, California State University, Fullerton; and Eric Zanot, University of Maryland.

Introduction

Here, we get some clues as to the personality traits of those most likely to flourish in this curious business.

What kind of person is apt to be happiest working in an advertising agency? Quite a few people have the notion that they should work in advertising because of their sparkling personalities. "After all," they chime, "I understand advertising is a people business, and I've been told over and over that I am a really good people person. I *love* to meet people, *love* to help people, *love* all kinds of social interaction, *love* parties—so I'm certain advertising would be perfect for me."

Well, let's put it this way: It certainly doesn't hurt to have an up personality. Obviously, it's a lot more pleasant to work with someone who isn't a sourpuss. But if for one nanosecond you think that a "have a nice day" personality is a guaranteed trip to the top, forget it. A megalomaniac grouch with talent and experience is worth a boxcar of bubbly space cadets, and every solid agency knows it.

Actually, it's dangerous to attempt to stereotype the attributes of the best advertising people, because you encounter some wonderful exceptions to all rules. But there are eight distinguishing characteristics worth mentioning from my experience:

1. Willingness to listen at length—without glazing over or dozing off. Some advertising people are superb talkers, but they can't stand to

listen to anyone else. They rarely wear well with clients or peers—and, all too often, they can't understand why their careers bog down.

2. Sense of humor. Ability to take oneself not *too* seriously. This is not to say one should be a court jester, but relevant humor can defuse combative situations and rally support to the agency's cause. If you're looking for a role model, try reading about an Irishman named John Fitzgerald Kennedy.

3. Team player. Another cliché, but the sports analogy still seems to sum it up best. It means spending a lot of time with other folks from your agency, praising, nagging, sharing, communicating, recognizing that some are more talented than others—in short, pulling together. There are some great solo creative players in this business, but those who wish to be managers must understand and relate to the whole-gang concept. If you think "only I can make it happen right," you're going to have trouble in an ad agency. An ego-trip management style is the inside lane to a career crash.

4. Being mentally big enough *not* to harbor grudges or fester over past mistakes. No matter how brilliant the agency and sensational the campaign, there are times when a colleague or client will screw up royally—and may even dump on you with purple majesty. It is impossible to forget those happenings totally, but don't dwell on past injustices. Such resentment will only bore small holes in the lining of your lower intestine.

5. Intensity. 'Tis better to be a bulldog than a St. Bernard. Couple this with conviction and you have an irresistible force. Winston Churchill gave a fabled "speech" late in his career. He glowered at his audience for several minutes without uttering a word. Then, slowly and very deliberately he said, "Never give in. Never give in. Never, never, never, *never!*" People like Churchill, *who hate to lose*, prosper in our business.

6. Enthusiasm. In his *Confessions of an Advertising Man*, David Ogilvy put it best: "I admire people who work with gusto. If you don't enjoy what you are doing, I beg of you to find another job. Remember the Scottish proverb, 'Be happy while you're living. You're a long time dead.' " Just be careful not to confuse enthusiasm with mindless effervescence. To be effective, enthusiasm must be rooted in substance.

7. Unflappability is another marvelous trait to possess. In Australia awhile back I heard the tale of the man who arrived home to find a "bit of a problem" under his bed. An eight-foot python had slithered in and wrapped itself around the man's dog. The animal's cries caught his attention, and he yanked the snake out from under the mattress, pried it loose from the mutt, tossed it out the door, and

"dispatched it with a garden hoe." Was he particularly distressed? Not at all. "I've seen bigger snakes," he said, helping himself to another Foster's Lager. *That's* the kind of attitude to have if you want to score points at an ad agency.

8. Thriving under pressure. (Close to but slightly different from unflappability.) Let's face it: Some folks love constant deadlines and the challenge of doing the nearly impossible, while others collapse when threatened with such conditions. This is also a huge arena of Walter Mitty self-delusion in my experience. I guess everyone wants to believe he or she is capable of handling pressure with élan. In truth it's a gross mistake for people to kid themselves or think, "I'll handle it better with practice."

To help weed out those destined not to succeed at an ad agency, I recommend two self-examinations. Neither is long and both have questions that are deceptively whimsical. I suggest you think long and hard about your answers.

Test 1

1. Are you the type of individual who enjoys thinking about—or, even better, doing—several things simultaneously?
2. Do you begin to twitch when there isn't much to do?
3. If the dinner party is set for 7:00 P.M., do you feel bad if you arrive at 7:10?
4. Are you interested in why and how things happen as much as what happens?
5. When other people attempt to mute out the commercials on TV, do you insist they stop? And, better yet, do you ask to turn up the volume?
6. Are you equally alert at 6:00 A.M. and 11:00 P.M.? Do you agree with Thomas Edison that four hours of sleep a night is enough for a healthy adult?
7. Have you sent signed letters to the editor recently or stood up in a public meeting and voiced an unpopular opinion?
8. When you were a kid, were you always the first to jump in the swimming pool on cloudy days?
9. Do you read? I mean *really* read: devouring, caressing, absorbing those printed pages? Can you simultaneously enjoy the Sunday comics, *Bonfire of the Vanities, Newsweek, National Geographic, People,* and the *Wall Street Journal*?
10. Can you laugh after a good friend has hit you in the face with a cream pie?

4 ♦ Introduction

Test 2

1. It's Friday, and you and the love of your life were planning to go to the beach on Saturday, but your second biggest client calls at 3:30 P.M. to plead that you bring the campaign creative proposal and budget to a special unplanned meeting of territory sales managers at 10:00 A.M. tomorrow. "They're not too keen on the approach," he moans. "It probably will take most of the day to convince them, and even then we might get shot down." Will you be there?

2. The client rejects the creative recommendation. The creative director, copywriter, and art director all beseech you to resubmit it. If the client remains adamant, you will have an impossible magazine closing date to meet. It is indeed good work. Will you return and win approval with a second effort?

3. You've labored overtime for a solid week preparing the media plan for the radio campaign. You've talked the stations into a number of concessions and stretched the budget. But the client objects because his two favorite stations have been left off the schedule. "My wife *always* listens to KSOP and KUGH!" Can you persuade him that using those stations would not be the best use of his money?

4. The four-color catalog must be delivered to the sales meeting on Tuesday. The production manager surprises you with the news that printing overtime will run up the estimated cost by $4,000. The client is in a foul mood, and he previously has complained about the job's cost. Can you call him right now and present him with the bad news?

5. You've written a business-to-business ad for a conservative client. You have this terrific idea, but it is far different from anything ever done before by the client. You've been told that the client *never* buys the unusual. You've also been told not to rock the boat. It would be far less traumatic to grind out another ad in the same old mold. Do you find a way to show your idea to the client?

6. You're in charge of production on a big annual report. It is scheduled to go on press at 4:00 P.M., and you are planning to be there for a final color check. At 3:00, the printer calls to announce a delay. "Should be on by 6:00." At 5:30, he calls to predict, "Probably by 9:00. Why don't we call you at home?" At 9:30, the phone rings at home. "Oh boy, this just isn't going well," the printer laments. "The best I can guess now is between 2:00 and 4:00 A.M." The report has to be finished tomorrow for the client's annual meeting. You are tempted to grab some shut-eye and let the printer make the final approval. Will you be at the press check?

7. You've convinced the client to approve the layout and copy. It's a magazine ad with a provocative headline, and it wasn't an easy sell.

But your creative team is awaiting your return to say that they have just come up with an even better headline. The production department is screaming to get the type set. Do you take the new headline to your client?

8. The rehearsal for tomorrow's 9:00 A.M. new business presentation is not going smoothly. It's your baby—you're leading the team. You recognize that several slides have to be redone. One of your co-workers must be told she is not needed even though she has been preparing her bit for the past week. The leave-behind packet is still being typed, but the typist's two-year-old has the flu and she has to get home. What do you reply when you're asked, "Will we be ready by tomorrow morning?"

9. Your job is to summarize the finding of a major market research study. In making the analysis, you quickly see that the client's products are given alarmingly low marks for both quality and reliability. The client is an older man who has always lectured the agency about how his products "are the best in the universe—light-years ahead of the competition!" He frequently complains about "negative media." You've been asked to present the bad news to him and to persuade him that it is not frivolous. You can defer the assignment to your boss if you prefer. Will you accept the task?

10. You are playing basketball before a huge, screaming crowd. There are only seconds left in the game, and the score is tied. The conference championship is on the line. There's barely time for one last shot. Do you want the ball?

There are a total of twenty questions on these two exams. If you could honestly answer seventeen or more affirmatively, an advertising agency just might be your kind of place. On the other hand, what if you prefer taking on one assignment at a time and seeing it through with great precision from A to Z? Does it perturb you to be constantly interrupted in the midst of important thinking? Does your skin crawl when revisions undergo modifications on top of adjustments as deadlines loom? Is going home at 5:00 P.M. important to you? Do you shrink from controversy? Do you abhor conflict? If so, civil service might be a happier career choice.

It's worth pausing a moment to ponder: Are folks who turn out to be extraordinary ad agency people the product of heredity or environment? Hard to say. Of course, some of these marvelous traits can be learned and nurtured. But I swear it often seems that the best have the right stuff *born* in them—in the same freakish way of poets, pianists, and hitters of curve balls. However, there are a lot of us who weren't gifted from the cradle, who had to find out the hard way, and to whom I respectfully dedicate the chapters ahead.

AN ANSWER FOR THOSE WHO SEE ADVERTISING AS THE GREEDY FOX IN THE LAZY HENHOUSE OF CONTEMPORARY AMERICA

Some tranquil evening or afternoon when you least expect it, a friend, neighbor, relative, or complete stranger is going to jab a finger in your face and announce that advertising is the curse of the Western world. While it may be tempting to lash back at these attacks with sound and fury, such a response rarely does more than fan the flames of accusation. Your antagonist is positive that Vance Packard was on to something when he wrote about "hidden persuaders" and that those con artists on Madison Avenue can sell anything to everybody.

David Ogilvy and John O'Toole, among other advertising industry giants, have written persuasive rebuttals to the critics of advertising, and it is occasionally useful to quote them. But, having made handsome sums of money in the business, they are seen as biased and tainted by many skeptics.

But Stephen Fox, the author of *The Mirror Makers,* is by no means a member of the inner circle of contemporary American advertising. He is a social historian who views advertising from some distance and has no vested interest in its success or failure. That's why I like to refer to his thoughtful comments at the close of *The Mirror Makers* when I encounter a citizen who suggests that ad agency people are cut from the same cloth as child molesters. Here are the two paragraphs that I urge you to remember:

> In regard to advertising's broader cultural impact—the power to create and shape mass tastes and behavior—outsiders are generally more impressed than those inside the business with the alleged influence of Madison Avenue. . . . Outsiders see only the smooth, expertly contrived finished product, often better crafted than the programming and editorial matter it interrupts. Insiders know the messy process of creating an ad, the false starts, rejected ideas, midnight despair, the failure and account losses and creative angst behind any ad that finally appears. In particular the insiders know that no successful ad can stray very far from where the audience already lives. The ad must be fitted to the audience, not the other way around. "Advertising doesn't manipulate society," said Carl Ally in 1977. "Society manipulates advertising. Advertising responds to social trends. Agencies respond to advertisers. It's that simple."
>
> One may build a compelling case that American culture is beyond redemption—money-mad, hedonistic, superficial, rushing needlessly down a railroad track called Progress. Tocqueville and other observers of the young republic described America in these terms in the early 1800s decades before the development of national advertising. To blame advertising now for these most basic tendencies in American history is to miss the point. It is too obvious, too easy, a matter of killing the messenger instead of dealing with the bad news. The people who have created modern advertising are not hidden persuaders pushing our buttons

in the service of some malevolent purpose. They are just producing an especially visible manifestation, good and bad, of the American way of life.

Those thoughts, coupled with the more pedestrian fact that without advertising, subscription prices for newspapers, magazines, television, and other media would be out of sight, are the best armament I have worn in mounting battles with emotional critics.

CHAPTER ONE

Understanding How Ad Agencies Live and Breathe

In this chapter we demystify advertising agency culture. We'll identify what differentiates the two fundamental types of agencies, probe the principal departments (and ways to work productively with each), discuss different kinds of bosses, and evaluate various kinds of accounts. We'll also look at pay and perks, job (in)security, ownership, and the differences posed by our stepsister, the PR agency.

SIZING UP THE CRITICAL DIFFERENCES: RIGHT BRAIN VERSUS LEFT BRAIN

Often someone asks, "Underneath all the hype, aren't all ad agencies basically the same? Except maybe for size?" No, they're more like snowflakes: From a distance they all seem to be a windy white blur, but under a microscope each is distinctly different. Ad agencies can, however, be lumped into two broad categories: those who are happiest worshipping at the "temple of creativity" ("Advertising should aim to be seemingly outrageous!") and those who feel more comfortable in the "church of marketing pragmatism" ("It isn't creative unless it sells!").

Ideally—and this is basically true of the best firms—an agency combines the intuitive/spontaneous with the explicit/analytical. But if you think they all arrive at a tidy balance, you are due for a rude awakening. Agencies, like all human beings, tilt either right brain or left brain in terms of operating philosophy and practice. (Credit for the following adjectives goes to Jacquelyn Wonder and Priscilla Donovan, authors of *Whole Brain Thinking*.)

Left-Brain Agency Mindset		Right-Brain Agency Mentality	
Positive	Active	Intuitive	Diffuse
Linear	Goal-oriented	Spontaneous	Symbolic
Analytical	Rational	Emotional	Physical
Explicit	Concrete	Nonverbal	Playful
Sequential		Visual	Holistic
Verbal		Artistic	

Totally left-brain agencies say, "Advertising is more science than art," and have big research departments. The head of client services runs this shop, and the account managers bully the creative department. Totally right-brain agencies say, "Creativity for creativity's sake will accomplish everything." They don't have research departments, and the creative director is king, pope, and grand dragon rolled into one. Account managers are little more than stylish messengers with orders not to return from the client unless the creative recommendation has been approved in toto.

It's fairly obvious that there are more left brainers than right brainers in this business (in any business, for that matter). And right there is a key reason why so much advertising is dull, uninspired, and monotonous. On the other hand, there is also a fair amount of outlandish right brainism around, too, resulting in advertising that costs too much to produce, is too mysterious for people to understand, and contributes to a widely held notion that creative people are woolly thinkers.

While there are numerous examples of extremes in the ad agency world—agencies that won't do anything unless the numbers are right; those that haughtily proclaim almighty creative powers—the majority of firms simply *skew* right or left brain.

To me, agencies that bend to the right have the most to offer—to you, to their clients, and to the world. Interestingly, even those far removed from advertising have been known to subscribe to this right-brain view. For example, Albert Einstein in speaking about the universal decrees of physics said, "There is no logical path to these laws; only *intuition* resting on sympathetic understanding of experience can reach them." (He also said, "Imagination is more important than knowledge.") Ferdinand Porsche said, "You have to take into consideration not only the technical calculations, but also the feelings that result in design." And John Naisbitt in *Megatrends* cautioned high-tech manufacturers that their products would face consumer rejections unless they included the human, emotional element.

In my highly opinionated opinion, it is absolutely critical to your future that you consciously decide which kind of agency you want to embrace. Now, I must add that if extreme left brainism appeals to you, I hope you will abandon the idea about a career in advertising and pursue a more suitable line of employment—something calling for studies of attitudinal paradigms, perhaps.

I'm not in favor of creativity without relevance or discipline, but given the choice, I want to work for an agency that does more than just move its lips in support of the creative product—an agency which deliberately, knowingly veers right brain. It's not necessarily an easier way to run a business, but it's a lot more satisfying for the soul and—given the incredible media clutter of our time—can also be appreciably better for a client's business.

The Challenge: Identifying the Creative-Driven Agency

"But," you say, "all agencies brag of their creative strength." (True, I must admit.) So how can a newcomer sort out "those that skew right," particularly in smaller markets? Fortunately, there are some universal characteristics:

1. Are there any creative people in the agency's ownership, or are they all from walks of life other than copy and art? If the latter is the case, pause and reflect.
2. Does the agency's best work win awards? Be careful, though, there are a lot of superficial awards around. It's far better to get an Award of Merit from the One Show (New York) or *CA* (*Communication Arts*) than to receive a Sweepstakes Award from something like the Association of Suppliers to Major Public Landfills in the West.
3. Check into the agency's recent history. Has it ever resigned a client because of "differences in creative philosophy"? Is it willing to put its economic life on the line rather than do bad work?
4. When you visit the agency's offices, do you see samples of their best work prominently displayed? If not, worry. If so, take a long, hard look at it and judge according to the professional standards you are beginning to establish.
5. Does the agency have the reputation of sticking up for its ideas, or is it known as "being real easy to work with"? Again, it's a fine line. You don't want to associate with pigheaded, arrogant prima donnas, but you certainly won't get consistently good work from a yes-suh, boss! outfit. I like the way mega-agency Leo Burnett once spelled out its position on this matter in a house ad with the headline "Born August 5, 1935. Reared on 12 Principles":

   > To fight for what we believe in, regardless of contrary client opinion, providing our conviction is based on sound reasoning, accurate facts and inspired thought; to be intellectually honest.

6. Find out if anyone subscribes to the magazine *Communication Arts* (*CA*) in the agency. Note if it's displayed in the waiting room/lobby. This lovingly produced publication appears eight times yearly and is revered by creative heavyweights.

7. In your interviews with agency honchos, feel them out as to their role models in the industry. If they admire Lee Clow, Hal Riney, Ralph Ammirati, Harry Jacobs, Nancy Rice, Ed McCabe, Carl Ally, Andy Berlin, and/or Tom McElligott, that is a very good sign. If they like David Ogilvy and John O'Toole, that's not bad. But if they rave only about faceless places "that are turning out okay work—not flashy, but seems to get the job done," look out.

You'll feel much happier if you land in an agency that shares your convictions about what constitutes good work. Of course you first have to have some convictions, a point that seems to escape legions of frenzied job seekers. It's little wonder they end up in equally ambivalent agencies where they can join the headlong rush to spew still more deplorable examples of what advertising shouldn't be.

By the way, this matter of convictions is of enormous consequence. I implore you to think about the subject as we spend the following pages delving more into the machinations of an advertising agency and its clients. Then, in Chapter Four, let's get serious about articulating your advertising philosophy. But, first, we will examine the organization of this curious entity, the advertising agency.

EXAMINING THE STRUCTURE OF AN AD AGENCY

Regardless of geography, size, philosophy, or assorted idiosyncrasies, an advertising agency must encompass five basic functions:

- account management (also called account service and client services)
- creative services (copy, art, radio/TV production)
- media planning and buying
- print production (including the "traffic" responsibility, which in larger firms is singled out as a separate job title)
- finance and administration (keeping the books and running the office)

Agencies also regularly offer research, direct response, sales promotion, and/or public relations services, but these are not obligatory.

While the operations list is steadfast, the organizational structure can vary enormously. Take, for example, my first agency employment. There were six employees, and the owner did not believe in job titles. He expected everyone, except the bookkeeper/receptionist, to work on *all* aspects of the business. At this agency, my boss, the owner, did most of the client contact and wrote most of the copy. But he also handled some production requirements and listened to media sales pitches. As for the other employees, it wasn't unusual for one of the artists also to do some client contact as well as handle production duties. At various times I was involved with copywriting, media buying, production estimating, publicity, and account service. It was a great way to break into advertising, but don't ask me to show it on a traditional organization chart.

When my partners and I formed BPN (Borders, Perrin & Norrander), our "organization chart" was the epitomy of functional simplicity:

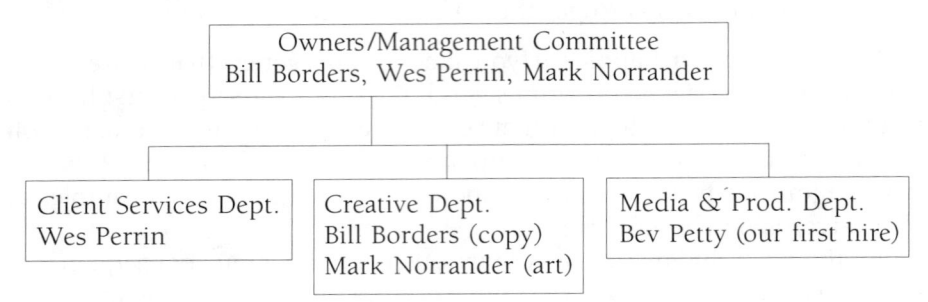

```
            Owners/Management Committee
         Bill Borders, Wes Perrin, Mark Norrander
         ┌───────────────┼───────────────┐
Client Services Dept.   Creative Dept.        Media & Prod. Dept.
Wes Perrin              Bill Borders (copy)   Bev Petty (our first hire)
                        Mark Norrander (art)
```

We had only four people, but, boy, did we have the bases covered! (As for "finance and administration," Bev also did the billing and answered the phones, although we all took turns at that.)

Larger agencies, understandably, have a more formal structure. To give some idea of the typical setup, Figure 1.1 shows an organization chart for BPN after it had grown to employ about seventy people with offices in three locations. Every different agency has its own organizational nuances, but this chart shows the basics and also provides a glimpse of career ladders in various departments.

Mainstream advertising textbooks cover this organizational material in detail, so it is not my intention to have you overdose on the subject here. Rather, I would like you to know more about the everyday operations of each major department and to gain an understanding of how they regularly interact. Let's start with the "suits" (the slang term for ad agency people—male and female—who work in account management or client services; harkens back to the time when a dark suit was the expected business uniform for an account manager/account executive).

The Account Management Department

While the job description for account manager—written or implied—may differ from agency to agency, the reason for being remains constant: to represent the agency and be the primary point of contact with the client. Account managers (also called account executives, or A.E.s) must grasp five golden batons in conducting their affairs:

- to act as an account team captain within the agency, marshalling, motivating, and monitoring the firm's resources
- to assist the client with strategic thinking and direction setting

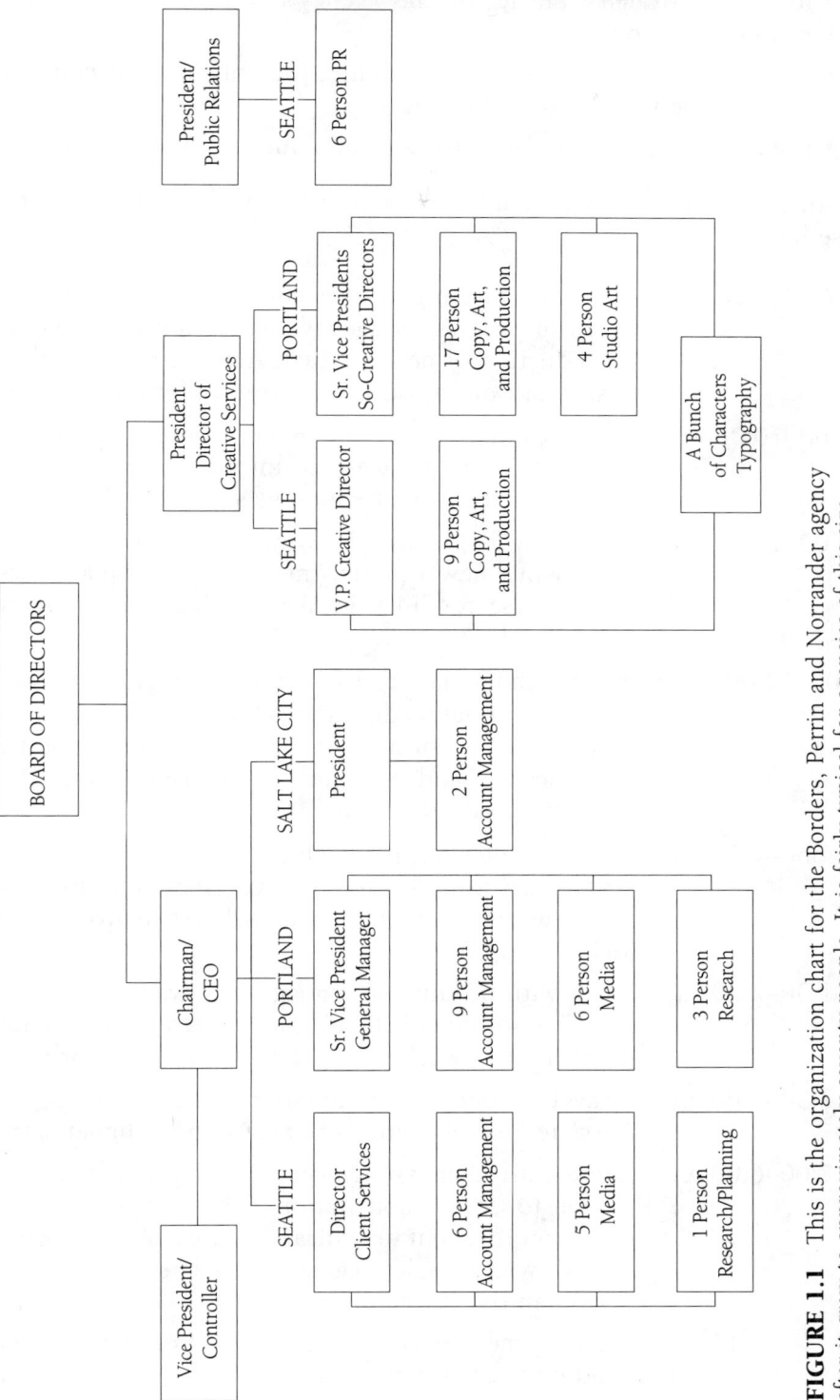

FIGURE 1.1 This is the organization chart for the Borders, Perrin and Norrander agency after it grew to approximately seventy people. It is fairly typical for agencies of this size, except for the in-house typesetting function ("A Bunch of Characters"). Increasingly, however, agencies are setting their own type, rather than buying it from outside suppliers.

- to be the primary oracle for the agency's strategic and creative recommendations
- to steward the economics of the account profitably, thereby contributing to the fiscal health of the agency
- to be a strong participant in the agency's hunt for new business

An average day for a reasonably busy account manager might run along these lines:

7:30–9:00 A.M.   Breakfast meeting with a client to check status of work-in-progress at agency. Discussion of needs for introduction of new product. Agreement reached to start work on introductory print ad for the trade.

9:00–10:00 A.M.   Back at office, write conference report on breakfast meeting. Write job start for introductory ad. Check mail and return phone messages.

10:00–11:00 A.M.   Meeting with creative department to go over strategy for client's new product introduction. Explain secondary research findings. Amplify job start information. Emphasize deadlines.

11:00–12:00 Noon   Meet with media director and junior buyer to answer questions about media choices for new product introduction. Then, sit in with them at a presentation by the sales rep and publisher of *Wow!* magazine. Decline invitation to lunch.

Noon–1:30 P.M.   Meet in conference room with other account managers and agency president to discuss current opportunities for new business. (Lunch is ordered in from local deli.)

1:30–2:30 P.M.   Meet with production manager to review cost overruns on printing of client's catalog pages. Arrange for meeting next week with color separator and printer.

2:30–3:00 P.M.   Travel to client's headquarters while listening to cassette tape of agency's newest radio commercials.

3:00–6:00 P.M.   Meet with client's engineering and product design people to see a demonstration of the new product and learn more about technical features. A discussion follows with the sales manager about latest competitive moves in the marketplace.

6:15 P.M.   Drive home, carrying a briefcase full of materials for reading after dinner.

Are there any shortcuts for gaining the respect and confidence of your clients and colleagues? No, not unless you consider "work *hard!*" a synonym for shortcut. However, as David Ogilvy has said, "You must not be so nakedly aggressive that your fellow workers will rise up and destroy you." Even the brightest and sweatiest of new account people can unwittingly shoot themselves in the foot with co-workers. The following guideposts can help you avoid this calamity:

1. Don't be too full of yourself. Account managers, like football quarterbacks, are often center stage, in the spotlight. They get accolades and perks, eat at better restaurants and wear nicer clothes, so it's fairly easy for them to get swell-headed. Remember, there may be others in the agency who resent you because (a) they believe account people are always getting more credit (and bigger paychecks) than they deserve or (b) deep down, they want your job. If you go in for grandstanding, they will redouble their efforts to toss sand in your gears.

2. Let the others on your account team know *fully* what's going on. "Well, of course!" you say. "After all, I pride myself on the detail and pungency of my conference reports. And I always tell the creative people *exactly* what the client said."

    That's a good start, but it's not enough. Take a page from Peters and Waterman's *Excellence* books: Use "MBWA, or Management By Walking Around," and take time to give the latest scoop personally to everyone on the account (especially if you work for an agency spread over several floors). Don't limit your input to whether the newspaper ad was approved or rejected. Describe what the new regional sales manager is like. How are the new products doing in field testing? Why was the St. Louis distributor canceled? Why are sales up or down for the quarter? And mention anything else relevant to the client's world. The account should be a living, breathing persona, a member of the family whose health is of concern to all. But it won't be unless you make it come alive.

    Some account managers convene a weekly progress meeting with media, production, research, and creative to discuss all the latest happenings on the account. In small shops it may be simply a case of making the maximum use of coffee breaks or lunch gatherings. However you choose to do it, just be sure the word gets around promptly.

3. If you make a mistake, stand up and shoulder the blame without asterisks and disclaimers, *even if it isn't all your fault.* It's so rare for a person to admit error these days, you will immediately stand out from the pack. The worst thing you can do is to deflect the responsibility to others: "If only Mary had stayed on top of this, we

wouldn't be in this mess." Hogwash. Harry Truman was right: The buck stops on your desk. Period.

Conversely, when things go right, distribute praise widely and publicly—to *everyone* involved. An advertising professor once told me, "My greatest-boss-ever absorbed everything that was my fault, but gave me (and others) full credit for jobs well done, no matter how small a role I or they played. I would have died for him, had he asked."

4. Once you are invited to join in the heady pursuit of new business, you have to walk a communications tightrope. You must keep a zipped lip on some of the details to which you will be privy. ("This is no business for blabbermouths," declared Ogilvy.) But don't be too mysterious. Tell what you can to your associates. Otherwise, they will feel left out, and the new business arena becomes rife with rumor, jealousy, conjecture, and misinformation.

5. As you progress within the agency's ranks, don't be afraid to let go, to delegate, not only the menial tasks but the meaningful ones as well. The agency will never grow if you insist on doing everything important (and fun) yourself.

6. Don't overlook the value of the old-timers at your agency, even if they seem mossbacked. Jo Foxworth, who ran her own agency in Manhattan, put it this way in her book, *Wising Up*: "If you're the new gang, remember that the people who've been around awhile know a lot that can be useful. Even though you don't plan to use any of it, listen respectfully. You may hear something that will change your mind."

The Creative Department

This is, without question, your greatest challenge and the springboard to your future. "Everybody in advertising is mixed up, but especially the creative people," wrote Jerry Della Femina in *From Those Wonderful Folks Who Gave You Pearl Harbor, Hard Line Dispatches from the Advertising War*. "Few great creators have bland personalities. They are cantankerous egotists," wrote David Ogilvy in *Confessions of an Advertising Man*. Nevertheless, if you can work well with, and feel good about, writers and art directors, chances are you'll enjoy life in an agency. If you have trouble understanding creative department residents, consider them rather juvenile, and resent their celebrity status, the odds are you'll be happy only at an extreme left-brain agency.

The most prominent inhabitants of the creative department are the copywriters and art directors. As you might expect, the former are principally concerned with words and the latter with visuals. There was a time in American advertising when the copywriters ran the show and the art people were merely "wrists" who sketched out the writers' ideas. Today, at most agencies the two work closely together, and in the best of teams, the writer might suggest the look of the ad and the art director (or A.D.) could come up with the headline.

Their boss, and an extremely important person in the agency culture, is the creative director. He or she will approve every creative recommendation before it reaches any client's desk. Some C.D.s are harsh and overbearing and impose their thinking on all the agency's work. Others are less threatening and give more freedom to their staff. Regardless of their style, it is imperative that you begin to establish a level of respect with this creative czar.

The configuration of any creative department depends on the size and requirements of the agency's clients. Small agencies generally are limited as to creative staff. They can't afford much of a payroll, so they must rely on outside, freelance talent to provide copy and art. Larger agencies may have a number of writers and an art department that includes: several senior art directors and junior assistants; a mechanical artist who specializes in pasteups, an airbrush artist who does photo retouching, an illustrator who does a variety of different styles of drawing/sketching for both layouts and finished art; and perhaps a designer who concentrates on logos, corporate identity, packaging, and signage.

Also in larger shops you will find radio/TV/video specialists who work exclusively on the production of electronic media advertising. They handle all the myriad ramifications of making commercials, watching over budgets, and worrying about such things as talent casting, locations, props, special effects, and the like.

How to Work Well with Your Creative Colleagues Many stories exist about the donnybrook clashes of will and ego that can occur between account management and the creative department. As with all business folklore, there's both truth and fiction in these narratives. Certainly, such hostilities can and do exist. (When Andrew Kershaw was chairman of Ogilvy & Mather, he described such strife as "artificial war . . . silly, unproductive and unprofessional.")

Will you be swept up in such conflict? It all depends on the people running your agency. If you are fortunate enough to join an agency where a common vision is held by both creative and business management, you will be free of the eternal conflict of right brain versus left. Dealing with the creative forces will be open and above board. But if you happen to end up at an agency where commitment to a common vision is only tokenism, look out: The creative personnel will be primed to regard any outsider as an adversary, and it will take some supreme efforts to overcome this perception.

Some of the best advice I've read on getting along with creative folks was written by Jack Foster, then senior VP/creative director at Foote, Cone & Belding, San Francisco, in *Adweek*:

If you're having trouble getting along, realize first of all that it might not be your fault.

There are many prima-donnas, overblown egos, and me-me-me people in creative departments, and their hypersensitive reactions to legitimate requests and questions sometimes makes working with them a trauma instead of a treat.

There are also many account people who don't have the slightest idea how to deal with people, how to gain their respect and loyalty, how to get them to attack projects with alacrity.

And no matter how smart you may be if you can't do those things, you'll never make it in this business. Never.

So, if you are having trouble getting along with writers and art directors, and you suspect that a part of the reason is you, here are some suggestions:

Care about them as people. If you do, they will forgive your weaknesses. If you don't, they will not even acknowledge your strengths.

Get rid of the word "I." If there was ever a "we" business this is it. Make writers and art directors feel as if they're part of the team. Learn "we" and "us." . . .

Never flaunt your education. It bugs writers and art directors when you assume your degree gives you some kind of elevated status. Hell, they're probably better educated in their fields than you are in yours. After all, they've been writing and drawing since kindergarten.

Don't live in a paper world. Talk. Of course you have to put it in writing. But, don't stop there. Discuss every assignment with the writer and art director. And do it before the paperwork arrives. . . .

Challenge them. Present them with a problem, say "Solve it" and walk away. Then, after they've solved it, challenge them again. Ask them if there isn't some other way to do it better. Ask them if they thought about this point or that point. Ask them how they would solve the same problem five years from now. Raise the bar. The good writers and art directors will find a way to jump over it.

Question everything they do. If you don't understand something, ask them why they did it that way; they know. Don't wait for the client to ask you why they did it; you don't know.

React. *For God's sake, don't just sit like a glob of oatmeal—say something.* Do you like it? Do you hate it? Does it confuse you? Is it off strategy? Is it unconvincing? Unclear? Muddled? Trite? Poopy? Great? Say it right away. You can always change your mind later. Creative people don't mind if you change your tune. They mind if you don't sing. [Italics mine. I think this is a particularly wise suggestion. Kindly take it to heart.]

Praise their efforts. Baltasar Gracian wrote: "Praise is to talent what the west wind is to flowers—life and death itself." Don't be stingy with it either. It is impossible to praise too much. Or too often. Or too many people.

Trust them. Doubt them, and they will start doubting themselves. And nothing breeds failure like self-doubt.

Allow them the freedom to fail. The best writers and art directors swing for the fences every time. Criticize them when they strike out, and they'll start trying to punch the ball into right field. "Go for broke," says John O'Toole [former CEO of Foote, Cone & Belding and current president of the American Association of Advertising Agencies]. When they do, praise them, whether they hit the ball or not. [It's interesting to note that David Ogilvy also used a baseball metaphor when writing on this subject: "Discourage bunting," he advised.]

Be receptive. You're looking for a fresh approach. When they bring you one, don't fight it because it's not what you expected. Welcome it. Then kiss it.

Never ever lie. About anything. It is the unforgivable sin. If something is due on the 21st, do not say it is due on the 19th. If the client thinks their ad is lousy, say so. If you forgot something, or neglected something, or screwed something up, admit it. In every case, tell the truth. Even when it hurts.

Listen. That's something you can't do when you're talking.

Never refer to them as "my writers" or "my art directors." They aren't. They are people who work with you, not for you. You don't hire them. You don't fire them. You don't give them raises. You are neither their boss, or their mentor. Don't act like it. . . .

Report. Immediately. Nothing bugs creative people more than having to wait to hear how the client liked their work. So tell them. . . .

Simplify. Be enthusiastic. "Nothing great was ever achieved without enthusiasm," wrote Emerson. "Get rid of sad dogs who spread gloom," wrote Ogilvy. If you see something you like, shout. Your fire will ignite others.

Have fun. "When people aren't having any fun, they seldom produce good advertising," wrote Ogilvy. And if you aren't having any fun, it's hard for the people who work with you to have any. So loosen up.

To those nuggets I add: Show your colors by making a tough sale. Anyone can gain the approval of a sure-thing creative recommendation. But it takes guts, guile, and first-rate persuasion skills to convince a client to take a chance on something far from the expected or the norm. It also takes creativity, of the type that cannot fail to build bonds with a writer or an art director.

Here are two examples of this kind of creativity and persuasive ability (you'll find others in the section entitled "On Selling When They're Not

Buying" in Chapter Two). When one of our account managers failed to gain the client's okay for a series of unusual radio spots, he returned with a "radio story board." "Now these commercials are going to play in the theater of the mind," he said, "and here are the mental pictures these messages will conjure up." Then he read the scripts while the client looked at the illustrations on the story board. An odd approach? To be sure. But it turned the tide. The client said yes, the spots were produced, and they turned out to be loved by all.

On another occasion the same client (but a different individual) was torpedoing a trade print ad because it was "so unlike our industry." He suggested some copy that would "point out that we're the biggest and best in our field." The account manager then reached into his briefcase, pulled out an eight-by-eleven-inch mirror, and replied, "You would only be talking to yourself and your staff and your friends." He put the mirror in front of the client. "Do you think your market would be most interested in a version of 'Mirror, mirror on the wall, who is the fairest of them all?' or the intrusive message we recommend? I'll bet they would pay more attention to an ad that offers a benefit to them." The client harrumphed, smiled, and said he would think about it. The next day, he approved our recommendation.

It's hard for many account managers (and clients) to understand this thing called the "creative process" which involves words (the copywriter) and pictures (the art director). They're not alone. In fact, social scientists are hard pressed to find adequate words to describe the phenomenon. Explaining how it works in an advertising agency is about as easy as catching sunbeams.

The best hands-on depiction of the creative process I have found is in Jerry Della Femina's *From Those Wonderful Folks* .... It's an uneven pot-boiler of a book for the most part, but in the chapter "Fights Headaches Four Ways" we are told just how Della Femina (then a writer, now the chairman of Della Femina McNamee, Inc.) and Ron Travisano (his art-director partner) figured out a campaign for the institutional investor market one morning between 7:00 A.M. and 9:20 A.M. (the client was due at 9:00, but he was a little late). In an explosive burst of inspiration, they discovered the idea and wrote and finished layouts for five ads in a little over two hours.

> The excitement in the room is fantastic. Now we can't sit down. We're jumping up and down because we've a deadline to make and now we've got it and we know we're going to make it. There is an electric feeling in the room and this is what this business is all about as far as the creative person is concerned. ...
>
> The feeling in that room between 8:30 and 9:00 is like insanity. Ron is drawing as fast as he can, throwing papers around, and I'm chattering like a maniac. That's when an ad comes together, this is how it happens. No

one has ever written about it. No one's ever come close . . . describing what it is. They talk about it as though it's magic.

If you explain the creative process to your clients in those words, they probably *still* won't understand, but Della Femina's words do indeed "come close" to capturing the essence of the happening.

Now, before we probe the media, print production, and research departments, I realize there could be a temptation to gloss over these sections. Frankly, they don't command the attention lavished on the account management and creative functions, but you'll be shortchanging your career if you fail to know them inside and out. You owe it to yourself to be acutely aware of all three for three selfish reasons: (1) How well you work with these teammates will have a major bearing on your progress in the agency. (2) These may be the only departments offering employment in the early years of your career. As you are forever being told, getting a toe in the agency door is the supreme challenge when you have little or no experience. Therefore, seriously consider openings in departments other than account service or creative—that is, media, production, and/or research—even if it isn't your first or even second choice. (3) These may not be the most glamorous jobs, but they *are* indispensable at an agency, and they do represent solid career opportunities. And it's not inconceivable that you will like the job so much you'll change your mind about striving for any other position.

The Media Department

In agencies of all sizes, you'll see people working long hours here. The person in charge is titled media director, and in smaller shops he or she may indeed be the "department." (In fact, media people may handle other assignments as well, ranging from account service to secretarial duties.) In larger agencies, the department is staffed by professionals who tend to specialize: those who concentrate on buying and negotiating; those who concentrate on planning, analysis, and strategy (generally the more senior people).

Media professionals are mainly involved with the "major media": radio, TV, newspapers, magazines, and outdoor. On many occasions, however, they also probe such less-mainstream media as airport displays, buses and taxis, ballpark fences, shopping carts, sports and theatrical programs, and—in Israel—fresh eggs. Yes, eggs! Recently the Golden Eggs company in Jerusalem found a way to print ads on ordinary grocery store eggs. Eastman Kodak ordered nine million imprinted with its logo and the copy, "Take a picture with Kodak." "You can't ignore the message when you open your refrigerator," declared the president of Golden Eggs. "It's shouting at you 'here I am!' "

In this department, you will soon be in trouble if you don't enjoy a meaningful relationship with computers and calculators. Much of the work for any new hire in the department involves checking rates, ratings, schedules, cost efficiencies, and other sticky data wickets. When a cost estimate is prepared for a client, there is scant room for error. A person who despises detail is not welcome here.

It also helps to have a knack for patiently gleaning pertinent information from oral sales presentations. **Media mavens** (those who are extremely knowledgeable about planning, buying, and negotiating media) are constantly asked to listen to sales representatives touting the validity of individual radio and TV stations, newspapers, and magazines. Hearing them out is a prerequisite for the business, and while it can be informative, it is not always fun. (This becomes abundantly clear when the 300-pound sales rep with bad breath comes calling for *Upland Archery and Wildebeeste Tracking*.)

At smaller shops, the media openings often encompass a lot of grunt work. In the long haul, that can work to your advantage. My first assignment after joyously landing a job with a five-person agency was to look up rates, type space orders, and mail ad mats/slicks to 240 weekly newspapers across the United States. Zounds, but it was tedious! However, when I finally took the last bundle to the post office, I understood more about the quirks of SRDS (Standard Rate & Data Service, the company that produces the "bible" of the business for media info) than I ever wanted to know, and I could answer basic questions about newspaper production. That rudimentary knowledge served me well for the next twenty-five years.

To put it bluntly, ad agency personnel who babble media jargon, but don't really understand the basics, are not worth their keep. Conversely, those who know the fundamentals can really shine when a client interrupts the meeting to ask questions like: "Would you explain this page from the latest Arbitron TV ratings book for me?" Or, "If I want to reach 50 percent of my target audience with a weekly frequency of four, how many television GRPs [gross rating points] do I need to buy?" (Two hundred happens to be the answer.) Or, "What does Simmons say about in-home readership for *Sunset*?"

For starters, learn the fundamental services used by the industry to measure media effectiveness. **Arbitron** is a widely used source of audience measurement for radio and television. The reports are based on diaries kept by a precise demographic sampling of each market and are updated several times yearly, depending on the market size. **A. C. Nielsen** is another well-regarded monitor of television viewing. The firm pioneered the use of the "audimeter," an electronic device that attaches to TV sets in sample households and records use minute by minute. The Nielsen Television Index reports on network and national cable audiences while the

Nielsen Station Index covers spot market viewing. Nielsen supplements its data in certain areas with diary reports.

If your agency is too small to purchase Arbitron or Nielsen reports, you can usually borrow copies from leading radio and TV stations in your market. Sales reps from these stations can be invaluable in explaining how to wade through the data and interpret them intelligently. Just understand that they will always find ways to manipulate the figures in their favor.

For magazine data, you should be on friendly terms with both MRI (Mediamark Research, Inc.) and SMRB (Simmons Market Research Bureau). Curiously, MRI always goes by its initials, while SMRB is known simply as "Simmons." Both cover product usage patterns and media habits to a faretheewell.

Then, there are the two media data base hulks: **Telmar** and **IMS (Interactive Market Systems).** Each offers subscribers an avalanche of media information including MRI, Simmons, **ClusterPlus,** a resource used primarily to determine market potential and pinpoint mailing targets; and **VALS** (Values and Lifestyles Survey), a state-of-the-art analysis of the relationship of lifestyle to buying patterns and media habits. VALS categorizes people broadly into four groups:

1. "Need-driven," people whose buying is influenced more by need than choice.
2. "Outer-directed," men and women who are very concerned with what others will think about them.
3. "Inner-directed," those who seek to satisfy their own inner priorities rather than responding to what others value—a group dominated by "baby boomers," people born between 1945 and 1964.
4. "Integrateds," a very small percentage of the U.S. population (perhaps 2 percent) who live with an inner sense of what is meaningful and self-fulfilling.

In the late Seventies and early Eighties, the trend was for agencies to access this information via "on-line" connections (telephone modems) to their computer terminals. But with the emergence of lower-cost personal computers (PCs), all the major data base sources (Telmar, IMS, etc.) began selling software to agencies. Now, if an agency is large enough to afford the investment, it much prefers to buy the software, save the data in its own PCs, and wave goodbye to on-line charges. (In fact, both Telmar and IMS have stopped updating on-line data, and are placing their biggest marketing eggs in the ever-expanding software basket.)

With each passing year, the sophistication of the available software grows at a mind-boggling pace. For example, a program called "Media Resources Plus" allows an agency to do radio and TV rankings, schedules, reach and frequency analyses, even color graphs of findings. Media professionals expect that shortly TV station avails will be available electronically, creating a major time-saving advantage for those agencies able to procure the software.

Are you now in clover by mastering the above? Not quite. You also should be intimately familiar with the following basic buzzwords:

Print Media (newspapers, magazines, periodicals)

Agate line At newspapers this is an ancient way of measuring space. It takes fourteen lines to make one column inch (i.e., one inch in depth; the width is that of the newspaper column, which is rarely identical for any two papers). Newspaper advertising rates were historically quoted in *lines,* not inches, as common sense might indicate. To calculate the cost of a half-page newspaper message, you needed to know the number of lines constituting one-half page of ad space and then had to multiply that by the price per line. For example, if it took 1,250 agate lines to make a half-page ad in the *Ferndale Bugle* and the rate was $.84 per line, the space cost was $1,050. Today almost all newspaper rates are quoted in column inches. (The *Wall Street Journal,* however, continues to charge by the agate line.)

The frequency discounts allowed by newspapers are also based on lines or inches used. In other words, an advertiser running 5,000 lines a year with the *Bugle* would qualify for a rate of, say, $.75 an inch, whereas a one-time advertiser using only 500 or so lines would be charged the higher "open rate," which might be $.84 an inch. Ideally, your client will approve an annual media budget that forecasts the amount of newspaper space to be bought. Armed with that figure, the agency can contract with the newspaper for the most favorable end rate. For example, if the plan calls for ten ads totalling 1,000 inches to be run during the year, the client will qualify for the 10,000-inch rate. However, if the client cancels part of the program and doesn't run those 10,000 inches, then the newspaper will bill for a "short rate" at the end of the contract period.

Here's an example of short rating:

Your client contracts for 10,000 inches at $1.00 per column inch.

Your client runs only 8,000 column inches during the year.

The newspaper's next lowest frequency discount is for 5,000 lines at $1.20 per column inch.

Your client has paid $8,000 (8,000 × $1.00), but he hasn't qualified for that end rate. Rather, he should have paid $9,600 (8,000 × $1.20). Therefore, the newspaper will bill a short rate of $1,600.

In figuring newspaper space costs, be sure to determine if the rates are "local retail net" (do not include agency commission) or "national/gross" (15-

percent commission included). It's incredibly easy for an agency rookie to use the wrong rate card when making an estimate, and that kind of error can haunt a relationship for months.

ABC (Audit Bureau of Circulations) Just as financial institutions need periodic audits, so do publishers when it comes to circulation figures. The ABC was organized by agencies, advertisers, and media to regularly verify circulation statements of member magazines and newspapers. It currently has a membership of over 5,000.

ABP (American Business Press) This association boasts 650 domestic and 120 international publishers of business periodicals. Members agree to abide by the ABP code of publishing practice, which includes regular audits of circulation by a nonprofit tripartite auditing bureau.

Bleed This is a favorite of agency art directors and has nothing to do with red or white corpuscles. Rather, it means that the ink on a printed page extends to the edge of the paper (there is no white border around the advertising material). Depending on the layout, it can enhance the graphic drama of the message, but often at additional cost for the space. Many magazines charge an extra 10 or 15 percent for bleed coverage, and this can play havoc with a tight budget.

BPA (Business Publications Audit) This organization specializes in verifying the circulation of business-to-business periodicals and medical journals.

The professional auditing process is costly and time consuming, so many smaller publishers forgo the service and simply offer "sworn statements" or, in the case of *really* small periodicals, copies of post office receipts showing the number of copies mailed. As a general rule, mentally turn on the yellow caution light whenever you see an unaudited circulation statement.

Circulation This is the number of copies distributed to readers. "Paid" circulation means the readers bought the periodical either on the newsstand or via subscription. "Qualified" circulation indicates that the publication has documentary evidence of their recipients' mailing addresses, evidence that they meet the definitions of the "field served" and "recipient qualification," are correctly classified in "business/occupational breakout of circulation," and have received continuous service for at least six months. (You see this frequently in the circulation statements of business-to-business magazines that do not solicit paid subscriptions.) "Nonpaid" readers receive the publication without paying for it; "non–qualified" recipients receive it without any documentary evidence. Obviously, those publications with paid circulation command greater respect.

Closing date This is the industry's way of saying "deadline." If you don't deliver the order or the materials to the publication by the stated closing dates, your client's ad will not appear in the issue ordered. However, these dates are often stretched, with extensions commonplace.

Cost per thousand (CPM) This is what it costs to reach 1,000 individuals with a particular advertising vehicle. For example: If one page of advertising costs $3,000 in a magazine with 100,000 readers, the CPM is $30. If the space costs $500 in a publication read by 1,000, the CPM is $500. CPM can be used to quickly show the relative cost of one publication to another (or one medium to another, for that matter).

Demographic editions Some magazines offer special editions or sections that are directed to specific types of readers. For example, if an advertiser purchases space in *Newsweek Woman,* the message will appear only in those copies going to female subscribers.

Hi-Fi and Spectacolor These are two types of full-color preprinted inserts in newspapers. Hi-Fi is on a continuous roll and the pages are not trimmed as evenly as in Spectacolor. Both are printed on a better-grade paper than newsprint.

Issue life This term describes how long it takes for the periodical's maximum audience to see/read the issue. Daily and weekly publications obviously have shorter issue lives than do monthly or bimonthly vehicles.

Make good Should a publication foul up your order, it may offer to "make good" its error by running the correct message free. Your clients will expect you to press hard for this adjustment if it is the publication's fault. (Term is used for electronic media, as well.)

Primary and pass-along readers The primary folks are those in the household of the magazine purchaser. Pass-along readers are those who see the magazine outside of the primary household (barbershop, dentist's office, auto repair shop, etc.). Most media gurus give higher value to in-home readership, but of course it varies by publication. Business magazines, for example, are likely to be read more intently at the office than at home. Some periodicals with relatively low primary circulation (and high CPM) can get pretty creative with their pass-along reader statistics, as this is an area that defies pinpoint auditing.

Psychographics This is a research catchword widely used by print (and electronic) media sales reps. It relates to studies of individuals' lifestyles and personality characteristics, information that frequently guides editorial direction of a magazine (or program content of a TV show).

Rate base This is the circulation figure on which a publication bases its cost of advertising space. Some publishers guarantee delivery of those numbers; others do not.

ROP This signifies "run of press" on a space order and means it's okay to run the advertisement anywhere in the publication, as opposed to requesting a fixed position (e.g., in the sports pages of a newspaper or on the inside back cover of a magazine). As you might expect, publications can charge dearly for fixed positioning.

Short rate When an advertiser fails to meet the frequency discount requirements of a space contract, a short rate is charged. See "agate line" earlier for a detailed example.

Spread   This is the name for any print ad covering two full, facing pages. Newspapers used to refer to it as a "double truck," but that expression is rarely heard anymore.

Electronic Media (radio and television)

ADI (area of dominant influence)   Arbitron uses this term to describe TV markets. (Nielsen labels TV markets as DMAs, or "designated market areas.") There are approximately 205 TV markets in the United States, encompassing more than 3,000 counties.

AM   Here's one for trivia buffs. Everyone knows of AM radio stations, but few people realize that AM stands for "amplitude modulation" (and probably even fewer know what *that* means). Roughly, it refers to the way sound is transmitted by these stations: The power (amplitude) of the sound waves is modified (modulated) to simulate original sound.

Availability, or "avails"   The time slot (ten-second, fifteen-second, thirty-second, etc.) in a program, or between programs, that is available for purchase by advertisers. One of the first steps in building a TV buy is to ask the stations for a list of avails with prices.

Barter   This is a practice that frequently sounds better than it proves to be. Essentially, broadcast time is exchanged for merchandise, rather than sold for cash. It's hard for an agency to make money on these transactions, and my experience has been mostly negative. Still, it does represent an opportunity for a cash-starved client to obtain some broadcast visibility. If you get involved with barter, proceed with double caution.

Cume persons   This is the total number of different (unduplicated) persons who listen or watch during a defined time period. A station's weekly cume is its maximum reach potential.

Cume rating   This is determined by dividing the number of cume persons by the market population. In radio this is the percentage of the population that listens within a defined period of time.

Drive time   The hours when radios are most heavily used in automobiles: 6:00 to 10:00 A.M. ("morning drive") and 3:00 to 7:00 P.M. ("afternoon drive"). Not surprisingly, avails during these times carry the highest price tags.

Fixed position   In broadcasting, this means a commercial slot purchased with the guarantee that it cannot be "preempted," or moved. Obviously, you must pay a premium for "nonpreemptible" spots. If you choose to purchase the cheaper, preemptible positions, you run the risk of having to give up your slot to someone willing to pay more.

Flighting   This is the name for a strategic ploy calling for periods of heavy media exposure interspersed with short spells of nonactivity, or "hiatus."

FM   Stands for "frequency modulation," a process of adjusting the frequency of the transmitted sound waves to achieve a clear radio signal, free of static or fade.

Frequency This is the number of times individuals or homes are exposed to an advertising message.

Fringe time This is TV jargon for the time periods surrounding the highest viewing evening hours ("prime time"). They vary some from market to market but are generally 4:30 to 7:30 P.M. and 11:00 P.M. to 1:00 A.M.

Gross impressions This is the total number of times a commercial is seen or heard. It is calculated by multiplying the total number of persons exposed by the number of exposures.

GRPs (gross rating points) This is probably the most bandied about expression in the media business. "How many GRPs is that buy going to deliver?" Yet, for all that overuse, it is interesting to observe how some agency people squirm when asked to provide a succinct definition of "a rating point."

Basically, one GRP is equivalent to 1 percent of the market's population. To calculate GRPs, you multiply the percentage "reach" of the message by the average "frequency" of exposure. In other words, if a TV buy will reach 20 percent of the market and be seen an average of five times during a week, it will deliver 100 GRPs. If it would reach 50 percent of the population an average of five times, the schedule would be worth 250 GRPs. When evaluating media proposals, be careful to note whether the GRPs are for weekly or monthly periods. Four hundred GRPs a week is going to have far more impact than 400 spread over a month.

HUT (homes using television) This is the percentage of homes in a market using TV during a specified period. If four out of five homes are watching a television program at 8:00 on a Friday evening, then the HUT level is 80 percent. The percentage varies by season, time of day, geography, and cable penetration. For example, one A. C. Nielsen study showed HUT levels for the 11:00 P.M. to 1:00 A.M. period to be 30 percent in New York City, but only 11 percent in early-to-bed Portland, Maine.

PUT (people using television) Why the initials for the TV term, but not for the radio (there's PUT, but no PUR)? Beats me. At least the definition is the same for each: the percentage of people using TV or radio at a given time.

Prime time In addition to being the nickname of a highly paid professional football player, this designates the time period when TV watching is the highest: 8:00 to 11:00 P.M., Monday through Saturday, and 7:00 to 11:00 P.M. Sunday. (One hour earlier in central and mountain time zones.) Naturally, commercial time here commands the top prices, locally and nationally.

Pulsing Another strategic approach in media buying. In this case, messages are run continuously and augmented periodically by a burst of heavy activity. Your client has to have deep pockets to favor this technique.

Rating This is the percentage of individuals (or homes) watching or listening to a particular television or radio program. For example, if you have ten homes owning TV sets in a market, and two of them are watching Program X, then that show has a 20 rating.

Roadblocking *See* Simul-buy below.

Scatter plan This is the name given to a media buy that calls for commercials to run in many different time slots and programs.

Share Another particularly hot buzzword, it means the percentage of homes using TV (or radio) that are tuned to a particular program. For example, if 30 out of 100 homes in a given market are watching "Monday Night Football," that program has earned a 30 share.

Simul-buy (also called roadblocking) This type of media buy occurs when fixed position commercials are purchased to run at the same time on several TV stations in the same market. For example, Nissan might buy a thirty-second spot at the 9:00 P.M. break in Portland, Oregon, on channels 6 (CBS), 8 (NBC), and 2 (ABC).

TAP (total audience plan) This is a package of commercial avails that radio stations offer as a "good deal" for general audience advertisers. The advertiser's commercials will run in different dayparts with the total buy calculated to deliver a majority of the market's "total audience."

TSA (total survey area) In measuring the audience of a radio market, this pertains to all of the counties in which there is significant listenership to the market's stations.

Weighting This is the practice of assigning greater importance (or "more weight") to a particular group of people or market segment when developing a media plan.

Wild spot In calculating residual talent payments, this applies to spot market buys in unsponsored programs on noninterconnected programs.

Outdoor/Transit

Kings and queens No royalty involved here; these terms refer to the relative size of posters used for advertising on the exterior of buses (transit advertising, in other words). The king-sized units are the largest and appear on the bus sides. "Queens" are available on fronts and backs of buses.

Override This is what happens when the outdoor advertising company doesn't sell all of its space. Rather than having a blank board staring at the public or carrying a nonpaying public service ad, the company simply lets the current advertisement "ride" past the end of the contract period. This can result in several weeks of free exposure for your client, if the paper doesn't deteriorate from weather exposure.

Painted bulletins As the name indicates, these outdoor advertising modules have the message painted on them (as opposed to having paper pasted on them). They are larger than thirty-sheet boards, averaging about fourteen by forty-eight feet. The message is painted on large panels in the outdoor company's shop, then trucked to the bulletin's location and installed on the existing framework. Often, special cutouts extend beyond the borders of the bulletin in the quest for greater visual impact. Space contracts are usually for three- or six-month periods.

Typically, the painted bulletins are sold as either "permanent," meaning the message stays at the same location for the length of the contract, or "rotating," in which case the painted panels are physically moved to different locations at thirty-, sixty-, or ninety-day intervals.

Showings Posters are usually purchased in multiples called "#100 Showing," "#50 Showing," "#25 Showing," and so on. These are supposed to equate with gross rating points for one day, so a 100 showing would potentially be seen by 100 percent of the market's population. However, audience measurement is far less sophisticated than for radio and TV, so verification of reach and frequency isn't commonplace. Generally, all showings are for a minimum of thirty consecutive days, but in smaller markets advertisers can sometimes purchase posters on a weekly basis.

Thirty-sheet posters Still called "billboards" by many average citizens, these are the standard outdoor advertising "boards" of today. It originally took thirty sheets of printed paper to cover the space, hence the name. The area for copy is approximately ten feet high by just under twenty-two feet long.

Becoming familiar with these terms also prepares you for survival when, despite your highest hopes, you end up working with a so-so media director. You'll be able to evaluate the recommendation and push for appropriate adjustments before exposing anything to the client. This is far better than merely transporting a half-baked proposal to a reasonably knowledgeable client who will delight in pinning your ears back.

It's an appalling fact of life that media professionalism receives almost apartheid treatment at some hack agencies. Media decisions are dictated by the client or the account person (aka the agency owner), and the "media department" is nothing more than a young woman who looks up rates, calls for TV avails, and types orders when she's not acting as the agency receptionist.

How to Work Well with Your Media Colleagues Regardless of the strength of your agency's department, the account manager is going to receive phone calls galore from media sales reps. Why? Because they fear that the account manager holds the hole cards on media recommendations (which he or she does in some situations, as I mentioned above). This means many offers of lunch, drinks, and occasionally dinner, in addition to the normal business-time requests for opportunities to convince you of the merits of their media vehicle. For a time this can be a pleasant diversion, but it rapidly wears thin. Some media reps can be highly informative, not to mention highly entertaining, and time spent with them can be fruitful.

Others are simply various shades of exasperating. In choosing the ones you see, be sensitive to the feelings of your media teammates, who could feel they are being victimized by a sales end run.

My policy is never to have a meeting, lunch, or dinner with a media salesperson unless someone from my media department is also there. (Okay. I confess that I have broken this rule occasionally for an old business friend—but only on extreme, guilt-ridden occasions.) And my public utterances are always the same: *all* media decisions are made *only* after our media department makes an analysis and recommendation.

In summary, you want two things to occur media-wise. First, you want the sales reps to call your media people, not you. Your colleagues can then alert you to the upcoming meetings, lunches, or whatever, and you can be suitably selective. Second, you want your media department to feel they have your full support and confidence.

Here are five other points to keep in mind when dealing with the media department:

1. Spend the time with your client to pin down primary and secondary target audiences. A regular complaint from media professionals is that audience targets are too broad or not well thought out, then changed in midstream!

2. Every client has prejudices about favorite and unfavorite media, either by category ("I think radio is a waste of money!") or by specific property ("Channel 6 has lousy news coverage. Always has. Always will."). Be sure your media people know about these prejudices so that you can work together to alleviate the ones that are unreasonable.

3. If it's a fairly decent budget, make sure every "merchandising" extra is brought to light. (This can include such goodies as reprints of print ads, counter cards, hangtags, in-store broadcasts, prize drawings, hot air balloons, and the like.) A harried media person might overlook these in the heat of making a good buy. In the end these extras can make you both look good. (Refer also to "Making Small Budgets Look Huge" in Chapter Three.)

4. Encourage original thinking. Memorize what media guru Jim Surmanek (senior VP at McCann Erickson) said in his book, *Media Planning: A Practical Guide:*

> Sometimes the quantity of numbers generated prevents planners and buyers from spending the time to look into the numbers and see what made them happen in the first place. Sometimes the numbers become the rationale rather than the guideline. Sometimes the human element is lost, and creative thinking is subjugated to an almost nonexistent role. And that is a pity.

5. Unless your media folks are loose cannons, don't hide them from the client. They certainly don't need, and don't want, to attend every meeting, but they should be at major input sessions and should have carte blanche to call the client directly whenever a quick answer is needed. They also should have the opportunity to present their recommendations personally, rather than always having you do the honors. If their presentation skills are weak, you may be able to help with some coaching and rehearsal—and, in the process, knit an even more effective working relationship.

The Print Production Department

Despite the production department's unquestioned value—without wise production people, great advertising would never come to be—it is arguably the most ignored of all agency functions. In David Laskin's book, *Getting Into Advertising,* he spends twenty pages on "Account Management," thirty pages on "The Creative Team," but only six pages on production. A nationally used, 795-page university textbook, *Advertising: Its Role in Modern Marketing* by Dunn and Barban, lists 29 chapters with 494 subject headings. In the table of contents, the word *production* occurs twice: "mass production" and "production services" (outside of the agency).

Yet production offers some incredible opportunities for a newcomer to become instantly immersed in the swirling waters of agency work flow. Yes, it requires some capacity to understand technical matters—particularly when it comes to full-color printing—but you certainly don't have to be a nuclear physicist. You do, however, have to have a head for details, a true sense of urgency, and a ringmaster's flair for coaxing different personalities to work in concert.

Trying to sum up the work of the production folks is almost a book in itself. Here are some of the basics. Once the account manager opens a job, the production person has to keep one eye on the clock and determine when the creative work must be ready to present to the client and when the finished material must be either delivered or shipped. Piece of cake, eh? Well, it can be a nightmare.

In larger agencies, there generally is a "traffic function" associated with the production section. In theory, traffic checks with all departments and makes sure that jobs are moving along smoothly and meeting due dates. In reality, the person must become a nagger/cajoler/motivator of the first order, and the best ones are frequently the least popular. This is a terrible job for someone new to the agency business, as this person simply will not have the clout to keep things moving. In the 1960s, *Advertising Age* ran a series of poetic vignettes on agency life by Draper Daniels. This is how he portrayed the "traffic man":

Alone, unloved, here he perspires,
Caught between two spreading ires,
The eagerest beaver of all the clan,
The pittering, pattering traffic man.
The ogre before him called copy resists,
The ogre behind him called contact insists.
Bewildered he stands, his heart all a-flutter,
Wondering which bread carries the butter.

Work flow in an agency doesn't move forward by automation and robotics. It takes the human touch of the dedicated production department. If the copywriter and art director aren't reminded when their work is due, they might not get to the assignment in time to meet the deadline for the account manager's meeting with the client. Once the meeting happens, revisions may be requested and more creative work is required.

After the layout and copy are approved, production's work is compounded (see Figure 1.2). Cost estimates have to be prepared. Type has to be set and proofread, photography scheduled. **Stats** (short for "photostats"; also called **PMTs**) have to be ordered, then a **mechanical** or pasteup prepared. Proofs in the form of **dyluxes** or **color keys** or **signature prints** or **match prints** must be produced by outside suppliers, checked with persnickety art directors, shown to clients, revised, resubmitted, and re-revised. Everything has to be checked and rechecked, with the chances of error running high because of the time pressure. (If you are unfamiliar with any of these boldfaced terms, you should refer to the Glossary at the end of this book.)

If the job involves a print advertisement, production must worry about getting the reproduction material to the publication on time. The closing dates are printed in Standard Rate & Data Service directories, of course, but deadline extensions are commonplace and obtaining them is often a task for the department's newest member. Then there's the whole briarpatch of publication specifications to wade through. What is a half-page ad size in *Zow* magazine may bear no resemblance to a half-page in *Pow* magazine. And that's only the beginning, as each publication has its own detailed mechanical specs involving everything from halftone screens to whether the emulsion should be up or down on the color film negatives.

If it's a printed piece such as a sales brochure or catalog, competitive bids have to be obtained from printers and the job awarded on the basis of the best combination of price, service, and quality. This means talking to several sales reps, making sure the specs (type of paper, number of folds, number of color separations, etc.) are clear and making sure they can deliver on their promises.

How Long Will It Take . . . ?

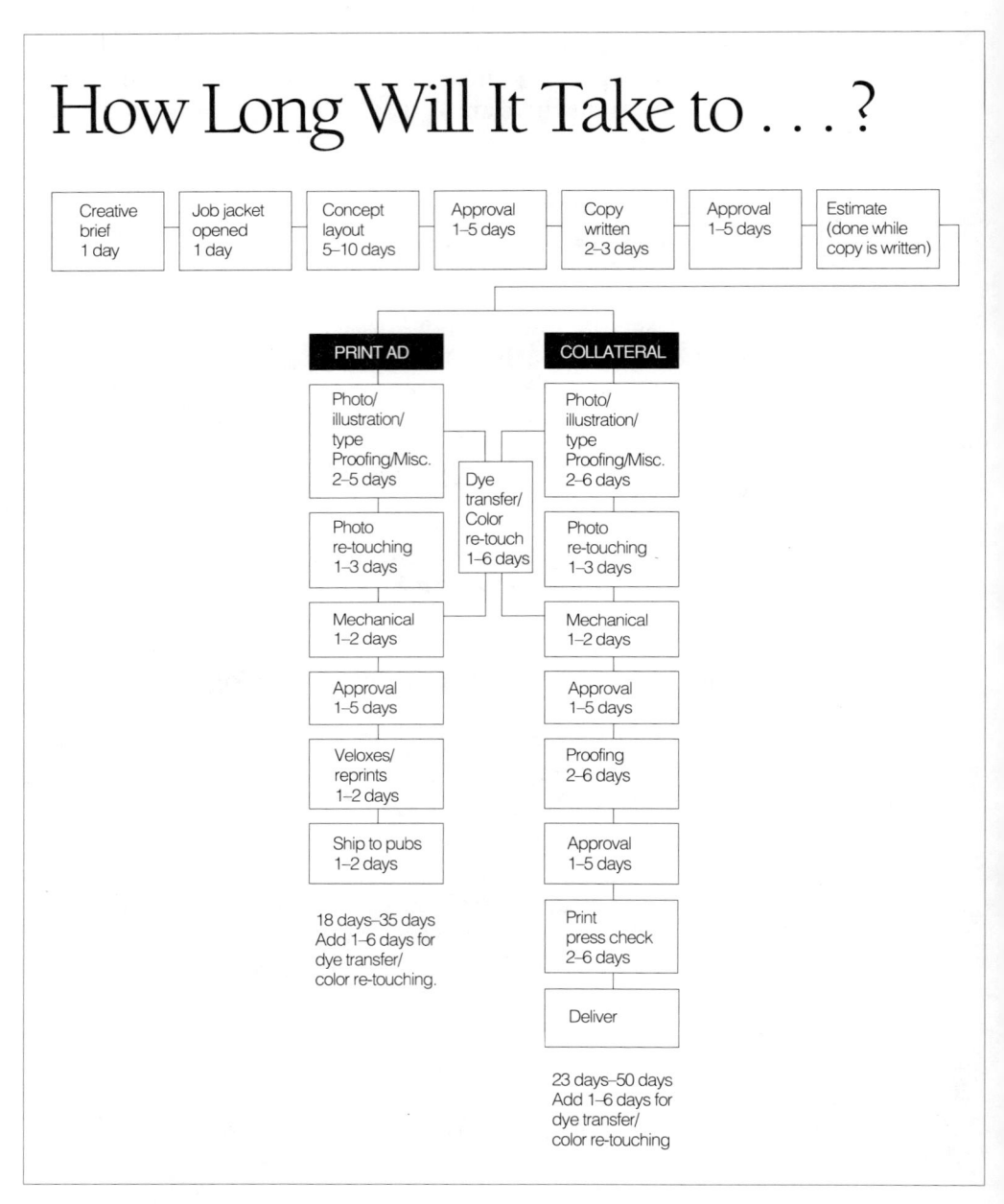

| Creative brief 1 day | Job jacket opened 1 day | Concept layout 5–10 days | Approval 1–5 days | Copy written 2–3 days | Approval 1–5 days | Estimate (done while copy is written) |

PRINT AD

- Photo/illustration/type Proofing/Misc. 2–5 days
- Photo re-touching 1–3 days
- Mechanical 1–2 days
- Approval 1–5 days
- Veloxes/reprints 1–2 days
- Ship to pubs 1–2 days

18 days–35 days
Add 1–6 days for dye transfer/color re-touching.

COLLATERAL

- Photo/illustration/type Proofing/Misc. 2–6 days
- Photo re-touching 1–3 days
- Mechanical 1–2 days
- Approval 1–5 days
- Proofing 2–6 days
- Approval 1–5 days
- Print press check 2–6 days
- Deliver

23 days–50 days
Add 1–6 days for dye transfer/color re-touching

(Dye transfer/Color re-touch 1–6 days)

FIGURE 1.2 Estimating the length of time it will take to complete an advertising project is far from an exact science. The best production people have a keen grasp of the critical variables, but even then it's impossible to know for certain how many hours or days it may take for each step. This flow chart provides guidelines for typical workflow timing in a medium-sized agency.

When jobs are completed, production has to wrestle with all of the outside bills, checking to make sure they are accurate and in sync with estimates. Or, if the bills aren't, they consider why and then work with the account manager to explain everything to the client. Finally, production works with whoever does the agency's billing, to be sure the clients are invoiced correctly.

Production staffers must accept a life under the gun, knowing that mistakes can be devastating for a small agency—for example, a glaring typographic error on the final summary page of the client's annual report. If it isn't the client's or the printer's mistake, it's going to fall hard into the lap of the agency. Paying for one such screwup can wipe out the profits on ten other jobs. People who are error-prone, rattled under fire, and habitually late to dinner should never take a job in a production department.

How to Work Well with Your Print Production Colleagues A production department that is ferocious on detail and imbued with a finely honed sense of urgency is wonderful to behold. Time after time these are the people who will be of inestimable value to agency and client: Like finding a printer who will work on Sunday and not charge double time. Or locating a source of fresh orchids for mailing in the dead of winter. Or finding a cheap source of used bowling balls for the sales meeting themed, "We're Bowling Over the Competition!" Or being at the printer for the press check at 2:00 A.M. and finding the nasty typo on page 23 of the six-color job. Or getting the slides redone overnight because the presentation has to start sharp at 8:30 the next morning. Is it any wonder I urge you to keep on the best of terms with this department?

Here are seven ways you can improve your relationship with production people:

1. When you return from a client meeting with any kind of printer's proof sheet for a job with a tight deadline, don't scribble a cryptic note and run off to your next meeting. Take time to explain personally every needed adjustment.

    What if you have no choice but to leave a note? (For example, everyone has gone home, and you won't be coming into the office the next day.) Then take pains to be sure your notes are readable. It's just as bad to leave words that are indecipherable as it is to leave none at all. Then call the production department as soon as you can to confirm that all is understood.

2. When the project involves printing a large quantity of, for example, a product catalog or an annual report, realize that minutes are precious. The moment you learn of a surprise change at the client's office, reach for a phone and alert your production co-workers. If you're under a fierce deadline, take the final corrections directly

from the client to the printer's plant. Arrange to meet the production person there, and skip dallying at the agency.
3. Be tactful but relentless with clients who procrastinate. There are account managers who believe they are doing the right thing when they let the client "have a little extra time for a final review." But if the brochure absolutely has to be delivered at X hour on day Y, that "take your time" approach is poison.
4. Do your homework and learn the basics of print production. Then, if a client makes a bizarre correction request, you can immediately point out the consequences in time and cost. It's deadly when you have to wait back at the agency for the production experts to explain it to you and then call the client back and try to relay the explanation.
5. As in the case of media, clear the way for production to have direct access to clients. Don't act as a filter when time is of the essence.
6. If a printer or color separation house or other supplier asks you to lunch or a ball game or another social event, make a habit of including the production worker on the account.
7. If there's a serious squabble over cost with a vendor, offer to get bloodied. Go in arm-in-arm with your production colleague and fight the good fight together. But ask first, rather than assuming that your presence is always the answer (you might simply get in the way). And be fair when trying to resolve cost disagreements. It might be a case in which the agency and the client—not the supplier—should absorb the cost.

The Research Department

This is another plausible way to segue into the agency world, but it's unusual for smaller market agencies to invest much in staffing this resource. If they do use research, it is far more common for the agencies to buy these services outside on an a la carte basis from firms specializing in market research or public opinion polling. Large agencies, on the other hand, invariably will boast of substantial in-house research capability.

Traditionally, agencies emphasize research addressing two areas: (1) to find out more about the market to which the advertising is to be targeted, and (2) to attempt to measure the effectiveness of creative efforts. To me the first concern is of enormous importance, and I am continually amazed to see advertisers racing ahead *without* market information. "Why should I pay to learn what I already know?" they bellow. What they really mean is "I prefer to learn the hard way." Even such a nonadvertiser as baseball great Casey Stengal wisely advised, "If you don't know where you're going, you could end up somewhere else."

To pry loose relevant market input, a researcher must quickly grasp the basics of both projectible and diagnostic techniques. Projectible studies are apt to involve large, carefully calculated audience samples and sophisticated interviewing tactics, and the results should be rather precise. Diagnostic research refers to such activities as **focus groups,** in which a relatively small (generally eight to twelve) number of people from the target audience are sequestered in a single room and guided through a range of topics by a moderator. They are useful for finding clues to market truth, but the findings are by no means projectible.

I am less impressed with the second concern. The pretesting of a creative recommendation still leaves much to be desired, in my experience. Bill Bernbach said it best: "Research is very important, but I think it is the beginning of the ad, not the end. To find what the problem is does not solve the problem." Hall of Fame Copywriter Ed McCabe is even more emphatic. He says, "No piece of successful advertising I've ever done has ever been tested." Tom McElligott has insightfully pointed out, "Commercials that test well are commercials that consumers have seen in some other form." John O'Toole echoed that thought in his book, *The Trouble with Advertising,* when he wrote that creative pretesting "is misused when deductions made from commercials that have tested well are allowed to dictate rigid formats to which all future commercials must be written." Still, many clients view creative testing as "insurance on their investment," and agencies are in great need of researchers who can deal with the challenge.

It's worth noting that even such an avowed proponent of advertising research as Ogilvy felt the field had some serious glitches. In *On Advertising* he writes, "Grateful as I am to the researchers who have helped me to produce effective advertising, I have nine bones to pick with them." Two especially hit home for me: 1. "Advertising research is full of fads. In the sixties we saw Eye Cameras, Latin Squares, Facturals, Randomized Blocks, Greco-Latin Squares. Some of them were useful, but all went out of fashion." 2. "Worst of all, researchers use pretentious jargon—such as *attitudinal paradigms, judgementally, demassification, reconceptualize, suboptimal, symbiotic linkage, splinterization.*"

A relatively new research-related function called account planning is slowly arriving on the scene after years of use by agencies in Great Britain. In the United States it seems to be taking two slightly different directions. At left-brain agencies, an **account planner** uses the latest marketing research resources to aid account managers to develop strategic plans; in other words, it's a hybrid research-account management role. At right-brain agencies, the account planner still employs research techniques but works for the creative department and is charged with "bringing the feel of the marketplace" to the entire account team. The planner takes the position of the targeted consumer in the development process and is responsible for the message being relevant and effective. Chiat/Day/Mojo, a consistent winner of major creative awards, has been using and advocating this method since the early 1980s, but to date few other U.S. agencies have found favor with the practice. The biggest complaint is that account planning seems mostly to duplicate services already provided by the research and account services departments.

How to Work Well with Your Research Department Colleagues   As mentioned before, you will be fortunate to have this service housed under your agency roof. But whether you employ an outside firm or rely on fellow employees, the same five rules apply:

1. You can't be expected to be an expert on research, but you can still push hard for *actionable* results. Too many times the findings are interesting but impossible to implement. As a result, the study gathers dust on a back shelf and is of little value in making marketing decisions. It's not that researchers have their heads in the clouds; they want action, too, but they can get wrapped up in the nuances of methodology and neglect to ask the right questions. An account manager should go over every questionnaire with a critical eye to make sure the potential answers can lead to concrete action. Any vague or extraneous questions should be weeded out. For example, it will do a fast-food client little good to find out that consumers like specially cut french fries if he does not have the resources to install such equipment in his restaurants. However, if he learns that consumers want cleanliness even more than convenience or menu variety, he can put extra emphasis on that operationally (and perhaps in his advertising).

2. I'll echo what I said earlier: Clients need to understand the limitations of focus group research. It is stimulating to observe but is not intended to, and cannot produce, projectible information. The group sessions are useful for gaining clues and insights but cannot be substituted for full-bore field research with a statistically reliable sample. You and your research associates must educate clients so they do not have inflated expectations about focus group results.

3. Ogilvy told fledgling researchers in *On Advertising,* "You must also be able to work sympathetically with creative people, most of whom are stubbornly allergic to research." A sensitive account manager can play a strong role in smoothing that working relationship. You can help the creative team interpret research reports and can be a conduit to ensure that their concerns are covered in future surveys. You can also help the researchers to understand the "You're killing my baby!" fears of writers and art directors. And you can guard against clients putting too much blind faith in creative pretesting.

4. Keep abreast of all the latest research techniques and discuss them at length with your research partners. Be conversant with new developments in psychographic (or lifestyle) research such as VALS (Values and Lifestyles Survey). The more you know, the better equipped you'll be to answer research questions inside the agency and at the client.

5. Contrary to what you might guess, many clients are reluctant to spend money on research. They view it as either "too academic" or "too expensive and sophisticated for us." Consequently, if you see the true worth of a research project and can be instrumental in selling it, you will significantly boost your standing with the research department. Look for these opportunities and make the most of them.

The fifth basic function, finance and administration, is the only one that is not indigenous to advertising agency culture. It is part of the routine of any business: answering the phones, handling correspondence, keeping the files, billing clients, paying bills, keeping employee records—in short, traditional office management. Its importance cannot be denied. Obviously, without a solid business manager at the helm, any agency will struggle to keep afloat. But the generic aspects of this subject are covered exhaustively in other books and classes, and this book isn't out to add to that body of knowledge—with two exceptions: cost accounting and compensation for agency services. These special topics are complex enough to deserve several pages of explanation in the next chapter. Steel yourself—it is not easy reading.

"It's a delicate balance," wrote Ogilvy about working relationships within an advertising agency. And so it is, much like the fabled high wire act of the Flying Wallandas. That's why anyone aspiring to run an advertising agency must master all the inner workings of this curious creature. Those who falter in this business often are individuals with tunnel vision. They understand all too well their narrow specialty, but they've never bothered to learn the nuances of the other departments. Small wonder that these people are passed over when it comes time to select the men and women who are destined to run important account groups or satellite offices. Over and again, I have seen agencies in turmoil because the new general manager simply didn't understand what made the media department tick, or (much more often) he or she could not cope with the unorthodox culture of the creative department.

How can one avoid this narrow-mindedness? I have no one-sentence answer but suggest that the key is for you to make extra efforts to reach out to other staffers in your shop. Some basic knowledge can be acquired by reading trade books and articles, but the most complete education comes from dialogue with those master pilots in departments down the hall, up one floor, or across the street. Ogilvy was fond of saying that the best hobby for anyone working for him was *advertising,* and to that refrain I would add "and advertising agencies." I submit that pound-for-pound there exists today no more fascinating business culture on this planet.

ASSESSING THE ACCOUNTS

Should you covet assignment to certain kinds of accounts when you finally are hired? Yes, but more than likely you'll have little voice in the matter. Initially, you'll be placed on either (a) the busiest or (b) the most troubled account in the agency. And for very logical reasons: That's where help is needed—sometimes desperately.

Once you manage to prove your worth, say in a year or more, it is time to prepare a personal game plan for the future. It's a cold-eyed fact of life that all accounts are not regarded with equal favor in any agency. Most folks on the outside would say, "Well, of course! Everyone knows that the biggest accounts are the most important. Conspire to work on those, and you're on the inside track."

Sounds like a foolproof approach, right? There are, however, a couple of notable snakes in this seemingly tall clover. For one, big accounts can equate with big committees and bureaucratic approval procedures. This can be deadly to the health of first-rate advertising, not to mention the agency account team. Early on, you owe it to yourself to be involved and associated with the best work possible. 'Tis far better to labor on a smaller piece of business that makes heads turn, than on a monolith that continually produces just okay advertising. However, if the account is large both financially *and* creatively, by all means do whatever you can to work on it.

Second, the biggest clients are not always the most profitable. They ought to be, you would think, but the advertising world is rarely a 2 + 2 = 4 kind of business. Large clients demand large chunks of agency services and don't always feel beholden to pay for them. It's not uncommon for the account compensation to be based mostly on media commissions, and when a sizable budget is suddenly severely cut back, the agency's main source of income disappears. They've invested the talent time, but unless these costs can be recovered via fee income, there's not much that can be done except to wait for next year's program and hope it doesn't suffer the same fate.

Now, a fair question at this point would be, Just what kinds of accounts *should* you angle for?

1. Try to work on as many *different* accounts as the agency allows. The more varied your total experience, the better off you'll be later on. And *don't* duck those "industrial" or business-to-business clients. Maybe their products seem boring compared to consumer goods,

but the chances are frequently greater for doing standout work and making the sales charts jump. From the beginning, try to avoid being typecast as a "package goods," or a "financial services," or any other narrow-specialty account person. That can happen when you are placed on a single big piece of business which consumes all of your time. You end up knowing that industry to a faretheewell but know zip about any other market category.

2. After you have logged enough time to have some say about your account assignments, seek to work on ones with these attributes:
   a. Consistently approve noteworthy creative work and are a favorite of your agency's top copy and art people.
   b. Have a large enough budget that the ads have decent visibility in the marketplace.
   c. Are committed to growth and eager to capture more market share.
   d. Have savvy client marketing and advertising management—people you can learn from.
   e. Either make money now for the agency or possess a legitimate opportunity for money to be made in the near future.

Realize that you will never know enough about your client's business if you restrict your learning to business hours. Even to begin to understand it you need to be "on call," spending evenings and weekends reading relevant trade journals, studying competitors' ads, calling on distributors and retailers, talking to actual users of the products or services (plus using them yourself), and being ever alert to items of interest in all media. "Their business is your business," said William E. Phillips when he was president of Ogilvy & Mather. "The most successful account managers at virtually all major agencies owe their success to deep involvement in the business of one or more major clients." (Incidentally, that kind of involvement includes total allegiance to the client's products or services. For example, if you're working on a Pepsi distributor's account, never order a Coke in public. If you're assigned to the area Burger King account, don't ever be seen munching a Big Mac. How do clients react when they spot such an infidelity? *Adweek* recently carried a story about the day a new agency man paid his first visit to the Champion footwear headquarters while wearing Nikes. " 'Let me take a look at those,' barked the Champion president. The next thing [the agency guy] knew, the Nikes were flying out the third-story window, and he was fitted with a pair of Champions." In my experience, he was lucky the client allowed him to remove the shoes before they were tossed out the window.)

Be leery of playing the role of Captain Marvel. There are situations in which your presence might indeed help convert a shaky account into a solid one. But let's face it: Miracle turnarounds are rarely achieved on this planet. In Ogilvy's words, "Some [clients] behave so badly that no agency could produce effective advertising for them."

If you sense that the current account manager is a bumbler, then by all means go for a "savior" assignment on an account that is in hot water. However, don't overestimate your ability to effect change. Accounts that have bad people calling the shots are going to make even the best and brightest newcomer look bad. In the words of Jerry Della Femina, "The advertising business is full of thick-headed guys." If you confirm that this is the case, strive mightily to dodge the valley of death assignment. Unless the client's people reform, you are essentially doomed. Account management labor of this kind is detrimental to your reputation (and your digestive tract). Will ducking such a task hurt your chances for other advancement in the agency? Short-term—depending on your boss—it might cast a cloud. But longer range, you will be far better off to sidestep grim reaper accounts.

SORTING OUT THE BOSSES

Volumes have been written by business gurus about the importance of mentors, and I echo their basic sentiments. Unfortunately, the chances of having a free hand in picking your boss are decidedly limited when you're chasing those first jobs.

Bosses, like agencies, are not all created equal, and it will pay enormous dividends to your career if you can spend time early on with someone really good (as opposed to someone really average). The reasons for dwelling on this are obvious: You can learn a lot from blue-ribbon people, and you can pick up a lot of bad habits from the also-rans. That's one of the shining advantages of working for a highly regarded small agency: Because there are relatively few employees and no layers of management, the track is cleared to associate with the top performers. There's generally a limited window of opportunity here, though, because the good small agencies do not remain small for long.

Regardless of the agency's size, you should seek out, scheme, and connive to work for the men and women who are leading the charge. The situation closely parallels setting up your course schedule in college. It was common knowledge who the best profs and instructors were (and who were the easiest and most obtuse). The challenge was to find some way to get into their classes. Ditto in the agency world. It won't take you long to identify the best of breed. Just remember that human brilliance follows no fixed physical or emotional formula; you cannot gauge mental depth on the basis of looks or personality. In his book *The Effective Executive,* Peter Drucker made the point that

> among the effective executives I have known and worked with, there are extroverts and aloof, retiring men, some even morbidly shy. Some are

eccentrics, others painfully correct conformists. Some are fat, and some are lean. Some are worriers, some are relaxed. Some drink quite heavily, others are total abstainers. Some are men of great charm and warmth, some have no more personality than a frozen mackerel.

This learning experience will not likely be an easy one. When David Ogilvy wrote in *Confessions* about "men of genius in advertising agencies," he remarked, "Almost without exception they are disagreeable." He compared employment in great agencies with the elation and agony of working for Winston Churchill:

> He drank like a fish. He was capricious and wilful. When opposed, he sulked. He was rude to fools. He was wildly extravagant. He wept on the slightest provocation. His conversation was Rabelaisian. He was inconsiderate to his staff. Yet, Lord Alanbrooke, his Chief of Staff, could write: "I shall always look back on the years I worked with him as some of the most difficult and trying ones in my life. For all that, I thank God that I was given the opportunity of working alongside of such a man, and having my eyes opened to the fact that occasionally such supermen exist on this earth."

Compounding all of this is the fact that many of the best agency leaders are not ipso facto terrific teachers. They are not equipped to give you the kindly professor routine, much as you might crave it. For one thing, the best ones seem always to be slightly overbooked. They're running hard, sprinting from meeting to meeting, skipping lunches, catching planes, and making sure clients aren't lonely. They simply don't have time to conduct a formal training program. Then, too, there is an intuitive touch possessed by the best agency leaders that is extremely difficult to put into words. It's a combination of innate understanding and trial-by-fire experience that defies pat explanation. To expect this to be transferred to you with mere words is like asking O. J. Simpson to tell you how to make open field cuts carrying a muddy football.

"Hey, wait a minute," you say. "If that's the case, what's the point of straining to work with and for these folks? I might be better off going to some *Ad Age* workshop." No. It's a matter of opening yourself up to what's going on around you. You can learn a lot just by watching and listening to the best agency people. Plus, on the bright side, there are many strong agency geniuses who *are* also good, straight-on mentors. Perhaps you'll be fortunate enough to latch on with one of these Plato types.

Now, let's consider another darkside possibility: You discover that your newly assigned boss is less than spectacular; in fact, he or she is pretty ineffective. You can't turn your back on this person and pretend he or she doesn't exist—that's job poisoning. I suggest you make the best of what you have, but simultaneously begin to employ a simple, two-pronged guerrilla strategy. First, in your spare time find ways to be in the vicinity of your mentor-elect: coffee breaks, lunches, and beers after work, for example. Or come up with a suitable excuse for hanging around after hours when this individual is rehearsing a major presentation. Hone your listening skills and be a sounding board if needed. And don't be too sophisticated to run errands, find props, and deliver things. Stretch your imagination to find new ways to be invaluable to this person.

Then, once you've got your assigned responsibilities covered, make it your personal crusade to learn everything possible about the accounts of your heroes and heroines. This will have to be above and beyond your regular workload, or you'll quickly tick off your less-than-spectacular supervisor. Talk to the media planner/buyer about the radio buy rationale on these accounts. If there are research reports, read them, and probe the conclusions with the research people. Understand the creative strategy and get to know the writer and art director responsible. Scan the trade press for tidbits that might be of interest to these clients. In short, become the unofficial backup person. Then, when the need arises to have a new person added to your preferred mentor's accounts, *voila!* who else could it be but you!

As you hunt for jobs, remember that bosses represent a crucial one third of the holy trinity of career accomplishment. If you really want to make a mark in advertising, be *very* selective about (1) the agency you work for, (2) the accounts you work on, and (3) the people you work under. If you get that trio right, only your own lack of talent will keep you from leaping tall buildings with a single bound.

PREVIEWING THE CAREER PATHS

Ah, the eternal quest for more responsibility and bigger raises. Just what are the typical rungs on the career ladder at an ad agency? Not too surprisingly, advancement opportunities are directly related to the size of the agency and the magnitude of the accounts involved. In the smaller shops, there is the basic 1-2-3 upgrading scheme: Initially you join the firm in a junior or entry-level capacity. In the account management area this is sometimes labeled junior or assistant account manager (or executive), sometimes account coordinator. Don't fret about your first title—what matters is *you've been hired*! If you're any good at all, soon (say, within a year) you will be bumped up a notch, certainly with more responsibility and generally a better title (but not always—some agencies move with great caution because they fear client reaction: "It's nice that Ellie has been promoted to account manager, but does that mean I won't see Ben, our senior person, anymore? I mean after all, she's just a *kid*!"). Pay no attention to that stuff—believe me, sooner than you like, you will have too many gray hairs to be called a rookie anymore.

Stage two is to be a full-fledged account manager. In some firms, that later is boosted to senior account manager, a signal that you have more experience.

The third rung in a small agency might be president. After all, if you have a dozen people total on staff, it doesn't make any sense to have a lot of layers. In larger agencies, you will become an account supervisor (curiously, advertising is one business in which being a "supervisor" is higher status than being an "executive" or a "manager") and, later, a management supervisor or perhaps director of client services. This indicates that you have one or more people working under you, but it doesn't mean you can abdicate responsibility or lighten your workload. In fact, the job pressure will increase with each upward move on the organization chart.

As for the other departments, predictably each has its own litany of job titles. In the print production department, neophytes are called assistants or coordinators and, with seasoning, advance to become production (or traffic) supervisors. The top title is production manager, although in bigger firms there may be more than one person carrying this business card, each responsible for a different group of accounts.

Media, on the other hand, offers a smorgasbord of titles. Rank beginners again are either assistants or coordinators. The next notch up is to be a buyer (first as junior, then full-fledged, and finally senior buyer). If the agency is good-sized, then another promotion might be to planner, but in smaller shops buying and planning are always rolled into one job. Some agencies like to have their media people specialize so that one individual is in charge of print only or television only. There are media managers and media supervisors in the upper reaches of the department, but generally the top spot is media director. However, it's not unusual to have assistant media directors and co-media directors as well.

Research departments for small and medium-sized agencies, if they exist at all, are thinly staffed. It's unusual to have more than two or three people in this area with the boss having the title of research director or research manager. His or her assistant is labeled just that. If anyone else is in the department, they probably are handling clerical or statistical duties.

In the creative department, one travels either the copy track or the art trail. Fledgling scribes are initially junior copywriters and progress to senior copywriter or even copy chief (a title not much in vogue anymore). Graphics men and women generally start as "wrists," people who do layout and pasteup work at the behest of the senior folks. The best of the lot evolve to the art director stage, first as junior and ultimately as senior art director. If there's a good-sized department, the person in charge will likely be called executive art director. The next bump up is to become a creative supervisor. These people can emerge from either copy or art, but they must be multidimensional—able to deal equally well with words and pictures. They are second only to the high priest of the area, the creative director, who can be the single most important person in the entire agency. There are all kinds of group titles (e.g., "Creative Director, High Technology

Group") in the big shops, but since this book is not intended to be a compendium on big agency life, I'm not going to mention the many possible additional job titles.

In any department, a further form of annointing is to be named a vice president. This should be a hard-earned reward for years of commendable performance, but some agencies have twenty employees and ten vice presidents. The title has been ladled out so generously that it doesn't always have the same meaning as in other fields. (This can grate on clients, too, who live in organizations where one labors for fifteen years to be named an assistant vice president and the only folks appointed vice president are five years away from retirement.) If becoming an officer means crossing the threshold of ownership—in other words, acquisition of some agency stock is tied to the promotion—then, I submit, you can genuinely feel the VP title is something to crow about. (More about agency ownership later in this chapter.) Down the line come senior vice president and executive vice president appointments, plus department management or general office management designations. And, as I said earlier, in the big agencies, there are all kinds of group titles to contend with.

While the various job titles are captivating to newcomers, I wouldn't worry about making sure you have them committed to memory. What I would worry about is consciously monitoring where you stand with your employer. Since the management of any vibrant agency is almost always on the run, many bosses are remiss in letting staffers know how they're doing on a regular basis. It doesn't mean they are ducking the issue; it just keeps getting pushed aside as flash fires flare up. When you encounter these conditions, you must professionally press for regular reviews of your performance. If you don't know for sure how your boss regards your work, you can only guess about your chances for advancement.

Above all, if your lot doesn't improve within a reasonable period of time, don't be lulled into thinking, "It'll all work out if I work hard and hold up my end of the bargain." That's what Chamberlain thought when he visited Hitler in 1938. Take Jo Foxworth's counsel, "Don't sweat out a mismatch. . . . Living is now—the only time you are ever sure to have."

EVALUATING JOB (IN)SECURITY

At business functions when others learn my occupation, they respond like a stuck record, "Boy, there's sure a lot of anxiety in your field. Did you ever lie awake nights wondering if you'd have a job the next morning?" No, I've always slept just fine. But there is some truth in the stories about the unpredictability of ad agency staffing. If you are the kind of person who dotes on job security and wants the tightest of pension and retirement plans, life in the ad agency lane may fray your nerves.

On any given day an agency can lose a major account and that means a major reduction in income. The only way to compensate for such loss is to add other business or to reduce expenses—that is, cut staff. Because that kind of news frequently makes headlines in the trade press, it is little wonder that advertising agencies are stereotyped as having about as much job security as do ice cubes in the tropics. And, I have to admit, accounts can be lost for the most out-of-the-blue reasons. For example, in the spring of 1988, cigarette maker R. J. Reynolds–Nabisco took away $70 to $80 million (yes, *million!*) in billings from Saatchi & Saatchi DFS Compton because the agency created a TV commercial announcing Northwest Airlines' ban on smoking. The trade press reported, "Executives of several other major advertising agencies expressed surprise at the move, especially because the agency was handling no tobacco products. They said the move seemed to reflect a broadening of conflict-of-interest concerns among more agency clients."

Horror stories aside, though, I don't think the situation in ad agencies is far different from that in most other walks of business life. While people once joined companies as "lifers" and planned to spend twenty-five, thirty, or more years building a "comfortable retirement," today's professionals are experiencing a much more volatile work place. Mergers and acquisitions in all fields have caused unexpected consolidations, cutbacks, layoffs, and early retirements. Offshore competition and periodic soft economic conditions have forced even large corporations to trim departments and dramatically change hiring practices. Maybe the current state of American business can best be summed up in the quote by professional basketball coach Hubie Brown: "These days no matter what you do for a living, you're always one step away from the street."

And, as with all myths, there is a great deal of exaggeration in the tales of how "cutthroat and insecure" life is at an advertising agency. Jerry Della Femina fanned these fires considerably when he wrote *From Those Wonderful Folks Who Gave You Pearl Harbor* in 1970. Among many dark tales of advertising life in New York, he recalls an agency president who once told him, "I start worrying about losing an account the minute I get it. The minute I sign the contract, I'm one step closer toward losing it." Some other stellar doomsday comments include:

Most account guys live with fear in their hearts.

You've got to be afraid. You spend every day knowing that if you blow it, you're out for a year.

Usually the large agencies have a **killer** to do the firing. Most agencies have one killer; the bigger agencies might have two killers. . . . If every new guy who shows up doesn't start producing immediately, the killer wants them taken care of.

Della Femina declares "You go to work in this business and if you last for five years the chances are you're going to be fired the next day. Seniority means nothing. This is not the railroads."

Close inspection, though, will reveal that good accounts at good agencies do not move all that frequently. To cite just a few at the national level: Kellogg's has been with Leo Burnett since 1949; AT&T first hired N. W. Ayer in 1908; Kodak dates from 1930 at J. Walter; and GE and BBDO have been married since 1920. Strong and profitable account relationships lasting five to twenty years are commonplace. And agencies with the best reputations rarely undergo wild gyrations in staffing.

Are there any ways to enhance your chances of survival when your agency is facing a layoff? Sure, but it's no great mystery: Just be first-rate at your job. The wagging mouths in the industry are always crying about people losing jobs, but isn't it interesting that some people never end up on the beach? Good times and bad, their careers move brightly ahead. Either they're too valuable to be handed a pink slip when the Glitzo account goes South or they'll be hired presto by someone else (maybe even by Glitzo's new agency).

Of course, the best job security of all is to move into an ownership position—where you are the hirer and firer, not the hiree and firee. This is especially true as you find yourself aging past fifty. A 1989 survey of 400 companies by the American Association of Retired Persons found that older workers in many companies felt "subtle pressures to make them feel uncomfortable and unwanted." You'll find even more of this prejudice in the advertising industry where people constantly harp about "being *with it*."

The bottom line about job security is that it is not as bad as frequently rumored, it's easier to land a job when you're under fifty, and it can have its moments of madness. For example, even a highly creative, "hot" agency can occasionally lose a major client, as when Fallon McElligott managed to lose the $8 million (!) US West account in early 1988 (see Figure 1.3).

PROBING THE PAY AND THE PERKS

What! You mean you're not going into the business for eleemosynary reasons! And, you actually harbor notions of making *big bucks*? "Well, good luck." That's what you will likely hear if you confess your ambition to older members of the agency club as you make your job-hunting rounds. (In a 1986 survey of advertising professionals by *Esquire Magazine,* the "worst" aspect of their work was "the pay.")

The truth is harder to pin down, but here are the general rules of the road: Entry-level jobs tend to pay poorly—in many smaller markets, worse than teaching or social work. Forget what you've read about bright MBAs getting $50,000 and up in their first Big Apple job. That's Planet Wall

'Creative' letters cost ad agency big client

By PAULA FROKE
The Associated Press

MINNEAPOLIS—An award-winning advertising agency has drawn the wrath of feminist groups and lost an $8 million client after it sent a photograph of an African boy kissing a cow's backside to a woman who called one of their ads sexist.

"My reaction was almost disbelief that in this day and age anybody could be so insensitive and so contemptuous of a member of the public," Kay Taylor of the Minnesota Women's Consortium said Wednesday.

She said the consortium had mailed copies of the photo to other clients of Fallon McElligott, which has gained national recognition in the advertising world for its often-offbeat campaigns.

Agency chairman Patrick R. Fallon has apologized, saying agency executives had "allowed our reaction to your criticism to sweep us beyond the bounds of judgment, taste and common decency," but the incident has cost the Minneapolis-based agency its sixth-largest client.

The dispute began when Neala Schleuning, director of the Mankato Women's Center, wrote in October to Charles S. Anderson of Duffy Design Group, a Fallon McElligott affiliate, criticizing parts of a presentation he had made to a marketing conference.

Schleuning also objected to a poster ad for the television show "Dynasty" that prominently features the phrase "Bitch, Bitch, Bitch."

Anderson responded with a Nov. 7 letter and a photograph of a naked African boy kissing the backside of a cow.

"As the enclosed photo clearly illustrates, the Dinka tribe of East Africa has a rather barbaric ritual that has apparently been going on for centuries," Anderson wrote. "I pass it along to you believing that you will be able to deal with these people in the same firm, yet even-handed manner in which you dealt with us."

When Schleuning objected, Fallon wrote that he was "appalled" that Anderson had not made arrangements to pay for an African visit and offered to pay the full cost of a one-way trip.

Creative director Tom McElligott wrote Schleuning on Dec. 7 to say her "amusing" letter had entertained 150 people around the company bulletin board, and he called her the company's "brave missionary to the Dinkas."

US West, one of the regional telephone companies formed when the Bell System was broken up, announced last week it would drop an account with Fallon McElligott worth $8 million to $10 million annually.

US West spokeswoman Robin Baca said her company had been pleased with Fallon McElligott's performance. The agency, founded six years ago, won Advertising Age magazine's agency-of-the-year award after just two years in business and has won 46 industry Clio awards.

"But US West has a strong and longstanding commitment to pluralism and equal opportunity," she said.

FIGURE 1.3 The news of the US West account departure startled the ad world but showed dramatically how agencies can lose clients even when the work wins awards.

Street, light-years away from the ad agency galaxy. Salaries—even in larger firms in larger markets—start *low* at advertising agencies. Some of this is due to tradition ("In the old days you always started in the mail room," etc.), but mostly it's a matter of supply and demand: Most years there are more applicants than jobs, so beginning pay suffers accordingly.

That's the bleak side. The shiny side is that—unlike teaching or social work—if you're good, you can, in relatively few years, make a lot more money. This is dramatically true for creative people, but next in line would be the account service folks. Regrettably, those in the media, research, and production departments are on a slower track.

The two keys to bumper-crop remuneration are (1) doing first-rate work on accounts important to the agency and (2) making significant contributions to the winning of new clients. Now here's the catch: It is rare for an account manager to make the grade on points 1 or 2 until he or she hits that magic age of thirty, or at least *looks* like that magic age. Interestingly, this does not hold true for early-blooming writers and art directors, who are less visible on a daily basis. In the account service area, however, clients have a decided tendency to downplay agency people who don't look as though they have enough experience. (And let's face it: You *will* be a lot more knowledgeable at thirty-four than at twenty-six.) Ogilvy, in *Confessions,* says in his typical all-knowing manner:

> However hard you work, and however knowledgeable you become, you will be unable to represent your agency at the client's policy levels until you are at least thirty-five. One of my partners owes the rapidity of his ascent to the fact he went bald when he was thirty, and another had the good fortune to become white-headed at forty. Be patient.

That seems a bit strong to me, but, alas, for young agency people, there are more than a few grains of truth in his statement.

It's typical to be underpaid until you're approaching thirty, and then to make some pretty good bucks. The old saw for account managers was to be sure to earn at least their age (i.e., $27,000 annually at 27; $30,000 at 30, etc.). In smaller markets, when you first start out that might still be a reasonable objective, but in larger markets it certainly wouldn't hold true anymore. In all major cities, the cost of living—especially housing—has driven salaries wildly upward in the past few years. For what it's worth, the annual salary survey conducted by *Adweek* gave these salaries as average for 1990: copywriter—$39,000; art director—$37,700; account manager—$35,600; media buyer/planner—$24,500. Typical salaries for the top people in each department are much higher; for example, vice presidents in creative departments average $66,400 and VPs in account management $63,200. On the client side, advertising managers average $42,600 and public relations directors $44,600.

Between ages thirty and forty-five (but *especially* between thirty and forty), you will find the greatest opportunity to multiply your income by moving from one agency to another. Ideally, your employer will reward you to the point where you don't need to even think about switching. But all too often in reality, internal salary increases will not match offers from other agencies. This is a critical time in your career, not just from a compensation standpoint but also in determining where you want to end up at age fifty and beyond. (Jerry Della Femina told his readers in *From Those Wonderful Folks* . . . , "The average age of the account executive is thirty-two, thirty-three, and then *they start lying about their age* [italics mine]." Later he talked about an account person who'd spent six months looking for a job. "Age 52. Chances, zip. Who's going to hire him?")

Even during the early years of your career it's smart to press for regular performance reviews with your boss to determine exactly where you stand. If you don't know for certain how management regards your work, you may badly misjudge your salary potential. Such performance critiques don't have to be stiffly formal with a checklist published by a human relations guru; they can be conversations over an early breakfast, or over a beer or fruit juice after a long day. Just be adamant that they occur at least twice yearly and that you take careful note of what is said.

A streetwise rule of thumb: In your first decade of agency work, if you aren't progressing/growing/advancing to your satisfaction every three years, take a hard look at moving on. Of course, if the place is sensational, you love it, and you're stretching your mind, maybe the rule doesn't apply. But don't allow yourself to mold in a dead-end situation. Jo Foxworth in *Wising Up* advises women, "If you haven't had a raise or praise in a year and a half or if your raise is a routine one passed along without comment, it's about time to move."

Incidentally, some men and women have interviewed at our agency with the mistaken idea that account managers are paid like hard goods salespeople: on a commission basis for work sold. This is way off base for any truly professional shop. Likewise is the notion that you will get overtime or comp time. Not likely. If you're looking for something that pays well by the hour, longshoring is a far superior elective.

In addition to straight salary, however, there are a couple of extra means of compensation that should not be discounted. Bonuses are the number one add-on. Agencies that are doing outstanding work and making strong profits can offer some very attractive bonus programs. (Of course, it helps a great deal if these agencies also have generous owners.) Generally, bonuses are paid once a year, and the (again beware of generalizations) payment guideline is equivalent to five to fifteen percent of annual salary. The most important people are again going to receive from the most important bonuses.

The other key benefit is profit sharing. This is rarely offered until after you've been with the firm for a year or two, and then it takes three to ten more years to "vest" fully (i.e., until you have rights to 100 percent of the money in your p/s account). Hard to warm up to at an early age, because the money is locked up until late in life (or until you bail out to take a job elsewhere), but it can be very meaningful in the longer haul. And, in addition to being an attractive retirement security blanket, a p/s plan also shields money from income taxes, which will be increasingly important to you as your salary rises. The tax laws are constantly in flux, though, so you need to weigh the value of your plan in light of the latest rulings.

Some employers offer a special savings plan labeled by the U.S. government as a "401(k)." It offers three attractive benefits: (1) You can invest up to approximately $8,000 in the plan and defer taxes on the whole amount. (2) Any earnings you gain are also tax-deferred. Typically, you'll have a choice of three investment options, although some companies have offered as many as seven. (3) Most employers will match part of your contributions, usually 50 cents on the dollar up to 6 percent of your pay. The money is locked up until age 59 1/2, however, and you can make withdrawals only in case of hardship.

Other perks are in the long-term picture, too, such as autos or reimbursement of auto expenses, extended health care, liberal expense accounts, and club memberships, and these in time can add up nicely. These are all carrots dangling in the future, though, as fledgling account managers are rarely offered more than a basic medical plan for starters.

Now, as to ultimately being featured on "Lifestyles of the Rich and Famous"—in my dour view, your chances aren't so hot. You can make a very handsome living as the valued employee of an advertising agency, but there is only one way to make good money *and* end up with some job security in your advancing years. That's spelled o-w-n-e-r-s-h-i-p and is the topic discussed in the next section.

LOOKING TOWARD OWNERSHIP

When it comes to total compensation packages, I'm not big on pension plans and retirement benefits, and I'm skeptical about Social Security. I acknowledge the value of medical/dental coverage, but they don't stir my deepest emotions. Even good pay and profit sharing fail to move me in comparison to the greatest agency carrot of all: ownership. Oh, certainly it is unrealistic to fret about this when you are first starting out. Obviously, it is not a subject to dwell on when you are finally offered that first decent job. But once you feel in your bones that the advertising agency business is for you, then *immediately* set as your highest long-term priority the goal of being more than a hired hand.

To make such a big deal about this may be puzzling to some of my colleagues. After all, ownership of anything brings a whole Pandora's box of responsibilities, not to mention gastric distress. It's not for everyone, thank goodness, because opportunities for latching onto a piece of the action are definitely limited.

"All right," you say, "then just *who* is best suited to withstand the slings and arrows of agency ownership?" Actually they're fairly easy to spot. It's those few who possess a classic entrepreneurial mentality—individuals who (borrowing from Webster) "organize, manage and assume the risks of a business." In other words, men and women who always spend a client's money as though it were their own. People who consider risk to be a natural element of business life—something to be treated with respect but not with trepidation. These are the adventurous souls, who are happiest when making the tough decisions that mean the future for them and their agency.

As your career rolls along, you'll be busy fending off the evil spirits of mediocrity that beset the advertising agency world. You'll be working for an agency of consequence—that's good. What's not so good is that such agencies become tempting targets for big shops on an acquisition prowl. The bad news is that if your shop is gobbled up, there go your chances to snare meaningful equity. But if your agency of choice is not afflicted by the merger/acquisition mania sweeping the land, maybe—just maybe—there is a signal opportunity flashing ahead. Some persons *on the premises* own this shop, and your goal should be to join them.

You will also have to face up to your own personal financial temptations. For example, what do you do when you have the option of either making a lot of money for a good, big agency owned by a holding company or making not-so-big bucks with a good independent offering you a legitimate chance to own stock? Don't think twice, I say. Unless vultures are circling low on your horizon, and you *have* to have that money right now, sign on with the independent.

"Wait a minute," you respond. "Don't the big agencies offer stock ownership plans as well?" Yes, some do, and some are not at all bad. But there is a *huge* difference between being one of 1,000 shareholders and one of 20 shareholders. It's nice to own some shares in the agency, but my counsel is to be in a position to eventually own enough voting stock to have a say in running the company. Only at that point will you feel completely in control of your working life.

"Well," you shrug, "it's all very well to preach, but how in the world can a younger agency person even consider buying into an agency unless he or she has a rich uncle? Why, previously in this very book, it was pointed out that salaries are not all that fantastic in the early career years." True, this whole section falls into the "plan ahead" category. But it's not too early to begin to identify those agencies whose management believes in the concept of employee ownership. Sad to say, many smaller agencies are essentially feudal kingdoms with one principal owner—all too frequently without a succession plan in place. Over the long haul you should be wary of these situations. This business is rife with stories of good people being promised an equity position by a sole owner who later changed his or her mind or somehow just never got around to it.

Fortunately, there are other independents with broader-base ownership. These are the frigates on which you should book passage. The agency I helped found, Borders, Perrin and Norrander, is one. Cole & Weber was another prior to acquisition by Ogilvy & Mather. There are other similarly enlightened agencies that have plans in place to provide an opportunity for good people to join the ownership family. Generally this is accomplished via some kind of bonus program. Either the stock is offered as a pure bonus in lieu of cash or a cash bonus is provided with the understanding that it will be used to purchase stock. Sometimes, options are available in which the employee receives some stock as a bonus and has the chance to purchase more on his or her own hook. (Incidentally, the stock bonus seems less succulent when you realize that it is treated by the IRS as income and you must pay taxes on it.)

Also bear in mind that most of these agencies are closed companies and the stock cannot be traded on an exchange. It therefore has only book value, not market value, and you must relinquish it at book prices if you leave the agency. If the agency is doing well, the stock *will* appreciate, but I don't view it primarily as a short-term investment vehicle. Instead, I see it as the best means to achieve a position as a managing partner within the firm. And, *long term,* it can be a terrific investment.

A few agencies have solved the issue by adopting government-regulated ESOPs, or employee stock ownership plans, which offer some significant, but complicated, tax benefits. Unfortunately, ESOPs can be costly to set up (legal fees and an outside appraisal of the true market worth of the agency can run thousands of dollars), and government requirements can be stressful to deal with. But in the right situation, an ESOP can be the perfect answer. For example, in the fall of 1990, the daily *Oregonian* reported that the eighteen employees of the Young & Roehr ad agency—an $18 million shop with a nice roster of high-tech and transportation accounts—used the ESOP method to buy out co-founders Jerry Young and Frank Roehr.

Yes, my "absolute admonition" to become an owner is too simplistic. There are many problems and complications about the process. And it is only too true that many who seek ownership are going to be denied the chance because the existing owners just can't let go. But all that aside, I urge you to keep one thing in mind. If the agency is doing great work and making money, and you have an opportunity to share in the ownership, *jump on it!* even if short term it means less cash in your pockets. Nothing's certain in this business, but owning a piece of the mother ship certainly gives you a rare chance to steer your own destiny.

OBSERVING THE STEPSISTER, THE PUBLIC RELATIONS AGENCY

"Are public relations agencies the same as ad agencies?" you ask. No, agencies specializing in PR services are distinctly different from their advertising counterparts. Their role covers all communications that influence public opinion. They focus on publicity (or "editorial placement")—getting their clients featured in media news coverage—and in a host of related public exposure activities, including speeches, press conferences, community forums, special events, and the like. PR agencies frequently deal with government agencies, shareholders, labor unions, employees, neighborhoods, and other appropriate "publics." They do occasionally resort to paid advertising as a weapon to attack certain public awareness problems (such as communicate their client's side in a nasty labor strike), but advertising per se is not their primary thrust.

It is uncommon to have a PR account person who cannot write news releases, and most seem to come from a news media background. In fact, it appears that the training ground for most PR agencies is not under their own roofs but outside in the news departments of radio, TV, and print publications. If you really hanker to work in PR, that is the place to cut your teeth. The exception to the rule seems to be in the computer technology industry. Wild-eyed growth has fueled the need for people who can communicate the esoterics of this field, and if you know and love computers, doors will open. This is the only conspicuous area where smaller agencies are talking about "doing our own training, because we can't find enough knowledgeable people on the outside."

There is a vociferous divergence of opinion as to whether advertising and PR services should be offered by the same agency. Back in 1963, when David Ogilvy first published *Confessions,* he proudly declared, "We have no Public Relations Department. I take the view that public relations should be handled by the manufacturer himself, or by specialist counsel." Today, however, now that he has retired to a baronial chateau in France, the Ogilvy organization *does* include PR on its list of services.

Certainly, many agencies attempt to stable both disciplines under one roof. In the larger offices, the two functions are still scrupulously separated, with clients served by one account manager for advertising and another for public relations (including product publicity). Thus, in theory, an *advertising* account manager shouldn't have to worry much about having PR or news media knowledge. In reality, however, such know-how is highly worthwhile, as the best laid marketing plans call for a close interaction of both kinds of mass communication. At the very least you should cultivate an appreciation of PR and be ever alert to ways it can extend the visibility of a campaign. For example, often in the process of making a TV commercial there are publicity opportunities in both consumer and trade news media. If the spot involves celebrity spokespeople, there can be interviews before and after the shoot. There also may be ramifications for the client's upcoming sales meeting: perhaps an "outtakes" video showing some of the scenes cut from the finished spot or a scripted personal appearance by the on-camera talent. Still photos taken during the filming will be useful for the client's company magazine or newsletter and also may be perfect for selected mailings announcing the campaign to retailers.

Then, too, you may find yourself employed at smaller agencies with smaller clients who want account managers to help with *everything*, including public relations. If you find yourself suddenly called on to be an instant authority on PR, consider this crash course:

1. Speed-read a couple of the best basic books about the field. I'm told that *Strategic Public Relations Counseling—Models from the Counselors Academy* by Norman Nager and Richard Truitt, published by the Public Relations Society of America, is a great start.

2. Go back to square one and look hard at the economics of providing this service. It's rarely very profitable in smaller shops. All too often unsophisticated clients hope it "can be tossed in for free." If you discover it isn't paying off, show the figures to your boss (who at the very least is bound to be impressed). Discuss the alternative strategy of working in tandem with a local PR professional who doesn't dabble in advertising. You can learn from him or her, and there is a good likelihood you can help each other gain accounts. In the days when my agency was small and deliberately *not* offering PR services, we gained several good clients from friendly PR firms to which we in turn referred prospects. The only catch is finding a firm you respect, run by people with similar values and standards.

3. Seek out people of your age and experience who work for the news media. For one thing, it's not too early to begin to build your own old boy or old girl network. But more importantly at this stage, you will have a chance to learn firsthand just what newspeople want, need, and will accept. (Bear in mind that PR practitioners are often held in low esteem by newshounds. They're regarded as press agents or con artist flacks willing to go to any extreme to sell a story.)

    If you can talk with the more senior editors that's even better, but generally they're too busy and, frankly, are edgy about spending time with a junior PR person. The challenge would be to convince them you honestly want to learn and are not resorting to some backdoor legerdemain in the hope of peddling a story about one of your clients.

4. Many clients have unrealistic expectations when it comes to news coverage of their companies. What seems to them worthy of the front page is often relegated to a paragraph on page 16. They can't understand why and want to know "how come you can't do a better job with our PR?" You can head off some of this client exasperation if you remind him or her of the time-honored definition of "news": *Man bites dog.* In other words, those activities judged by editors to be the routine, the everyday, the commonplace are not going to get

much play. The promotion of Arlie Snip to sales manager may be a big deal to your client, but it's only an ordinary dog-bites-man item to the news media. You'll be dancing over tiger-traps if you acquiesce to your clients' personal feelings, rather than giving them the cold shower of news reality.

5. If your client does have something genuinely newsworthy, bear in mind that the television folks want something that *moves*. Older clients in particular continue to think in terms of press kits and the same old press conference format where some hoary exec drones on, reading from prepared comments. The beauty of TV is its dynamic quality, so provide something that takes full advantage of the medium. If it's an important new product, show it in action, or have someone demonstrate how it's made or tested or marketed. Don't simply hand out a glossy photo and have a pontificating company spokesperson.

   Back in the 60s when I worked for the company that made Oregon brand cutting chain for power saws, we were opening a number of branch offices around the country but not getting much TV coverage. The local stations, even in towns like Lansing, Michigan, just weren't interested in "another ribbon-snipping ceremony." We solved this by wrapping a large, brightly colored ribbon around a six-inch-diameter oak log and cutting it with a high-horsepower chain saw. The noise, combined with sawdust swirling—and sticking to the dark suits of visiting dignitaries—was just right for TV, and our coverage vastly improved.

6. You'll do your clients a real favor if you can convince them to have a written plan for handling *bad* news, but it's far from an easy sell. A crisis PR plan is something that you never quite have time to finish. Then one night, your client's general manager is awakened by a call from a TV newscaster. Seems he heard that one day's supply of the company's product was mislabeled and anyone taking it might get severe food poisoning. Would the manager care to comment? Caught by surprise and unprepared, it's incredibly easy to say the wrong thing and to have the wrong person saying it. At the very least your client should have a clear understanding of who (and it should be a single voice) will speak for the company and who will decide the legal implications.

7. When other educational avenues lead to dead-ends, you might try this approach: Become friends with someone who works at a *real* PR agency, and help each other learn about your respective businesses. Personally, I also found it helpful to have worked summers with a weekly newspaper. At the time, it was just a job that didn't pay beans, but in retrospect it was experience that put me half a step

ahead of my fellow account folks. Time logged on a decent college paper is also worthwhile *if* you have a chance to work with a knowledgeable advisor.

Bottom line, you should determine beforehand if PR *or* advertising is your career expressway, and journey accordingly. But, along the way, you may find it necessary to blend the disciplines. This book is for *advertising* types, so you won't see much more about public relations, but that doesn't mean you should ignore the field. At the very least, take time to understand the fundamental differences. One of the better ways to torpedo a job interview is to casually comment that you feel "advertising and PR are pretty much the same."

CHAPTER TWO

Coping with Clients

If you happen to think managing clients is a walk in the park, consider these daily tasks: convincing a vacillating product manager to approve a most unusual creative approach, justifying your agency's fees, explaining why a project cost more than originally estimated, collecting a past due bill, and, oh yes, picking up the check for lunch.

SCOPING THE BASIC TYPES OF CLIENTS

About sixteen hours into your new job, someone is bound to mutter loudly, "This would be a wonderful way to earn a living if it weren't for those lousy clients." Well, let that run off your back, because without those dastardly clients the agency's world stops. David Ogilvy was dead right in *Confessions of an Advertising Man*, "Do not make the common mistake of regarding your clients as hostile boobs." Even creative maverick Jerry Della Femina has written, "Too many agency guys spend their time complaining about their clients. . . . It's a lot of crap."

When you first enter the business, there's a temptation to view clients as either Dodge City marshalls or horse thieves—you know, the Old West rides again. But the reality is that most—like heroes and villains the world over—are rarely all wonderful or all terrible. They're not black and white, merely innumerable shades of gray. The saving grace is the fact there *are* legions of people connected with advertising who are great to work with. These are the kind of clients that agency founder Ralph Ammirati once described as those "who notice, who know the difference, who appreciate the difference, who get involved, who respond." Jane Maas, in *Adventures of an Advertising Woman*, said they "always ask for that extra mile and always say thank you for the effort."

At the top of the heap are the *ne plus ultra* ("the highest point of perfection") clients. A rather rare breed, *NPUs* are distinguished by seven salutary characteristics:

1. They respect the agency's professional judgment and expect objectivity and independent thinking. They deplore sycophants. Peter Drucker in *The Effective Executive* relates the story of his first big consulting assignment (for General Motors). On one occasion he was called into the office of the CEO, Alfred P. Sloan, who told him:

    > I shall not tell you what to study, what to write or what conclusions to come to. This is your task. My only instruction to you is to put down what you think is right as you see it. Don't you worry about our reaction. Don't you worry about whether we will like this or dislike that.

    NPU clients ask the same of their agencies. They do not take the agency's proposals and attempt to, in the words of Jack Wagner, my boss when I was at Cole & Weber, "beat to fit, and paint to match"—a phrase that refers to the tendency of some clients to change the agency's creative recommendations without regard to the core strategy; they are more concerned that the ad will please their bosses than if it is relevant to the marketplace (typical examples include adding extra clichés such as "highest standard of excellence" to the copy or crowding another product in the main photo). If the recommendation is wrong strategically, or otherwise clearly in error, *NPUs* reject it. But they do not try to manipulate it into something closer to their comfort zone.

2. They regard their agency as an extension of their corporate family and treat it accordingly, not as some suspicious outside supplier. They are in accord with Dr. Robert Davis, a professor at Stanford's Graduate School of Business, who has written, "In short, the agency is your right arm. It is a key part of your marketing department and deserves to know how you think and act."

3. These clients are not afraid to take reasonable risk. The thought of making a mistake does not cower them. ("*Shipai wa seiko no moto*," chant the Japanese. "From mistakes come success.") They realize that eggs must be broken before a great omelette can be made. They do not believe in having their agency running scared. ("Emancipate your agency from fear" is Ogilvy's phrase.)

4. *NPUs* do not water down the agency's recommendations by subjecting them to tiers of approval and review. Several years ago in an *Adweek* interview, the Ally & Gargano agency revealed a prime

reason for the success of their TV ads for Federal Express: "All the decision makers are together at the [approval] meetings. We don't have to go through layer after layer." In their best-selling book, *How to Advertise,* Jane Maas and Ken Roman agree that "the longer the approval process, the more opportunities to make those 'little changes' that can ruin an advertisement. A few extra words may seem trivial, but they can overload the commercial and blur your message."

5. They are enthusiastic about the work and lavish it with praise if warranted. The ancient Greek author and soldier, Xenophon, long ago told his people, "The sweetest of all sounds is praise."
6. They are direct with criticism and do not play head games or emulate ostriches. According to Ogilvy, "Disastrous consequences can arise when a client pussyfoots." He urges, "Be candid and encourage candor." Once the smoke clears, they harbor no grudges.
7. *NPUs* are willing to invest heavily in the production of their advertising, understanding the analogy that great sculpture requires marble and granite, not putty and plastic (a metaphor borrowed from Dan Wieden, founder of Nike's agency, Wieden & Kennedy).

Are there a lot of clients like this? No. But there are enough to make working in an advertising agency all worthwhile. When you discover an *NPU,* treat him or her with the kindness and respect due any endangered species. Always remember that superlative advertising never appears in the public view unless wise clients approve the recommendation and sign the checks. Frank Lloyd Wright is credited for the line, "Behind every great building is a great client." This is doubly true for advertising.

Now, having gushed about all of those good specimens, let's look at the other side of the coin: those "grayish" types alluded to earlier. Here's a summary of some of the more flagrant varieties and a few thoughts on ways of coping with them.

Type 1: The Closet Creative Director

This kind of client wants an agency just to refine and upgrade his or her "terrific" concepts. Ogilvy once said, "Why keep a dog and bark yourself?" This client wants to bark. Creative giant Tom McElligott calls them "control freaks." He says, "They have to write the ad, to over-involve themselves to the point where they just destroy whatever enthusiasm a creative shop has."

Ways to Manage

- Find ways to keep these clients busy on right-brain projects within their organization. Let them vent their creativity on sales meetings, house organs, trade shows, and other important areas outside of the agency's sphere of interest. When these clients don't have enough to do, they often feel compelled to get into the agency's bailiwick.

- In presenting recommendations, make a point of referring specifically to the client's earlier input: "As you said, Charlie, . . ." Show that you were listening to all of Charlie's great notions, and make those points in front of his superiors. The best account managers can make the recommendation sound like a joint effort of Charlie and the agency. So what if Charlie gets some credit he doesn't deserve. What really matters is the approval to produce some very good work.

- In your own style and manner, have a good answer ready if the client huffs: "This isn't what I wanted! Weren't you listening to me?" You respond with something like: "Of course I was, Charlie. Let me explain again how your input helped us reach this recommendation. I'm sure you would agree there's more than one way to make this ad campaign work."

Type 2: The By-the-Numbers Client

These clients live and die by so-called hard data and regard computer printouts as aphrodisiacs. They are totally and blindly left brain. If something goes wrong, these people look slavishly to the numbers to find the answer. They always have a state-of-the-art pocket calculator. They hyperventilate at the possibility of complex research projects and, given the chance, will pretest ad headlines syllable by syllable. The late Bill Bernbach, founder of Doyle Dane Bernbach, characterized this type of client as "so busy gathering statistics [they] forget [they] can make them."

Ways to Manage

- Stay up nights becoming super-knowledgeable about research methodology and trends. To work with this client you must be able to demonstrate that you know almost as much about the subject as he or she does. Root through old copies of the *Journal of Advertising Research* and the *Harvard Business Review*. Seek out conversations with research people whom the agency regards with favor (on or off your staff).

- Include data from behavioral psychologists and other social scientists in your recommendations to add credibility. For example, look up the 1927 study by Bluma Zeigarnik, which found that messages are more memorable if they are slightly incomplete, leaving the audience with something to ponder. Called the **Zeigarnik effect**, this technique "makes the brain itch," according to its founder (from *Psychology Today* magazine).

  Or read the 1983 study by James MacLachlan and Pradeep Jalan, which showed unaided recall to jump significantly when the audience's curiosity was aroused early in an advertisement—a useful tidbit if you're trying to sell a "teaser" campaign. These and ten other intriguing techniques were detailed in the article "Making a Message Memorable and Persuasive" in the December '83–January '84 issue of *Journal of Advertising Research*.

- Look for precedent-setting examples of other similar creative approaches to show along with your recommendation. Resort to the old cliché "Nothing succeeds like success, and this sure has been successful for Federal Express."
- Delicately remind this client that research is not always fail-safe. Some of the most extensively researched new-product introductions ended up as embarrassments in American marketing history (Ford's Edsel automobile and new formula Coca-Cola, to cite just two).

Type 3: The Double Agent

Basically your age-old Mr./Ms. Two-Face. These clients adore everything you present, but it's a different story when it moves upstairs for final okay. Career advancement and/or job security are paramount to them, but they hate to "hurt the agency's feelings." These clients can blind-side you handsomely because they never turn down a proposal when there's just the two of you in a room. You leave the meeting thinking all is approved, and the next morning you receive a message that "a number of revisions are needed on the recommendation." This client type also loathes to break any bad news personally. Some will resort to sending a memo and leaving town on a quick business trip. Psychologist Robert Bramsom labels this type "super agreeables" in his book *Coping with Difficult People*.

Ways to Manage

- You simply cannot depend on this type of client to do justice to your recommendation. Somehow you must find a way to show the work directly to the final authority. Ideally, you can convince the chameleon to do it in concert with you. But if the joint presentation goes badly, you must be prepared to shoulder solo all the fire and brimstone. If this client as well as your recommendation are roundly criticized, he or she will be exceedingly reluctant to present again in tandem. Conversely, if the meeting goes well, be sure the client gets to bask in the applause. It's important that he or she feels this is a practice worth repeating. "The better your clients look, the better you and the agency look," said William E. Phillips when he was president of Ogilvy & Mather.
- What happens if you are totally stonewalled and not permitted to "go upstairs" with the client? (He or she may see the gatekeeper role as vital to job security.) Frankly, this is tough. Once or twice you may

be able to bring in your boss and thus force the issue of meeting with the client's higher-ups. Or, you can use opportunities when he or she is out of town, ill, on vacation, or otherwise occupied. Try to set it up, so the client says, "Look, since I won't be around, why don't you show the copy and layout directly to Ed. I'll let him know you will be calling." That way he or she can save face and cover tracks. On other occasions you can force the issue by turning to your advantage the pressure of imminent media deadlines. Explain that for reasons beyond your control, you have to get to the big boss for approval today, because ad material *has* to be shipped to the magazine in two days. (Sometimes you may be elasticizing the truth, but in most instances you really will be up against the deadline wall because the Double Agent is so sluggish.)

Type 4: The Obsessive Bean Counter

There's a fine line here. A strong ad manager patrols his or her budget relentlessly and properly monitors the agency estimates and bills. But there is a certain kind of client who feels duty-bound to question every item on a monthly bill, including the number of photocopies and why a delivery was made by cab instead of bicycle messenger. Ogilvy called these clients "pettifoggers" and advised, "If you allow them to haggle over payment of [the agency's] bills, you make a mistake."

It's a sad fact that this individual fundamentally doesn't trust the agency and is certain that with enough digging he or she will find scallawaggery. Account managers and media and production departments must spend an inordinate amount of time justifying each monthly billing, eroding the profitability on such accounts. Ironically, this client is frequently slow to pay.

Ways to Manage

- Document *everything* as the job progresses. Make notes on your calendar, on the job jacket, or on whatever works for you. But leave nothing to memory. If conditions change during the job—for example, three photos are needed instead of two as originally planned—submit a written revised estimate. Coax this kind of client to sign it. ("Wait a minute," you protest. "Are you saying that this persnickety client won't sign off on a routine estimate?" I am indeed. That's precisely what the Bean Counter conveniently buries on a crowded desk.)

- Learn to anticipate this client's questions and prepare a defusing letter to cover each monthly billing of consequence. Call out areas that might be disputed and explain your position in as much detail as possible. Never just send the bill and hope for the best. (For more help with this situation, see the section "Handling the Way-Over-Budget Project" later in this chapter.)

Type 5: The Ghost

Now you see 'em, now you don't. These clients love to fly. Given even the slightest reason, they're on the road. When you need a decision, they're in a meeting two time zones away. These clients will call you from an airport phone booth but can't give you an answer right then because the airline just announced the final boarding call. Or they approve some copy the day before leaving, then change their mind after landing in Cincinnati. Naturally, with the time zone change, they have to call you at home after everyone in the agency and all of your suppliers have headed home. These clients are gone so much, you begin to wonder if they are real. By being constantly in motion, numerous hard decisions are ducked and virtually everything is a last-minute crisis. To make matters worse, Ghosts are reluctant to delegate any authority to subordinates left at home.

Ways to Manage

- Forget about conducting business during normal hours. Outfox him or her by arranging to meet at dawn for breakfast, or at the airport, or over an evening drink or meal. Learn to make presentations in a car on the way to the terminal or over Sunday breakfast at a pancake house. At the extreme, lie in wait in this client's employee parking lot and snare a few minutes before he or she goes in the door to start work for the day.
- If the Ghost won't allow subordinates to make some approvals, seek ways to show the work to higher-ups in his or her absence. Watch for landmines here: Make sure you don't give the appearance of end-running this client. Persuade the Ghost that such action is (1) in his or her best interest as a manager and (2) necessary to keep programs on track.
- For an extremely important project, get on a plane and chase the client down. It may mean catching the red-eye from the West Coast so that you can meet for early coffee in a Chicago hotel—and then hot-footing it home before close of day. But what's a 28-hour day when you can sell some outstanding work!

Type 6: The Shopper

These clients are always looking for a better cost alternative, particularly on the creative end, and like to hand out side projects to freelancers and other agencies "to keep my shop on its toes." (*Adweek* magazine once described this type as "like the little kid on the block who pulls wings off flies.") They rarely have much taste and lack patience with subtleties. They like to point out to superiors that they have ways to get advertising work done "a lot cheaper than if our big-time agency does it."

Ways to Manage
- It's virtually impossible. Once in a great while, through patient education and meticulous service, you can modify such behavior. But in most instances it's hopeless, because all that matters to them is how much something costs. (They really belong in the purchasing department.) Pray that a transfer is forthcoming for this client. Use your boss's influence with the client's marketing management to seek ways to keep such types very busy with nonagency assignments.
- One of my former mentors once advised me to take one of these types out in the parking garage and deliver a hard punch to the kidneys. (At the time I laughed. Now I'm not so sure he was kidding.) Bear in mind that there may be times when you have to exercise extreme restraint not to take his advice!

Lastly, be forewarned that once in a purple moon you will encounter Type X, a genuine bum of a client who will cheat, lie, scream, intimidate, and drink beyond reason. Fortunately, most do not last long. When confronted with one of these, do not fool yourself, as rehabilitation and attitudinal adjustment are most unlikely. If your bosses insist on trying to keep the account, don't martyr yourself—life is too short to waste on these people. Pick your spot and bail out as soon as possible, remembering that it's always easier to land another job when you are employed than when you aren't. I agree wholeheartedly with Jo Foxworth's comments in her book, *Wising Up*, "Enjoy your job and if you don't, quit, no matter how much you're being paid. Life's too short . . . when you've got a job you hate."

If you were to profile an account employing a number of these six nefarious types, it would likely be very similar to the description of Atari that appeared in a 1983 article in *Adweek*: "The company is extremely erratic, with no focus, no continuity and no real interest in strategy. . . . Moreover, no one is in charge, or sure of his job."

It's no surprise that advertising people with world-class reputations are men and women who genuinely delight in dealing with all kinds of people. Almost anyone can do a decent job with a *ne plus ultra*. The challenge is to be able to persuade the less-than-perfect clients to accept more-than-ordinary advertising. It calls for a large dose of creative energy. I've always thought that is the ultimate fascination of this business—and a powerful motivation for getting into account management. For those who agree, a noteworthy future beckons.

ON SELLING WHEN THEY'RE NOT BUYING

If you're looking for magic formulas for selling ideas to clients, forget it—there aren't any. The key is understanding what makes your clients tick:

knowing their prejudices, nuances, and human foibles, and sensing the best time to present your case.

But, first you need to determine if the selling situation is Class A or Class B. Class A is the ideal. You and your creative team are totally in synch. This recommendation is indeed the Holy Grail. It reeks of greatness. It is strategically brilliant. The copy sings, and the visuals are mind-bending. This idea is bigger than life. Now, your mission is clear: Arm yourself with your most powerful weapons of persuasion, and spare nothing in your quest to gain the client's approval.

Then there's Class B, the one the textbooks seem to overlook. Here, you and the creative team are *not* in synch; in fact, you are light-years apart. To top it off, everyone is (once again) behind schedule. You don't see the layout and copy until thirty minutes before you have to present it. The ad is already on extension with *Field & Stream* magazine. If the client doesn't say yes, you could be running a blank page with the agency picking up the tab. You're half inclined to resign or call in sick. You don't see how any client with an IQ of more than 46 could possibly smile at this mishmash.

"Wait a minute," you mutter. "Why even bother discussing 'A'? Anything that good can sell itself. It's obviously duck soup. Let's just send it over by messenger and handle the whole thing by phone so we'll not miss our sailing lesson."

Sorry, approvals hardly ever happen that way. Sure, sometimes it *is* a laydown deal, when the client is the proverbial sharp cookie and buys the whole concept before you can stammer three coherent sentences. But a lot of times, the recommendations for breakthrough work are, well, downright scary—and harder to sell than clear cutting to environmentalists. It's what McElligott calls "the sweaty palms stage [which] most clients can't get past." Once in a great while, enthusiasm alone will carry the day. But you can't bank on it.

Persuading a reluctant client to okay an unusual and possibly risky concept is potentially the finest hour for an account manager. It calls for imagination and, yes, *creativity*. Those who do it well are the unsung heroes of this business.

For both situations, there are some fire-tested ways to increase your odds of making the sale. Let's look first at Type A scenarios.

1. Don't rush to show the creative materials. Begin by reminding the client of the objective of the message and the basic strategy required to accomplish it. (You both should be nodding at this point.) Take pains to establish the professionalism of the recommendation. Head off the client's natural tendency to grab the layouts or the **story boards** (large cards on which are drawn key frames of a proposed TV commercial) and react subjectively. (This sounds easy, but in reality it's like asking young children to defer opening their gifts until the day *after* Christmas.)

2. Remind the client of the communications environment that will surround the message when it appears. Regardless of the medium, it will be far different—and far noisier and more cluttered—than in their office or conference room. With print advertising it helps to paste the comprehensive layout in a sample copy of one of the publications recommended on the media schedule. Actually, this is a good down-home test to see if the message really does "jump out and grab you."

3. By all means refresh the client's memory of what the competition is doing and what must be done to out-think them. Also cover any special qualities—good and bad—of the specific market you are targeting. I have found it useful to quote from Harvard Professor Theodore Levitt's book, *The Marketing Imagination*, "To attract a customer . . . the seller must distinguish himself and his offering from those of others so that people will want, or at least prefer, to do business with him."

4. If you have any pertinent marketing research facts available, be sure to proclaim them. Any documented market information that supports your recommendation is going to increase your client's comfort level. Studies by behavioral scientists are next best (e.g., the Zeigarnik effect, cited earlier in this chapter under the heading "Scoping the Basic Types of Clients").

5. Think like a good trial attorney and use examples of precedent to reinforce your contentions. Show or describe other advertising that has achieved notable results by daring to be distinctively different (the best of VW, Levi's, Apple, Nike, John Hancock, etc., *and* the best from your own agency). Point out that some of the finest advertising in history received only lukewarm approval when it was first presented. The best story I've heard concerned the now historic "We're Number Two/We try Harder" campaign for Avis Rental Cars. In his best-selling book, *Up the Organization,* then–Avis president Robert Townsend wrote:

> Bill Bernbach [creative head of Townsend's agency, Doyle Dane Bernbach], came out to show Avis his recommended ads. He said he was sorry but the only honest things they could say were that the company was second largest and that the people were trying harder. Bernbach said his own research department had advised against the ads, that he didn't like them very much himself—but it was all they had, so he was recommending them. We didn't like them much at Avis either, but we had agreed to run whatever Bill recommended.
>
> The rest is history. Our internal sales growth rate increased from 20 percent to 35 percent the next couple of years.

6. Keep in mind that clients are human and subject to illogical idiosyncrasies. (It was Bernbach who observed, "The sad fact is that we human beings are a biological mess with all sorts of mental and physical hang-ups.") You may be asking for trouble if you schedule a tough presentation for Friday afternoon when the client is itching to leave for the lake. You're also likely to get a negative reaction if you present the morning after the monthly marketing report shows a sharp decline in sales. And, since some clients get grouchier as the day goes along, try always to see them before lunch. I don't want to overstate the importance of timing (most days you are at the mercy of the client's schedule, anyway), but don't totally disregard it either. It's tough enough for the average client to approve a breakthrough message on a *good* day, so it's doubly difficult if you have to face him or her on a day when the wheels are coming off.

7. If you're running into a barrage of "I don't think that's what we want," suggest that sometimes fresh ideas require a bit of time for digestion. Statesman Henry Kissinger once said, "Great men are so rare, they take some getting used to." The same holds true for barn-burning advertising ideas. Urge the client to sleep on the recommendation, to see if it grows on him or her. The late Andrew Kershaw, when he was chairman of Ogilvy & Mather, counseled, "Try delay. Often something turns up to save the day."

   If possible, *you* keep the creative materials. Explain that you want to review the client's criticisms with your creative department. This will prevent him or her from showing it to people in adjacent offices, who probably will reinforce his or her initial suspicions. The basic tactic here is to ward off an immediate kill. By buying a bit more time, either the client might change his or her view, or more likely, you can come forth with some new ammunition.

   For reasons that defy explanation, clients will sometimes react entirely differently when they see the creative materials the second time. Perhaps they have slept on it, or maybe they forgot something they objected to earlier, or it just looks better today. The key to the success of this act II tactic is the manner in which you make the return visit. If you reek of stubbornness and seem to delight in possessing a deaf ear, you are dropping sparks in very dry tinder. I've known short-tempered clients to tell such account people, "Get out of here and don't come back until you can show me you're listening to what I say."

   By all means, talk over the client's objections with your creative colleagues, and if any slight adjustments can be made, all the better. But with a magnum opus ad, it is doubtful much revision can or should be made. The only answer is to take a deep breath and dive back into shark-infested waters.

When you make your encore presentation, be sure to let the client know that you did not take lightly his or her comments of the previous day, that you are not being paid extra if this idea sells, and that you understand his or her point of view. Do everything in your power to impress the client with your intelligent tenacity and fervent conviction. Painstakingly review the reasons for the message and the obvious dearth of strong work in the marketplace. Finally—and probably most important of all—*bring some new bit of information or fact to the table.* This allows a prideful client to change his or her earlier opinion without appearing to have merely caved in to the agency. If you can induce a reluctant client to admit, "Well, that does put things in a little different light," you've got a big foot in the approval door.

The best example of this intelligent tenacity in my experience was a trade campaign for Code-A-Phone telephone answering machines. Our intrepid account manager, Michael Hoffman, returned to the client three times with the same highly unexpected recommendation. (The opening trade advertisement in the campaign was a two-page spread featuring a close-up photo of the *Battleship Missouri's* mammoth gun turrets and the headline "This Year Code-A-Phone Is Taking a Little Different Approach Toward the Competition.") He finally secured a less-than-enthusiastic approval but was told, "I think you guys [the agency] are going too far." The ad ran, and the response was overwhelmingly favorable. Then our client told us, "The only problem with this campaign is that it didn't go far enough. You guys should have pushed us harder." We took that as a classic left-handed compliment.

8. You don't have to be the Lone Ranger. A team sell is sometimes the best way to carry a tough concept forward. Call on the creative team, the creative director, the account supervisor, the agency president. The only caveat is to make sure it is more than window dressing: Don't bring along a person with an impressive title if he or she is not intimately aware of the recommendation and is prepared to make a legitimate contribution.

Also recognize that the heavy horsepower ploy can backfire. If the client is not familiar with other members of the account team and sees the management types only when there is a problem, he or she probably will go on the defensive when you come en masse. If you've built a foundation of confidence prior to these summit meetings, your chances of success are greatly enhanced. No client likes (a) to feel he or she is under siege by the agency or (b) to be surprised by some unknown agency person with fancy credentials.

9. Resort to pretest research—but only as a last-ditch effort to keep a great idea from being poisoned and *only* if you have access inside or outside

the agency to experienced research folks who understand your creative philosophy.

Don't get me wrong. I am not categorically bad-mouthing research. In fact, as stated earlier in this book, market research in advance of a campaign can be of inordinate value. The hang-up in my experience is the testing of advertising ideas in rough preliminary form. To me it is exceedingly difficult to obtain accurate feedback from a limited number of people looking at story boards, animated slides, comprehensive layouts, and the like. They simply do not have the impact of the fully produced message, and the artificial viewing situation does not reflect today's cluttered environment for mass communications. Even a research proponent like Ogilvy admitted its deficiencies in recognizing big ideas. "Research can't help you much because it cannot predict the *cumulative* value of an idea," he wrote in *On Advertising*.

Be wary also of clients who see focus group research as a panacea. Because of the fast feedback and the dramatic interplay, focus groups are widely used. And they can be very useful in providing clues and directions for marketing efforts. But they are intended to be diagnostic, not conclusive, and should not be confused with large projectable studies like those of Lou Harris or Yankelovich. With a weak moderator and a couple of overopinioned group members, it is easy to dump on a nontraditional advertising idea.

It's no sweat to fight the good fight when you *know you are right,* but, alas, there are days when the situation is much muddier. These are the "B" times I alluded to earlier, and my hints are conspicuously shorter.

1. Learn to submerge your personal feelings and emotions. Be coldly professional like a criminal defense lawyer. It is not necessary for you to *like* the creative recommendation. What must concern you is whether the materials are on target in terms of objectives and strategy. Even in the best agencies there are going to be frequent honest differences of opinion—that's a healthy par for the course. Ideally, there will be time to air these conflicting views and reach a meeting of the minds; unfortunately, this is not the modus operandi of most agencies. Therefore, sooner if not later, you will face a day when the creative recommendation arrives on your desk with no time for rework even if you could talk your creative partners into reconsidering. There will not be time to reschedule the meeting with the client. You are less than sold on the solution, but there are no viable options. You must go forward. Once again the advice of William E. Phillips, written in Ogilvy & Mather's pamphlet, "Principles of Account Management," is worth repeating.

    > You are speaking for the agency—not for yourself. Your client has hired [your agency], not you. The client assumes your recommendations are those of the agency. . . . It's okay to indicate that a

monolithic position does not exist. But it is only fair to your client to present the agency's recommendations as clearly and convincingly as possible.

Whatever you do, don't succumb to the temptation to be all things to all people. It's actually far more tempting than it seems from a distance. Let's say you have a difficult recommendation to present to a difficult client whose favor you would like to curry. How easy it is when he glowers to say, "I really didn't care much for this either. I have to admit that your criticism is astute. Sometimes our creative people don't have their feet on the ground." Then it's a snap to beat a hasty retreat to the agency's creative section where you breathlessly report, "I fought like a tiger, but to no avail. That blockhead of a client wouldn't recognize a good idea if he stepped in it." Now everybody's happy, right? Not for long, I assure you. Integrity and ethics aside, this chicanery is foolish. From a purely pragmatic standpoint, such double talk is almost always found out, and at that point your career can be severely damaged.

2. Bring in the creative cavalry—but carefully. I discussed the classic team sell earlier, in regard to Class A situations, and most of that advice applies here as well. In "B" cases, though, it is particularly valuable to have the *author* of the recommendation with you. After all, there is no one better suited to explain a challenging recommendation than its creator. Just be certain you don't take a "throw 'em to the wolves" stance. I literally have seen meetings where account people have introduced the creative person by saying, "Well, let's have George explain what's up his sleeve. Personally I haven't had a chance to review all the details, so I'll be as interested as you in seeing his thoughts."

There will be occasions, however, when the creative person simply does not have the personality to enhance the chances of selling the idea. If that's the case, substitute the creative director or the best management representative you can recruit. Fortunately, the majority of good creative people are articulate and persuasive. Pleasing recalcitrant clients, though, is not their strong suit, and it's up to account management to keep crunch-time meetings from disintegrating into a clash of egos.

3. Research to the rescue. A far from perfect solution, but perhaps it is the only one acceptable in this particular situation. Again, the comments made previously in this section (under "A") apply. The challenge is to attempt to measure the strategic impact of the message, rather than simply trying to find ways to make the client more comfortable. If you and the research people involved, either in-house or outside the agency, are not on the same wavelength, you may have the deck stacked against you from the start.

As a last resort, in either an "A" or a "B" situation, you should consider the infamous "rubber chicken maneuver." The expression has been in the jargon of advertising and sales for ages and basically refers to the use of outlandish theatrics to make a point, for example, the tossing of a war surplus dud hand grenade on the client's desk to emphasize "the explosive nature of this recommendation." Without question you have to be judicious in the use of this tactic. Go too far, and you run the danger of being viewed as a buffoon. Make a half-hearted attempt, and you may lay the largest of eggs. The hand grenade stunt worked a couple of times for me, but it also backfired nicely when it bounced too hard and scratched the client's $5,000 handmade conference table. Fortunately, the mark mostly polished out, but the memory haunted us for years.

When used for a clearly relevant reason, though, the old latex chicken ploy can pay off—and do a lot more than just produce some laughs. For example: A banking client was raining hard on us about the strategy behind a creative proposal. "I'm not sure you've really thought this through," he thundered. "I think you should go back and take this recommendation apart brick by brick. Maybe then you could convince me of its wisdom." Two days later while on the way to our second meeting with this client, I walked past a construction project and almost fell over a pile of used bricks on the sidewalk. I promptly emptied my briefcase into a large envelope and replaced the contents with four bricks (happily, an almost perfect fit). Then, prior to showing the proposal once more to our client, I said, "Rudy, we have taken your request completely to heart. Not only have we reviewed and analyzed this strategy from top to bottom, but we have literally torn it apart *brick by brick*!" As I spoke, I took the bricks one at a time from my now dusty briefcase and stacked them on his desk. He guffawed loudly and shortly thereafter told us, "I still question some of your homework, but let's run these ads and see what happens." (We did, and they brought in some $18 million in new CD deposits.)

Military surplus stores can provide an endless supply of props for hard-sell meetings. In addition to grenades, I've used steel helmets, gas masks, shell casings, and survival knives to good advantage. For example, we were able to enliven a lethargic session by stabbing a bayonet into a block of wood while declaring, "We're about to present some extremely penetrating advertising. Please note how the first headline cuts the competition to the quick." Stuntsmanship like this may help to carry the day, but *only* if all of the other components of your recommendation are strategically airtight. Don't confuse the sizzle with the steak itself.

Robert Cialdini in his book, *Influence: The New Psychology of Modern Persuasion,* writes about the "weapons of influence." He categorizes sales tactics under catchy headings, such as "social proof," "authority," "scarcity," and "liking" (the seller). As a social scientist—and self-confessed "easy mark"—he doesn't have a very high opinion of them (too manipulative, etc.). But, I disagree when it comes to dealing with difficult clients: The skillful application of such techniques is often the only way a controversial idea can be sold. To have a strong arsenal of these so-called weapons is not only proper but also quite essential if you are to win approval of nontraditional recommendations. Based on your personal style, you must determine which calibers work best, but it's suicidal to face major "A" or "B" battles without appropriate persuasive armament.

EXPLAINING AGENCY COMPENSATION

Of all the enigmas surrounding the practice of advertising, perhaps the most mysterious to average businesspeople is agency remuneration. A typical question from an unsophisticated prospect goes something like this: "I know you guys get a kickback from the media, but what else do you charge?"

It seems that most everyone has some foggy knowledge about the time-honored custom of media commissions, but even that is surrounded by confusion. "Is it 10 percent or 15 percent?" "Why is it sometimes 17.65 percent and other times 16 2/3 percent?" And so on. And, I must admit, agency compensation with its myriad variables is at best odd and at worst arcane. Nevertheless, a proper explanation of how and why the agency expects to be paid is fundamental to cementing a solid relationship. If you cannot explain it to your client's satisfaction, you will be laying yourself open for all sorts of assorted gnarly problems.

Here's an attempt to boil down just how the industry makes its money, and as you will quickly note, there are variables galore. Advertising agencies receive income from three principal sources:

1. *Commissions* from media (radio, TV, magazines, newspapers, outdoor) on orders placed by the agency. This is generally 15 percent of the cost of space or time in the United States, but it varies in other parts of the globe. For reasons beyond me, outdoor advertising (billboards) has traditionally paid 16 2/3 percent.

    Now, what happens if the agency is buying a page in the Altoona *Little League Guide* and the *Guide's* rates do not include the agency commission? Simple. The agency will mark up the net cost by 17.65 percent (equivalent to taking 15 percent off the gross amount).

    To complicate matters, newspapers have **net** (noncommissionable) rates for local advertisers and **gross** (agency commission included) rates for national advertisers (ditto for some electronic media as well). This means that agencies with local retail accounts must either mark up the net amount or find some other way of gaining compensation. Many a neophyte account person has wounded client confidence by mistakenly passing along net media estimates instead of those including the agency commission.

Incidentally, an additional discount of 2 percent has been historically allowed by major media for prompt payment of ten days from date of invoice. The trend in these profit-starved times, though, is to discontinue this discount. The mega-magazines—*Time, Esquire, Playboy*, and their ilk—continue the practice, but many other periodicals, as well as radio and TV stations, have run up the white flag. It's important to know what your agency's policy is for handling these so-called cash discounts. Some pass along to quick-pay clients; others do not, including many smaller shops, which need every dollar of income possible to stay in black ink.

2. *Hourly fees* for specific services in the manner of attorneys, accountants, and other professional service organizations.
3. *Markups*, generally 17.65 percent but occasionally as high as 25 to 30 percent, on the net cost of outside purchases made on behalf of the client. Why the variance? It depends on the market, the nature of the account, and the agency's fiscal policy. For example, political accounts, because of their tension-filled volatility and short duration, are often charged a higher markup percentage rate.

Outside purchases include such things as typography, photography, photo retouching, color separations, broadcast production, and so on. Where clients frequently get upset by markups is in the printing of a big run of an expensive brochure, especially with reruns of the same brochure. Often, special payment arrangements are negotiated just for those situations; for example, markups on reruns are to be a flat 10 percent.

Example A: Typically, This Is How an Agency Is Paid

Again with the caveat that generalizations almost always are full of exceptions, here is a typical compensation package that a small or medium-sized agency will have with an average account:

Compensation for all media services (planning, placing, creating, producing advertising for print or electronic media): 15 percent commissions of all space and time (16 2/3 percent in case of outdoor). Standard hourly fees are charged for all art department time (art direction, layout, pasteup, etc.). Markups of 17.65 percent are taken on all outside purchases for the production of the advertising. There is net reimbursement for out-of-pocket expenses such as long-distance telephone calls, deliveries, freight, and the like. Sometimes creative direction is also charged on an hourly basis. Generally, account service, copywriting, and media and production time are in effect paid for by media commissions.

Compensation for all collateral work (materials other than major media advertisements per se—catalogs, direct mailers, point-of-purchase materials, etc.—are lumped as *collateral* in this business): Standard hourly charges are imposed for all traditional agency services—account management, creative (copy and art), production—and markups are taken on all outside purchases, such as photography, typesetting, printing, laminating, illustration art, and so on.

Compensation for research and public relations services: Standard hourly fees are charged plus markups on outside purchases. (Outside research costs such as WATS lines for a telephone polling are billed according to the specific job agreement negotiated with the client—sometimes net, sometimes gross.)

Are there flaws in the system? Yes—many. For example, if the agency receives the majority of its income from media commissions, isn't it highly motivated to recommend a number of pricey media to the client? Certainly there are clients who suspect this. (Fortunately, the vast majority of agencies I have known are too professional to stoop to such sandbagging. Then, too, most clients are too knowledgeable about media buying these days to permit an agency to spend one dime more than necessary.) And what happens to the same agency when the client suddenly cancels the schedule, thus effectively killing that source of compensation? Usually there is a period of grief, followed by an aggressive effort to replace the income from another source. Depending on the size of the agency and the budget involved, such a cut can indeed trigger immediate layoffs of personnel.

Wouldn't it be better to have all agency remuneration come from fees and thus eliminate all of these concerns? That's what Ogilvy advocated when he wrote in *Confessions of an Advertising Man*, "The conventional 15% commission system is an anachronism." Twenty years later, however, he admitted, "I no longer care how I get paid, provided I make a profit."

There seems to be an increased acceptance of fees and retainers, but there are two big problems. First, what is to be the basis for the fee? Ideally it would be a determination of the estimated number of hours required to provide the right amount of service. But this is tough to spell out in advance. And marketing plans can change abruptly in midyear, thus tossing even the best-laid plans into a tizzy. Second, on the monthly bill, it makes the agency's income jump off the page. It doesn't matter that it's legitimate and fair and all that. On a sizable account, it's going to be a goodly amount of money, and over time that can rankle a client. Long ago, T. S. Eliot said, "Man cannot stand too much reality," and that applies to agency billing. Maybe it defies logic, but clients simply feel better when they pay gross media bills and smaller fees. They know the agency is getting a cut of the media, but somehow it doesn't hurt as much as seeing all of those fee dollars standing *naked* on the bill.

Cost Accounting: The Financial Linchpin for Agency Economics

Regardless of what compensation plan your agency espouses, the key to a happy relationship is a decent cost-accounting system. Whether you're using an IBM mainframe or an abacus, the important thing is to be able to discern if an account is profitable or unprofitable. Many small agencies still run their business with cigar-box accounting. "If we meet the payroll and have money left at the end of the year, we can't be doing too badly." That kind of thinking is deadly, and if your boss is bent that way, keep your résumé current.

By cost accounting, I mean a way to identify the income for each account with comparative data on the cost of servicing it, including both direct labor and an allocation of overhead. This is also the jeweled pivot that makes a fee-based plan work. If you can show the client in black and white where you stand profit-wise, and he or she is not the kind who enjoys holding your feet to the fire, you both can feel good about the justice of the fee. Or, if the fee isn't sensible, you can immediately take steps to adjust it or eliminate the conditions that are causing the imbalance. Once again, the situation is pretty clear-cut: If the agency's costs are outstripping income, either the fee must be raised or services reduced. If the agency's income is unreasonably high relative to its costs, more services have to be provided or (ouch!) the fee needs to be cut.

For reference, see the example of an agency cost accounting report in Figure 2.1. The column on the left, headed "11/89 current," covers figures for the current month, which in this example is November 1989. The column to the right, as its heading states, lists accounting details cumulatively for the year to date. (This report reflects BPN's fiscal year running from December 1 to November 30.)

By scanning this report, an agency manager can quickly know (a) what income the account has generated, (b) what it has cost the agency to service the account (in labor and overhead), (c) what the profit or loss is in dollars, and (d) how the account is faring in relation to the agency's stated profit target of 22 percent of income. This account was profitable but fell far below the 22 percent goal—a clear signal that in the future the agency would need to either increase income or reduce service costs.

Example B: A User-Friendly Compensation Plan

"Great," you say. "All of those compensation variables are certainly beguiling. But how about some straightforward hints as to what works best? Now, no doubt, you are about to reveal exactly what should be considered the ideal plan to recommend to all of our future clients."

Well, maybe. An absolute panacea has yet to be found, but I do think some combination of media commissions plus fees is the best plan. For example, have the client pay a set annual fee to cover account service planning and advertising measurement research. Allow the agency to take full commissions on all media placed. Use the standard (cited earlier) plan for collateral with the exception of account service; that would be covered by the fee. Monitor via cost accounting monthly and report semiannually to the client. Review and adjust annually if necessary.

	11-60 B1 JAN 22, 1990		BORDERS, PERRIN & NORRANDER, INC PROFIT & LOSS BY CLIENT REPORT			14:50 PAGE 1
CLIENT :BPN SAMPLE CLIENT CLIENT NUMBER :501		OFFICE :SEATTLE				ALLOCATION BASIS :CLIENT OFFICE DIRECT COST
			11/89 CURRENT	%	12/88 TO 11/89 YEAR-TO-DATE	%
TOTAL MEDIA			$ 0.00		$ 0.00	
RESEARCH			$ 0.00		$ 12,802.93	
COLLATERAL			$ 0.00		$ 1,274.44	
OFFICE SERVICES			$ 229.90		$ 2,998.45	
NEWSPAPERS			$ 0.00		$ 955.00	
OUTDOOR			$ 5,335.56		$ 5,481.57	
RADIO			$ 587.65		$ 45,436.89	
TELEVISION			$ 158,301.36		$ 478,891.72	
TOTAL PRODUCTION			$ 164,454.47		$ 547,841.00	
SERVICE FEES			$ 18,514.00	10.12	$ 203,654.00	
TOTAL BILLING			$ 182,968.47	100.00	$ 751,495.00	27.76 % OF BILLING IS INCOME
(a) AGENCY INCOME			$ 18,514.00	100.00	$ 208,628.00	100.00 % OF INCOME
DIRECT SERVICE COST			$ 8,038.04	43.42	$ 103,741.61	49.73
NONBILLABLE COST			$ 195.57	1.06	$ 4,663.19	2.24
TOTAL DIRECT COST			$ 8,233.61	44.47	$ 108,404.80	51.96
OVERHEAD ALLOCATION			$ 8,351.63	45.11	$ 85,090.53	40.79
(b) TOTAL COST			$ 16,585.24	89.58	$ 193,495.33	92.75
(c) CLIENT PROFIT OR (LOSS)			$ 1,928.76	10.42	$ 15,132.67	7.25 % OF INCOME (d)

FIGURE 2.1 An example of an agency cost accounting report.

All of this is just so much financial bilgewater without the all-important component of value. The best compensation plan in the world is meaningless if the client doesn't feel your work is worth the fee charged. Whatever else you do, don't get so hung up in the ramifications of proper bean-counting that you lose sight of your first sacred duty: helping to generate outstanding advertising. If you do that first, you will find it much easier to negotiate a final compensation package with even the toughest client.

Management consultant and former agency manager Charles B. Jones said it best in *Agency Compensation: A Guidebook*, published by the Association of National Advertisers:[*]

> It goes without saying that a necessary ingredient must be a healthy relationship between the advertiser and the agency. If the advertiser develops a lack of confidence in the agency's ability to produce the needed advertising, or if the agency lacks respect for the advertiser's judgment, dissatisfaction with the compensation plan is almost certain to occur. It would be obvious that no compensation plan would solve such problems.

I also vote for stating clearly the agency's profit goals. Clients understand all too well that an agency must profit to stay in business (if they don't, your agency is crazy to keep them). Figure 2.2 shows the compensation objectives for my agency (BPN). This page was given to every prospect so that all could understand that the agency's annual goal was to earn 22 percent of gross income with a resulting net profit equivalent to 3.3 percent of sales (capitalized billings, in agency lingo). We found that kind of blunt talk cleared the air quickly with prospects who otherwise would have remained suspicious about our money-making motives.

Fiscal Footnotes: Dealing with Billings and Errors

Be quick to see through one other widely held misconception about this business: "Billings are the mark of success." Hardly! *Income*, not billings, is the magic number. (Billings figures are almost always inflated anyway. It's characteristic of agency nabobs to round off to the next highest million when asked the size of a new account—and to round to the next lowest million when losing some business.)

The three words near and dear to agency controllers are *billings, income,* and *profits*. Despite sounding alike, they are distinctively different in meaning. *Billings* (always stated as a plural) are the total number of dollars that a client spends through an agency; they are roughly equivalent to "sales" in other industries. *"Capitalized" billings* refers to a formula used by agencies to convert income figures to billings when the account has a nontraditional

---

[*] This paperback is one of the best primers on the subject of agency finances. It is available by writing the ANA at 155 East 44th St., New York, NY 10017. Cost is $38.50 for non-ANA members. Much of the contents pertains to multi-million-dollar accounts, but the underlying principles are still appropriate in any situation.

> ## Compensation
>
> Our compensation is normally based on the following assumptions:
>
> 1. The agency will be responsible for all media planning and placement, and will earn the 15% commission. The commission will cover account management and copywriting charges on all media projects.
> 2. Strategic (marketing) planning will be accomplished by the client's organization, assisted by the agency. Depending on the level of our involvement in this area, a monthly fee may be required to compensate us for our time.
> 3. All outside purchases will be marked up 17.65%.
> 4. Agency compensation for all work done on non-media (collateral) projects and agency services not covered by media commissions will be compensated by hourly charges.
>
> Our compensation agreements are calculated to cover costs (people and overhead) plus a modest corporate profit goal of 22%—gross profit to income ratio. Expressed as a percent of sales (billings) the profit target is 3.3%.
>
> Our costs are monitored on an account-by-account basis by ADAM, our in-house computer system. We receive monthly profitability reports (sample enclosed) and will share them with you on a regular basis.
>
> Usually we review our cost/profit relationship after the first 90 days of working with a new client, with follow-ups at six (6) months and one year. (Thereafter reviews are annual.) Our profit guidelines are 20% at the low and 25% at the upper end. Anywhere between these two figures is an acceptable level of profitability from the agency's standpoint.
>
> Financial agreements are often hard to discuss between prospect and agency. But they shouldn't be. The "books" are available and we will always seek an open, candid atmosphere between ourselves and our clients even where dollars are concerned.
>
> We're comfortable working to budgets, we're used to estimating major projects in advance, and we will always keep the need for cost controls firmly in mind. We're confident together we can produce outstanding, *cost-effective* advertising we can both be proud of.

FIGURE 2.2 When the agency's compensation policy is reviewed with a new client at the beginning of a working relationship, chances for future misunderstandings are sharply reduced. This example is the candid statement used during my tenure at BPN.

compensation arrangement—for example, if an account purchases little commissionable major media. It's calculated by multiplying income by 6.67. *Income* is the amount of money retained by the agency after paying all of the expenses incurred on behalf of the client—media time and space, ad production, collateral printing, and so on. *Profit* is what is left after the agency pays salaries, overhead, taxes, and other costs of staying in business.

It's the one that really matters. (That's why BPN's general manager in Portland, Michael O'Rourke, has the word framed and hanging in a prominent place on his office wall.)

Keep in mind that any agency is involved with lots of pass-through dollars that do not contribute a cent toward paying the rent. If an agency spends $100,000 of a client's money (that is the billings figure) but receives income of only $10,000, that's the meaningful number, not the six figures that may make headlines in the trade journals. The companion thought to retain is that your agency's profit target should be a percentage of *income*, not of billings. If you are to achieve a reasonable pretax, preprofit sharing, prebonus number, you need to win 20 percent to 25 percent of income, *not* just that percentage of billings.

All good account managers also are aware of the fiscal cliff they patrol in terms of the danger of errors that the agency must pay for. Never forget that to break even after one $15,000 mistake (such as having to reprint a full-color catalog because of typos), you will need to find a client who will place $100,000 in media. Needless to say, in smaller markets and for smaller agencies, finding such a client is far from an everyday occurrence.

Lastly, I pass along several Ogilvy quotes that may provide a moment of inspiration when in the future you are having a rough time getting your client to pay what he or she should:

> Make sure that your agency makes a profit. Your account competes with all the other accounts in your agency. If it is unprofitable, it is unlikely that the management of the agency will continue to assign their best men to work on it.

> When a client frets about the price of his agency's services he ends up getting a low price and poor advertising.

> If you pay peanuts, you get monkeys. (attributed to Jimmy Goldsmith)

COLLECTING BILLS

In advertising lore, there are thousands of words devoted to strategic planning, market segmentation, positioning, the creative process, media trends, the analysis of multivariate data, and other similarly exalted matters. So this book isn't going to plow that same ground. Instead, this section covers the aspects of account handling that seem consistently ignored in the classic works: For example, what do you do with a client who doesn't pay up?

"Hold on," you say. "You mean that after four or five university years of sharpening my marketing and communications skills, I'm now going to be asked to dun clients for money? Why, that's the accounting department's worry!" Wrong. In all small agencies and many larger ones, the principal person responsible for keeping clients financially current is *you*, if you sign on as an account manager. Yes, it can be awkward and frustrating, but it *is* critical to the agency's business success.

Each agency has its own policy regarding client payment, but the best-run are adamant about prompt reimbursement: ideally within ten to fifteen days from receipt of invoice, but certainly thirty to forty-five days at the outset. In these cash-short, profit-squeezed times, many companies prefer to pay vendors (and this is how the financial hardnoses categorize ad agencies) as slowly as possible. We've had prospective clients who explain that payment in 90 to 120 days is "normal" in their businesses. Our response was that we considered ourselves an abnormal firm and couldn't live with that.

Ogilvy in *On Advertising* admonished agencies seeking new clients, "Watch out for credit risks. Your profit margins are too slim to survive a prospective client's bankruptcy. When in doubt I always ask the head of the incumbent agency."

There are two excellent fiduciary reasons for an agency taking a resolute position on the matter of payment. First, the agency is acting on behalf of the client in making purchases and is liable for meeting these obligations. The media, printers, typesetters, and so on, want and need prompt payment and are certainly more likely to provide stand-on-their-heads service to agencies who pay on time. The typical smaller agency does not have deep enough reserves to pay suppliers before it receives the client's check. Therefore, it is key that the agency be paid expeditiously so in turn its obligations are met pronto.

The second reason for taking a tough stand is that the longer an account stretches out the payment period, the more likely the agency will be dead in the water if the client surprises everyone by taking Chapter 7, 11, or 13 bankruptcy. Almost every agency president has a personal horror story about an account that looked solid, seemed in good shape, had been around a long time, and stiffed all creditors one morning totally without warning. For example, in 1983, when Britain's Laker Airways folded, a Miami agency, Hume, Smith, Mickelberry, was stuck with $100,000 in media bills. A spokesman for the agency said that the airline's flamboyant owner, Freddie Laker, "always paid his bills on time. He wasn't a sick patient who finally goes; his [demise] was more like a sudden heart attack."

Fortunately, you rarely have to take drastic steps to perform this keep-'em-current duty. In 90 percent of the past due cases, it's a situation where the agency's bill has bogged down on someone's desk. But unless the account manager raises the issue, that bill might stagnate there for additional weeks.

Persistence is the crucial ingredient. When your accounting department lets you know that your client is overdue, it's the signal to pick up the phone. And, if you don't get an answer that day, call again. Yes, be polite, but also be tenacious. Tell the client you'll be fired if you don't get an answer; tell him or her that you can't make payroll, that you're closing the books for the quarter—take some creative license. Simply put, make sure your bill gets to the top of the client's accounts payable pile.

If you sense something genuinely amiss—if your calls are stonewalled; if "the check is in the mail" too often—then *don't* delay alerting your boss. He or she will gladly put pressure on the client to pay an overdue bill. Waiting too long wins no friends and influences no fiscal enemies.

All of this may sound a bit as though the best agencies are a bit carnivorous and love to chew on clients. Not at all. Most clients respect an agency that is direct and forthright about finances. They understand that a company which doesn't get paid, doesn't stay alive. If you pursue payment with professionalism, you will not only collect but will win some quiet points for business acumen as well.

The key to fiscal peace of mind, though, is a hard, clear look up front before the client and agency tie the contractual knot. Here's what I think your agency should do:

1. When courting a prospective client, find out the company's past record for paying suppliers. With a bit of probing, you can uncover most of the "big hat, no cattle" types. Your agency can subscribe to *Dun & Bradstreet Credit Reports*, of course, but I've found personal networking to be more accurate and up to date. You and/or your boss can make some discreet inquiries to production vendors and the media. Your agency's banker also will have a conduit to credit information both formally and informally, and sometimes your attorney and insurance agent can help.

   If the credit record is poor, be wary. Unless either new ownership or new senior management is aboard, this company will not change its ways. "Once a four-flusher, always a four-flusher," counseled my former boss, Jack Wagner. If, for a variety of reasons, your agency feels it still wants the account (visibility, unique product, pathway to a larger client later on, etc.), then do whatever it takes to receive at least some payment in advance. Agencies tend to be skittish about pressing this proposition, apparently feeling it isn't professional, but there is ample precedent in the industry. For example, it is common practice for television production companies to insist on one-third or one-half payment of their bid figure in advance of any shooting. Agencies must learn to play with the same rules.

   Try mightily to avoid the benchmark weasels of all time: political accounts. These folks are quick to ask an agency to spend "on the come." "The money will be here tomorrow," and so on. All media wised up to this long ago, so it is strictly COD when buying print, radio, TV, or outdoor for a candidate or measure. No exceptions. Still, in the heat of a campaign some good-hearted agencies use their own money to make sure messages run on time. Sometimes their faith is paid in full (especially if their client wins). But after every election you read items in the daily press like this:

84 ♦ Coping with Clients

> A second creditor of Gary Hart's 1984 campaign obtained a court order Wednesday to try to block the Democratic presidential hopeful from getting $100,000 in matching funds for his renewed campaign.
>
> Attorneys for Semper-Muser Associates, a Culver City, Calif. advertising agency, served the Federal Election Commission with an order seeking money to pay $179,920 in debts and interest.
>
> Portland, *Oregonian*, Dec. 31, 1987

Needless to say, if your political client *loses* and still owes you, chances of collecting are even worse than normal.

Another alternative in these sensitive situations is to arrange for all media bills to be paid directly by the account. The agency's services will be charged totally through fees, and media commissions will not be part of the compensation plan. It puts the monkey on media's back, but generally they have broader backs to offer. Be prepared, however, to accept the fact that some radio, TV, and print folks may say no dice; and that's certainly their prerogative.

2. In the key new business presentations (or conversations, if you're fortunate enough to avoid competitive presentations), always include a segment on how your agency handles financial matters. This should explain how the agency achieves its profitability and simultaneously eradicate any misconceptions about profiteering. (Remember how I harped on this in the previous section.) Examples of how you bill should be shown along with information about cost accounting procedures. And your payment policy should be made crystal clear.

3. Be sure that your agency's chief financial person and his or her counterpart from the prospective client's company meet one another before the letter of agreement is signed. If these two see eye to eye, or even if they agree on what they disagree about, you literally and figuratively will be money ahead.

4. Lastly, don't be afraid to push for termination of the arrangement if it quickly turns sour on the balance sheet. It is deadly for an agency to have a financially irresponsible account. Your business should be driven by account management, not accounts receivable.

HANDLING THE WAY-OVER-BUDGET PROJECT

Despite one's best efforts, it seems that the accurate forecasting of creative and production costs is still much like predicting weather on the high seas. Just when you think you're sailing carefree in calm waters, an unexpected storm clobbers you.

Yes, we have years of experience and reams of data from previous activities. Yes, we frequently have computerized cost accounting. Yes, most agency people are dedicated to controlling costs. But the business is still beset by the unexpected, the unknown, and especially the never-tried-before. For example, how long will it take for a copywriter and an art director to come up with a great idea for the next magazine ad? Last time the creative juices were flowing, everything clicked and they finished in half a day. But this week, nothing makes sense, they're suffering from creative block, and after three days you have only a large pile of wadded-up layout tissues.

Even after the layout and copy are approved, there are dozens of tiger-traps in the production process; for example, rain washes out the scheduled TV shoot, but the models still have to be paid for waiting around in anticipation of the skies clearing. The photos need more retouching than anticipated because the natural lighting was off a tad. The type has to be reset several times because the client changed his or her mind, then the copywriter changed his or her thinking. Or, it's a half-page full-color ad in four magazines with each having slightly different production specifications. (The page dimensions are not alike, nor are the "screen" requirements. Screen refers to the number of dots per square inch needed to reproduce "**halftones**," or photos in lay language. Printing on coarse paper may call for 85-line screened photos, but on glossy paper stock your film must have something in the neighborhood of 133-line screens.) Instead of making one set of **color separations** (separate sheets of printing film, one for each primary color) and three identical sets of duplicate film, you end up providing different-size separations for each publication. And, since this takes longer to finish, you end up shipping via premium air freight to hit the closing date.

Are clients understanding about all of these variables? Depends. The very knowledgeable are, but often the client ad manager is not all that experienced. And even those who have been in the job for years can be ignorant of production mechanics. His or her response to these problems may be something like this: "For crying out loud. It isn't as though you haven't done this before. Why in the world is this (ad/catalog/TV spot/etc.) costing me twice as much as the last one? Don't you guys know what you're doing?"

Certainly, we've done that type of project before. Yes, we do know what we're doing (at least most of the time). But it's like the difference in building homes. On one hand you have the tract contractor who is using the cookie-cutter approach: Everything is reduced to common number, volume is very important, and the homes are all clones of one another. Then you have the custom house builder. He or she has blueprints and maybe an architect as well. But even though it, too, is a house by strict definition, this particular model has never been built before. And the chances are very good that either (or both) the owner and the architect are going to want some revisions after construction is under way. The custom home builder and the advertising agency are in totally different fields, yet in much the same boat when it comes to estimating costs.

All this means is that if you become an account manager, you will invariably be faced with situations in which the final costs have exceeded the estimate. Confronting the client with this news is about as much fun as doing your income taxes, but there are ways to keep it from happening:

1. Educate your client on the difference between *estimate* and *bid*. We are not in the generic products business, taking stock items from the shelf with a known, computerized price tag. Therefore, unless noted because of special circumstances, agencies do not submit fixed bid prices. Instead, they *estimate* the anticipated costs to the best of their experience and ability. When the job is completed, all actual, legitimate, documented costs are billed. This means there are occasions when the client pays more than originally estimated and times when he or she pays less. Every once in a while, you will encounter a client who thinks he or she is in the purchasing department and wants to hold you to what they see as a *bid* price—even if there have been many client revisions.

2. When the job is going through a lot of adjustments and revisions, try to submit revised estimates along the way. If the project is under the gun, it's tough for your production department to find time to do this. But I do urge you to find a way to get these revised figures to your client, particularly if it's a job involving some big dollars. This will substantially reduce the agony of the final billing. Remember, it is not so much the total *amount* that will be the problem as the unpleasant *surprise* factor. If you keep your clients apprised as the jobs progress, you will be in a far better position than if you assume they implicitly understand that costs are mounting.

3. Keep notes along the way, on your pocket calendar, on the job jacket, on your desk blotter, anywhere—just don't forget to do it. When a job drags on for several weeks, it is virtually impossible to reconstruct all of the twists and turns after it finally concludes. If you and the client later disagree over the billing, these notes can be your salvation.

4. Learn to sense potential problems on billing and try to defuse them. For example, if you review the monthly billing and see that the costs for some jobs are coming in higher than expected, find out why and write a cover letter of explanation to the client. Account managers who take the "ostrich approach" and send the billing to the client "hoping he won't notice" are asking for an angry phone call. Second best is to simply call the client, but if you don't confirm details *in writing*, it is still very easy to have misunderstandings.

5. Seek ways to get your client involved with, and knowledgeable about, basic production processes. Some could care less, and you won't get anywhere. But many others will welcome the chance to learn more about printing technology and the mysteries of color separations or how the sound is mixed for a TV commercial. The more they know, the more likely they will be understanding when costs are higher than originally estimated.

6. Be fair, but don't be a pushover when it comes to supplier costs. Learn what the going rates are for the best photography, illustrations, typography, separations, retouching, and so on. Then, when you see a cost that looks out of line, you can intelligently question it with your production or creative department—long before it ends up on a client invoice. You're spending the client's money, and if you can watchdog those expenditures, he or she will be very appreciative. Also, make sure your clients know what you're doing to monitor and control outside costs. (And don't be shy about tooting your horn when you save some dollars.)

7. It's easier for the agency to reduce inside hourly charges than to eat costs of services or materials purchased on the outside. Obviously, one maneuver involves an accounting adjustment while the other means paying hard cash. Thus, when the job costs must be absorbed by the agency, look first to inside time. But don't fall into the trap of thinking that such time "isn't that important." Some agency managers develop a knee-jerk reaction to client billing complaints. "We'll just knock off some inside hours," they smile. Well, watch out. Those hours are the agency's stock-in-trade and once erased from a billing card, they're gone forever. You can't re-box them for sales to another customer.

8. You might be incredibly fortunate and never have a messy billing situation to unravel. But I doubt it. It's in the cards that some jobs will be historically calamitous with liberal blame for everyone involved. In these instances, a council of candor is the best bet: Bring everyone involved into one room and thrash out a resolution. It generally means that agency, suppliers, and the client each have to give some. The value of the all-in-one-room stratagem is that the problem is attacked head-on and arguments and alibis don't drag on ad nauseum.

9. The key to maintaining your sanity is *anticipation*. The best account and production managers have highly developed olfactory organs; they can sniff out trouble long before it decays to the point where the whole agency knows it's a big stink. They know all too well what Peter Drucker pointed out in *The Effective Executive,* "The unexpected

always happens—the unexpected, is indeed, the only thing one can confidently expect."

Anticipation means keeping on top of the jobs as they move through the agency. If you see things bogging down in the creative department, you can quickly surmise that hourly charges are running ahead of estimate. If the creative solution requires such elements as helicopter photography, trained wild animals, endorsements from known celebrities, travel to Belize, or the like, then beware: The odds are piling up that cost overruns lie ahead.

Probably the single biggest storm warning is the number of revisions involved. For example, if a printed piece undergoes a host of changes—either because of the client or because your art director is not happy with the first go-rounds—you can be absolutely sure costs are leaping skyward. In the case of full-color work, the gyrations can be astronomical. Be especially wary about the printing of a large run of multicolor catalogs. Even if all has gone well through the various **cromalin** (fancy word for color proof) and **color key** (another kind of proof) stages, there still can be major problems when the piece gets on the press. It pays to attend those press checks with your production and art people even if they seem a real nuisance. (My production manager, Bev Petty, used to warn me, "Critical press checks are like childbirth; they never occur during normal, daylight hours.") Then you will have intimate knowledge of what really happened if there is a dispute later with the printer or color separator.

10. Sometimes the most practical way to resolve a contested bill is to fall back on the "Solomon's Baby" principle. Instead of painstakingly and painfully reconstructing all the details of a job, simply split the disputed amount 50-50 with the client. This assumes, of course, that the client feels that at least some of the blame is legitimately in his court. It's not the most sophisticated approach, but it can save a bundle of costly time for both you and the client.

11. Jack Wagner had a sign in his office reading, "Neither a Scrooge, nor a patsy be." That's good advice for these situations. Seek fairness and justice, and once resolved, put the affair behind you—don't carry a grudge. Be statesmanlike in your approach: Don't give away the agency store just because it's an easy way out; but by the same token don't press nonessential demands just to demonstrate how tough you are.

ENTERTAINING YOUR CLIENTS

Is entertaining clients a big part of your job? The best answer to that was put forth by William E. Phillips when he was president of Ogilvy & Mather.

Writing in the agency's pamphlet, "Principles of Account Management," he said, "Entertainment is the dessert, not the main course of your relationship with your clients. Good clients are distrustful of agency people who are big spenders. If you are not sensible with agency money, why should clients believe you will be sensible with theirs." Wise words. I urge you to heed them.

Occasionally you will encounter a client who feels that his or her role in life is to be stroked by the agency, who rejoices in sticking the agency rookie with a big entertainment tab, whose idea of a good time is to compare your entertainment offerings with those of other agencies openly chasing the account. Learn to identify these parasites early on. (By asking pointed questions of others involved with the account, you can quickly ascertain client personality traits.) Then play the necessary games to keep these clients at bay. For example, push to have meetings at any time except right before lunch or late in the afternoon. Project such a sense of urgency about getting the work done that only a fool would expect you to take time for socializing. Explain that you are on a strict diet for health reasons—anything to avoid becoming an entertainment punch card.

It's not as easy, however, to deal with a client who isn't a clear-cut Prince of Darkness. Heavy drinkers, for example, are almost endemic to this business. And many of them are otherwise decent people who will happily buy their share of rounds and contribute fully to the merriment of an evening. But they can also be tedious and quarrelsome and over time can intrude annoyingly into your private life. Here are a few suggestions for dealing with this type of client:

1. Don't feel you have to match the client drink-for-drink as though this were a test of manhood or womanhood. If pressured in that direction, get the waitress aside and have her refill your glass with mineral or Seltzer water.

2. Watch for clients who believe an "initiation ceremony" is necessary whenever a new account manager is assigned to them. My most extreme case involved a fascinating marketing director who always insisted that the agency account manager join him for lunch and "be sure to clear your calendar for the afternoon." "Lunch" would commence around noon and conclude shortly after 2:30 A.M. when the bars legally closed in Portland, Oregon. It was his way of sizing up new people.

3. If for religious or other reasons you do not drink alcoholic beverages, you will *not* be an agency oddity, as there are many agency people who share your views. The Mormon account managers I have known simply order soft drinks when out with clients. (I recall one occasion when a red-nosed client over the course of a long evening managed to down seventeen vodka martinis. The account manager matched him round-for-round: seventeen 7-Ups! This so

impressed the client, he never again subjected my colleague to that kind of ordeal.)

And one ironclad maxim: Absolutely *never* have entertainment charges appear on a billing to the client. All of the good agencies I know regard that as a cost of doing business and wouldn't dream of billing it back. But, somehow in the folklore of the business, there exist several oft-told stories of agencies not only invoicing the client for entertainment but actually marking up the cost by 17.65 percent! (I had a client at BPN who delighted in repeatedly telling how he had fired a previous agency for just such tactics.)

Of course, a certain amount of business-related entertainment is in order in serving clients. But if you are counting on this as an exciting fringe benefit, I'd say count again. In both of his books, *Confessions of an Advertising Man* and *On Advertising,* Ogilvy tells aspiring account managers, "Lunching in expensive restaurants is no fun if you have to explain a declining share of market while eating the soufflé." An occasional five-star lunch or dinner does occur, but more often than not, a working meal means a hurried ingestion of salami sandwiches brought in from the local deli.

CHAPTER THREE

About Surviving and Thriving in an Ad Agency

More counsel on subjects those big, thick textbooks tend to overlook. Some advice about dealing with collateral projects, maximizing the impact of small budgets, and courting new business. Plus, some tips on managing details and keeping in touch with clients and prospects.

DEALING WITH COLLATERAL PROJECTS

Ah, the glory of seeing the full-color spread in *Esquire*. The joy of viewing the new thirty-second spot in prime time. The ecstasy of hearing the campaign's radio commercials at drive-time. And knowing that you played a key role in the conception and delivery of this great material. That's the dream, isn't it? That's why you're going into this business. That—and the small stipend you receive monthly—makes it all worthwhile. That's advertising, right? Well, some days it is. But when you're working for a smaller agency, you soon find that the major media side of the game—the one that gets all the attention in those books about Madison Avenue—regularly plays second fiddle to the great Swamp of Collateral.

The origin of the term *collateral* is uncertain since it definitely reeks of banking and loan sharking rather than marketing communications. Loosely translated, **collateral** means everything that an agency does in addition to print and electronic media advertising per se. Thus it includes catalogs, sales literature, mailing pieces, envelope stuffers, point-of-sale materials, annual reports, corporate identity, exhibits, slide shows, and videotapes, among the more traditional assignments. Depending on the client, though, it can also have you involved in such odd projects as gifts and trophies for the annual sales meeting, gag photos for the chairman's birthday, matchbook cover designs, festival floats, and T-shirts for the company picnic. It's easy to sneer at such projects. After all, most of the larger agencies simply dodge this work, sometimes referring it to their sales promotion or design studio subsidiaries, sometimes merely referring clients to outside specialty firms. Smaller firms, however, do not have this option, as they need all the revenue they can generate. Plus, their clients expect this kind of ecumenical service. They, in turn, are not large enough to employ a variety of different communications groups to fill specialized needs.

My philosophy in dealing with collateral is, as usual, didactically simple: Full speed ahead! Take on the assignment with relish—and don't lower your standards just because it's "only" collateral. (The request for "quick-and-dirty" work, a constant menace to collateral projects, is dealt with later in this section.)

At the risk of maligning some remarkable people, I must say that the worst perpetrators of this down-with-collateral attitude are your creative department colleagues. How come? It depends. Some dump on collateral because it is too time-consuming and limiting. It requires far more effort for an art director to design a 24-page catalog than to lay out a couple of magazine spreads. And, let's face it: The ads get all the glory, visibility, and applause. At the major creative competitions, the big news is who has won the best of show for radio, TV, print, and outdoor. If they even have a category for collateral, it is given back-of-the-bus status.

When it comes to sales and application literature, the content is generally gone over with zeal by the client's engineering and technical people. As a group, these folks tend to be terribly myopic as readers of ad copy. (The plant manager of one of my clients once sent me a memo listing the fifty-two words and phrases he found objectionable in our copy for a product catalog.) They are also notorious for making changes on top of changes, frequently at the eleventh hour. They also are dubious of the value of subtleties and apt to quarrel about the lighting of photos, the spacing of copy blocks, and all of those things they don't know much about but think they ought to. And it is out of character for them to condone a generous production budget. The net result for many creative people is that these projects just aren't much fun, and this attitude is widely held in the agency world.

At this point, one note of clarification should be interjected: The anti-collateral feeling is far less evident when the elements are interwoven in a campaign context. In other words, it is far easier to get a five-star creative person interested in a catalog page when it relates to several print ads and a point-of-purchase poster than when it is just a single isolated assignment.

So, what words of wisdom might be offered to account managers faced with countless collateral projects? Try these:

1. Not every creative person shares the same impassioned dislike of sales literature, annual reports, and the like. In fact, there are even

a few practitioners who actually thrive on collateral. You, in concert with your creative director, need to identify these individuals and get them involved with your client's requirements. Often, they will not be in your art department but available as freelancers, which is okay as long as they meet your agency's creative standards.

2. Large collateral assignments such as multiproduct catalogs or corporate brochures take weeks, sometimes months to complete. Therefore, it is essential that you note *in writing* every change of signals along the way. Why? Because invariably there are going to be questions about costs when the job is finished. If you cannot document the reasons, your agency may have trouble collecting full payment. Ideally, there are revised estimates and punctilious conference reports issued as the project evolves, but when the heat is on to get it *finished*, this may not happen. Your notes may be the salvation if a cost disagreement arises after delivery.

To get an idea of a typical time-line for a complicated piece of collateral, see Figure 3.1, in which I show the production schedule for a 64-page, multicolor catalog that my agency created and produced annually for many years. You can instantly see that the number of separate steps and the number of weeks involved are invitations for glitches to occur.

3. In a complicated piece like an annual report, it is all too easy to overlook a typo on a dylux (or blueline) proof—and terribly unnerving when the client spots it after 20,000 copies have been printed in six colors. How can you guard against this calamity? I know of three ways:

First, don't even think about passing the reading buck. Proofread everything yourself, slowly and carefully. Absorb the words of William E. Phillips written when he was president of Ogilvy & Mather: "Assume that everything that goes wrong on your account is your fault, or could have been prevented if you were doing your job right."

Second, do everything in your power to make sure the agency's procedures for proofing are as airtight as possible. And this means that the people best suited for double-checking are indeed doing just that. There are times when a receptionist may prove to be a better proofreader than an award-laden art director.

Third, be nervously alert when you see copy changes being made repeatedly over several days on the same page. The danger is that the person pasting up type revisions to correction #3 might accidentally pick up old correction #2 instead of new correction #4. The chances of error are multiplied when all the type proofs are jammed into one file folder (or oversized envelope), which is an agency's normal way of saving all the materials pertaining to the job.

Omark SED Catalog
Production Schedule

July 29	Final layout and lead-in "color" copy to client
August 5	Approved layout and "color" copy revises at BP&N
August 11	Technical copy and final "color" copy to client
August 12	All photo props at BP&N
August 16	Approved "color" and technical copy revises at BP&N
August 16–20	Press proof 2/color bullet reproduction
August 19	Final technical copy to client for OK
August 24	Approved technical copy at BP&N
August 23–27	Photography/art
August 30	Copy out for type
Sept. 1	Photography/art to client for OK
Sept. 6	Approved photography/art at BP&N
Sept. 9	Type galleys to client
Sept. 13	Photography out for separations
Sept. 15	Type galleys with corrections at BP&N
Sept. 20	Approved type repos at BP&N
Oct. 4	Mechanical out for prep
Oct. 11	Loose color croms for OK at BP&N
Oct. 18	Color keys, dylux and croms to client
Oct. 25	Color keys, dylux and croms at BP&N for revise
Nov. 1	Revised dylux to client for OK
Nov. 4	Approved dylux at BP&N
Nov. 8	Film to printer
Nov. 15	Ready to ship partial

FIGURE 3.1 A complicated piece of collateral can take several months to produce. Here is the four-month production schedule for a 64-page, multicolor catalog that Borders, Perrin and Norrander produced annually for many years. The handwritten notes telling of scheduling adjustments were made by our production manager, Bev Petty, as the job progressed. *Croms* refer to cromalins, a type of color proof.

4. Don't allow clients to continually press you into producing quick-and-dirty materials. Once in awhile, this is okay, but both of you are asking for trouble if it becomes a habit. Any agency creative department with a smidgen of pride will want to spend the time to do a project right. And that probably means the job will cost more than the client had in mind. Avoid the alternative approach of cutting so many corners that the piece turns out a disfigured mutant, to the dismay of everyone, but especially your creative staff.

    On the other hand, advertising agencies are supposed to provide *service* to clients, and when a client makes such a request you will not cement the relationship by telling him or her to get lost. Instead, respond in one of the following ways:

    a. Explain forthrightly that it just doesn't make good business sense to have the agency do this kind of project. Underscore the economics of the situation, and be careful not to imply that the agency is too high and mighty to take on such a mundane assignment. Then, don't abandon the client dead in the water. Help him or her sort out sensible alternatives. For example, you might suggest a lower-hourly-rate freelancer who could get the job done directly, and then put the two in touch with each other, with you in attendance for the first meeting. (As stated before, it is important that you identify these freelance resources in your market and work to establish an ongoing relationship. And, equally obviously, it is critical that you don't put your client in the hands of someone who is going to undermine your agency's creative product.)

    b. An alternative to freelance assistance is to have the project done as a moonlighting job by one of your agency's junior creative people. You have better control here, but this works only if it's in accordance with the policy and philosophy of your agency's creative management. Certainly it cannot become routine.

    c. If the account is longstanding and nicely profitable, you may elect to handle the assignment as though it were first-class and simply absorb most of the normally charged fees for professional time. You might think that clients would be forever indebted to you for this loss leader approach, but regrettably, they tend to have pretty short memories. Instead of recollecting how much you absorbed, they just recall what a nice piece it was at such a decent cost, and "why can't you do that again?" As you might suspect, this variation can be used only for special cases—less than that if your agency's management is inclined to pinch pennies.

    d. For the occasional low-budget project of an unusual nature, consider having it done without the help of your creative department. This is the kind of counsel that rankles good creative people, but it is not meant as an act of war. In fact, the tactic is only meant to relieve them of some tedium. Take, for example, this actual situation in my career:

My client waited until the last minute to ask for help with a sales meeting. He needed a theme, a banner behind the podium and some signs on the walls of the meeting room, a few awards, and some kind of folder for each participant (one that would hold the agenda and meeting notes, etc.). He had to have everything in a week, and my agency's creative department was already working nights and weekends under incredible pressure on other projects. They simply could not get to the assignment in the time given.

Now, how you would tackle this dilemma. Take a minute to think about it. . . . Okay, got it figured out? Compare your thinking with my frantic solution:

For starters, I spent one evening at home filling several tablet pages with theme ideas. The next day I took the three "best" and showed them to one of the creative supervisors at lunch (I bought). He instantly offered some thoughts that improved what I had. I now had a theme.

I then visited with our production department. They knew a sign painter/showcard artist who could produce a banner on a tough plastic-impregnated paper to hang behind the podium. This simply stated the theme in bold lettering. For the wall signs, we looked up famous quotes relevant to the meeting theme (a typical one: "Behold the turtle. He makes progress only when he sticks his neck out." James Bryant Conant). Then we had them typeset and photostated up to 24" × 36" size and mounted on foamcore.

For awards we walked downtown to a novelty and rubber chicken store where we purchased such notable prizes as a pair of sunglasses fitted with battery-powered "windshield" wipers. These were awarded to the person judged to have demonstrated the clearest vision in forecasting future sales. We found an Einstein wig for the salesperson offering the hairiest ideas at the meeting, and so forth. (Never underestimate the power of corny gimmicks at gatherings of sales types.)

Lastly, we made thirty-five special folders for the participants by taking ordinary manila folders and running them through our photocopying machine. By carefully feeding them through one at a time, we found a way to have the meeting logo appear printed on each. They came out slightly curled, but we flattened them back to shape overnight under a stack of old Standard Rate & Data Service books.

It was now the day before the meeting, and we had met the client's needs with a modicum of time to spare, without a bundle of expense, and simultaneously had not infringed on the creative department's precious time.

Does that mean I advocate so-called creative bootlegging on a regular basis? Hardly. Only when you're pinned down under heavy fire. Use this maneuver very sparingly, or you're bound to be at odds with your creative teammates in short order.

Collateral projects can be moneymakers for a buttoned-down agency, but account managers must realize that many top-flight creative people regard such assignments as anathema. Managing this area profitably while still maintaining high creative standards is a bear. But, as a client once admonished me, "It's when you can hug the bear and live to talk about it that you know you've really accomplished something."

MAKING SMALL BUDGETS LOOK HUGE

In studying advertising, you are sure to encounter numerous scintillating case histories about GE, Ford, Xerox, Pepsi, Levi's, Apple, and other well-known brands. Reading them can be fascinating—inspirational, too, on occasion. But there's a basic catch, spelled b-u-d-g-e-t. While those textbook role models are working with media buys of seven figures-plus, thousands of American agencies are competing tooth and nail for annual budgets of $100,000 or less, often considerably less.

In 1989, the annual National Student Advertising Competition sponsored by AAF (American Advertising Federation) challenged entrants to come forth with a campaign for a new Kellogg's breakfast cereal. The budget: $40 million! Now this competition is in many ways a meritorious exercise. It requires students to think through a detailed real-world campaign and to present it to hard-nosed industry professionals. Many students regard it as the high-water mark of their university experience. And $40 million is by no means overkill to fund a national rollout. But it is a far cry from a typical working budget for the vast majority of America's ad agencies.

To put this in perspective, there are 5,000 agencies listed in *The Standard Directory of Advertising Agencies* (the agency red book), and less than 200 of them claim billings of $40 million or more *for their entire shop*. The 100th largest U.S. agency in 1990, according to *Adweek*, was Ackerman, Hood & McQueen of Oklahoma City with billings of $71.6 million. The hard truth is that unless you land a job with one of the majors, your first accounts are likely to have very small budgets.

Now it's easy to say, "We can't outspend 'em, so we'll just out-think 'em." But, when you're under the gun in Great Falls, or San Antonio, or Bangor, it's far from easy. Even in smaller markets it is *very* tough to accomplish much with only a few advertising dollars. In fact, when clients approach you with a plea to conquer the world, "but don't spend more than $35,000," you both may benefit if you counsel them *not* to advertise. If the account cannot spend enough to make a decent dent in the consumer's consciousness, chances are it will be a case of merely "spitting in the wind."

"All right," you say. "Assuming the situation isn't hopeless, and it is possible to make a decent dent, just what can be done to magnify a minuscule budget?"

The first and best way is, unfortunately, also the hardest: Do flat-out killer (i.e., outstanding) creative work. "Imagination is one of the last remaining legal means of gaining an unfair advantage over the competition," rightly said Tom McElligott, one of the founders of Fallon McElligott Rice, the Minneapolis agency that enjoyed spectacular growth and praise in the 80s. McElligott tells advisers, " . . . when everybody else is zigging, that's when it's time for you to zag. And the smaller the company is, and the bigger the competition, the more crucial that advice becomes."

If your agency creates advertising that captures the market's attention and is memorable enough to be *talked about*, oh, boy—suddenly, your little media budget seems bigger than life. For example, the Fallon McElligott Rice mini-campaign for a small hair salon in Minneapolis achieved near-cult status. (The most famous ad in the series featured a large stock photo of Albert Einstein looking typically disheveled with the headline: "A Bad Haircut Can Make Anyone Look Dumb.") *Photo/Design Magazine* reported, "[The campaign's] transit posters broke every record for being stolen, and have been seen as far afield as Stockholm, Sweden." Even though the ads haven't been in print for years, they are still vividly remembered in the Twin Cities and have even been featured in college marketing texts.

Or, from a more personal standpoint, I've seen great *radio* advertising cause consumers to tell researchers how much they liked the *TV* spots. In reality there weren't any TV commercials for our client, the Kah-Nee-Ta Resort in Central Oregon—we couldn't afford the medium. But the radio worked so strongly on the theater of the mind, the public was sure it had seen our client on television.

Other means of budget magnification are more mundane; three are discussed in the pages that follow.

1. The Merchandising Gambit

When you have few dollars for media purchases, don't trust to chance that key members of your sales/distribution network will see the advertising unaided. By key members, I mean your client's field salespeople—either factory-paid or manufacturer's reps—and those in the distribution chain. Depending on the industry, this might involve distributors, brokers, jobbers, and/or dealers or retailers, among others. Time and again these men and women will play a greater role in achieving your client's goals than will the end user.

If print ads are used, first be sure to send preprints to these important folk. Attach a note explaining when the campaign will run and where, and the fact that "we felt it imperative for you important people to receive advance notice." When the ad runs, talk your media sales rep into providing free sample copies or tearsheets. (Some publications "thumb-cut" the magazine so one can turn immediately to the appropriate page—a nice touch.) Again, attach a note touting what you are doing. Virtually every magazine has a **merchandising allowance** to provide additional support for its advertisers, but sometimes agencies overlook this. As you would expect, the more space you buy, the more goodies are offered, so smaller budgets are again seeing the short end of merchandising sticks. Still, some publications are more generous, especially with new advertisers, and it pays to work with your media person/department to negotiate for everything possible. Items routinely offered include the aforementioned tearsheets and sample copies, plus easel-back counter cards (sometimes nicely laminated) to use at point of sale, personalized letters from the publisher to your client's VIP customer accounts, and knick-knacks such as key chains, pens, and the like.

I advocate a third mailing about this same ad. Ideally it would include a counter card or other point-of-purchase item or an appropriate gimmick (such as a money clip). But if that's not in the cards, don't give up: Simply send another reprint or tearsheet and this time add a note saying, "We wanted to be sure you didn't miss seeing this dynamite message, which is appearing this month in publications reaching XXX,000 potential customers for you."

Regrettably, the cost of reprints can be a giant hang-up when you're coaxing a smaller client into this kind of effort, especially if it's a full-color advertisement. If the client can't or won't find the money to pay for reprints, the only option is to press one or more of the publications on the media buy to help out with tearsheets. For a small mailing list, you might use color photocopies, but the unit cost is still quite high. If you have time, it occasionally works to have the reprints provided by a label house (a printer specializing in big runs of color labels for consumer packages) or other printer of large sheets of paper. You can get a real bargain if they have room on the press sheet for your ad; otherwise, it would simply be blank paper trimmed off and trashed. You have to work with their schedules, though, and the paper stock generally is pretty lightweight. With black and white messages, reprints are much less of a problem—in a pinch, good photocopies will get you by.

The other media—radio, TV, and even outdoor—are also on the merchandising bandwagon, but obviously in different ways. You can send out radio scripts very inexpensively, but audio cassettes of the commercials are far better. (If your spot is announcer-read instead of studio-produced, arrange with the station for "air-check" cassette tapes of the message going out over the airways.)

With TV, you can send copies of story boards, but they have a fraction of the impact of seeing the live spot. So, I would push for meetings to show the finished commercial on good video equipment. Or, buy nonpreemptible spots at times when your vital audience can easily be in front of a TV set; then mail the schedule well in advance and lobby for them to host popcorn parties to see—and then record and replay on their VCR—this wondrous commercial. (For nonpreemptible times you pay a premium price to be assured of exactly when your message will run. "Preemptible" commercials cost less but can be bumped if a higher-paying customer wants that time slot.)

To achieve three meaningful mailing hits, you could first send advance word of the schedule's scope (calendar, number of estimated gross rating points, number of spots, anticipated audience size, etc.) and either a story board or a tantalizing single frame showing the creative approach. Second, send a detailed, day-by-day schedule showing precisely the time your spots will run and another visual page promoting the creative concept. Third, send a package of uncooked popcorn and a special "sell this one for the Gipper" comment from the sales manager.

2. The Big Bang Approach

Most small clients harbor delusions of being able to act like big advertisers. They have $40,000 to spend annually, so they try to spread it equally over twelve months. They rationalize, "I've got to keep in front of my customers year round; after all, that's what Coca-Cola and McDonalds do, and you sure can't quarrel with that kind of success!"

Sure, you can. There's an old Japanese proverb that goes, "Sparrows who emulate peacocks are likely to break a thigh." And so are clients who try to use the continuity advertising tactics of the national peacocks when they have only a sparrow's budget. I've yet to discover a client whose sales have significantly increased because he or she was barely visible on a regular basis.

Or, to put it in context of World War II, is it better to drop mediocre-size bombs monthly or a single atom bomb yearly? The A-bomb idea is high risk for a small account, but many times it is by far the best way to use a limited amount of money. "But consumers have such short memories," protest small thinkers. True, *unless* an honestly BIG idea is presented. Then, the residue—the fallout—will stick around and pay dividends for an incredibly long period.

It's tempting to cite the "1984" Apple Computer TV spot, run only once (during the 1984 Super Bowl) as the prime example of this big bang approach. But it isn't appropriate for this chapter because the production budget, allegedly $500,000, was decidedly *not* in the small category. Rather, my reference points are two clients, each with budgets of less than half of the production cost of that famous commercial. In the first instance, at BPN we finally persuaded Gerber Legendary Blades to put all of its remaining space budget into one full-color "spread" (two facing entire pages) magazine advertisement. Previously, it had insisted on 1/3-page messages. With this approach we could afford to buy only one insertion in each of two magazines. (The client was very nervous about the lack of frequency.) Naturally, we merchandised this ad to the veritable hilt before and after it ran.

The ad drew rave comments from the client's sales force, was credited as a major force in gaining important new distribution, and won several national creative awards. *Four years later*, the client was still receiving requests for reprints. As an added bonus, the photographs used in the ad were resized and utilized in the product catalog and for point-of-sale and packaging materials.

The second example involved a local real-estate firm that had traditionally spent all of its advertising budget in newspaper messages. It had flirted with radio but not with any enthusiasm. It had come to our agency (I was with Cole & Weber at the time) because it sought a brand image to differentiate the company clearly from its considerable competition. It had in mind a series of "classy" newspaper and magazine advertisements—in the mode of, say, Mercedes-Benz.

After wrestling with various options, the account manager, Pete Hatt (now the chairman of BPN), recommended that the entire budget be put into a series of three TV commercials and a concentrated schedule of approximately six weeks. At the time no other realtor—local, regional, or national—was using television. The client was dubious. Finally he reluctantly (against the advice of several of his staff) approved the notion, saying, "I'll accept your professional recommendation, but please understand, this better work, or *you're fired.*"

The spots ran and the phone rang off the hook. Calls were coming in not only from prospective customers but also from salespeople from competing firms who wanted to change jobs. Pre- and postawareness studies showed a phenomenal increase for the company's name and theme line. Shortly thereafter its sales volume was reported as number one among all realtors in the state.

3. *The Use of Celebrities*

From Nike's Bo Jackson to Jello's Bill Cosby, we are surrounded on the national scene by celebrities in advertising. And I guess we always will be, because—often flying in the face of logic—their endorsements do influence purchase decisions.

In general I am not a robust patron of the celebrity school of advertising, but I have to admit that on occasion endorsements can light up the marketing sky. Just be sure your target audience can clearly make the connection between the celeb and your product or service. "Sheer fame or memorability is not enough," wrote Jane Maas and Ken Roman in *How to Advertise*. "Choose a presenter who is *relevant* to your product." (Bill Cosby has been marvelous for some products, but bombed for others.) The two principal obstacles for me are (1) the price to obtain the services of a well-known actor or sports figure and (2) the creativity void displayed by advertisers who use these folk heroes. ("Hey, if we get Fats Russo to endorse our product, we don't need any fancy copy to make our point. Just have him hold up the package and say he likes it!")

Not too surprisingly, the cost factor eliminates most small-budget accounts from playing in this arena. But, you never know. There are occasions when a star is in between jobs or spouses or whatever, and just wants to work. And, in smaller markets, the celebrity tactic can be even more powerful since it is not a regular occurrence.

Some years back at Cole & Weber, we were able to coax the actor Robert Lansing to do a package of radio and TV spots for U.S. Bank of Oregon. He had been in a leading television series and some movies, but wasn't doing much of anything when we called. For around $10,000 we got a 110 percent professional effort from Lansing—and some noteworthy commercials. His presence made the campaign look far bigger and more expansive than it really was. Awareness soared, and deposits increased.

But, I would be remiss if I didn't add quickly some learn-the-hard-way words of warning: While celebrities can put more punch in your program, they also can cause rapid aging of agency personnel. If you run this course, look out for the following:

1. Dealing with agents. Some are just fine, but others are the stereotypical vultures: very unpleasant to deal with and ethically bloodthirsty.

2. Egos. Celebrities have big ones as a rule. They can be demanding, irascible, and petty, not to mention rude, pompous, and undependable. They also can be wonderful to work with. The best advice is to be ready for anything.

3. The quicksand of talent unions and residuals. Screen Actors Guild (SAG) and American Federation of Television and Radio Artists (AFTRA) are all-powerful, and if you employ entertainment talent you must be prepared to work within their policies for members. It's a subject worthy of a whole book, but by way of introduction, just remember that your client must pay for the use of SAG and AFTRA talent in thirteen-week cycles. Make sure your client understands that if he or she plans to use the commercials next spring or next year, there will be another talent payment due. Occasionally you can negotiate a personal services contract with the talent for an extended period—say, a year—with the proviso that you pay the union pension and welfare fees. Some try to beat the system by using Canadian

talent and shooting or recording north of the border. It can save money, but it certainly doesn't endear an agency to U.S. agents, talent, and studios.

4. Legal obstacles. Two decisions handed down in late 1989, by the U.S. Bankruptcy Court judge in Chicago, could dampen considerably a celeb's willingness to lend his or her name to an advertisement. The judge ruled that as "endorsers" the actors involved (in one case George Hamilton, in the other Lloyd Bridges) had a duty to the public not to make any "representation which would be deceptive" and that they must "independently substantiate the truthfulness of the words put in their mouths." At the very least this could raise the cost of celebrity endorsements, as they will want greater financial protection against this new risk of liability.

5. Fast fade. Celebrity status is fragile and uncertain. Today's hero can be tomorrow's yawn, and if the celeb goes downhill, so does his or her marketing impact. Athletes are notably risky because of the ogre of injury. William Perry, "The Fridge," of the NFL Chicago Bears was the hottest advertising property around one year, but then his team won fewer games and he was injured. All too soon, his value to advertisers evaporated.

To sum up, the right celebrity can help you maximize a limited budget. But bear in mind, working with these people is similar to skydiving. It can be heart-pounding, awe-inspiring, and crowd-pleasing, but it also can be nerve-wracking, unpredictable, and without much margin for error.

To see how complex it is to use AFTRA and SAG union talent, take a look at the "Quick Reference Talent Guide" in Figure 3.2. These guidelines are distributed by Talent Partners, Inc., a top organization in the area of coordinating talent payments with ad agencies. Suffice it to say, IRS regulations almost look simple by comparison.

Is there a trade secret for making an ad program seem bigger than life? Yes. It is summed up in the McElligott quote about *imagination* earlier in this section. Easily said, but not so easily achieved. It calls for brainpower and midnight oil. It's so much simpler to go with the first okay idea that comes along. As Thomas Edison allegedly said, "There are no lengths to which a man will not go to avoid thinking." If you happen to be an idea-sensitive, mentally tough agency staffer, it can be a golden opportunity to shine. You don't have to be a major league copywriter or marketing graybeard to help with ideas that expand the impact of a campaign. You just have to be street smart, work twice as hard, and carry a four-leaf clover.

SEEKING OUT AND WINNING NEW BUSINESS

Some say that advertising is an intoxicating experience, and I have to agree that it can be addictive—especially when you are in the midst of brilliant

Quick Reference Talent Guide

TELEVISION

Filming or Taping a Commercial

The use and payment of all performers appearing in television commercials is governed by the 1988–1991 Screen Actors Guild, Screen Extras Guild and American Federation of Television and Radio Artists commercials contracts. These are three-year contracts negotiated by the Joint Policy Committee on Broadcast Talent Union Relations of the AAAA–ANA and the unions. These collective bargaining agreements will expire on February 6, 1994. Accordingly, all commercials produced after that date will be governed by future agreements.

When a commercial is filmed or taped, the performers are paid a **"session fee"** as compensation for each day of work.

A session fee for an **"on-camera"** performer is $414.25 for an 8-hour day.

A session fee for an **"off-camera"** announcer is $311.50 for a 2-hour session.

Fees paid to performers known as **"extras"** vary depending upon the performance and skill requested from the extra. Extras are paid a single fee or buy-out entitling the advertiser to the use of the commercial for its life.

A **"commercial extra"** buy-out fee is $232.95.[*]

A **"hand model"** buy-out fee is $354.35.[*] [Someone who is hired for filming/taping of his or her hands, as in a commercial for a diamond ring or for bar soap.]

In the case of celebrity performers, payment agreements are individually negotiated often at rates over scale.

Note: All rates quoted herein are net and do not include Health and Welfare contributions, payroll taxes, and agency commission.

Program (Network) Use

If the commercial is scheduled on a network program, the performers are paid for each telecast during a **13-week cycle**. As an example, a commercial with one on-camera performer and one off-camera performer is telecast once during a 13-week cycle. The on-camera performer would receive $414.25 and the announcer $311.50.

If the same commercial were scheduled to be telecast 13 times, or once a week during the cycle, the on-camera performer would receive $1,607.80 and the off-camera announcer $1,247.35.

For network scheduling, as the number of uses in a cycle increase, the rate per use decreases.

[*] Extra rates will increase by 3.3% effective 2/7/93.

FIGURE 3.2 The "Quick Reference Talent Guide," distributed by Talent Partners, Inc., informs both talent and ad agencies about payment terms.

A discounted rate has been established for :10 and :15 commercials used on network programs.

Wild Spot Use [Commercials that will run as spot buys in unsponsored programs on noninterconnected stations.]

Compensation for the use of wild spots shall be for unlimited use within a cycle of 13 consecutive weeks and is based upon the number of cities in which the commercial is telecast.

For example, a commercial is used in Philadelphia, Boston, Detroit, and seven smaller cities. For one cycle, an on-camera performer's compensation for unlimited use is $789.15.

If the same commercial is used in New York, Chicago, Los Angeles, and 100 other cities, the on-camera performer would receive $2,532.95 for one cycle. An off-camera announcer in this commercial would receive $1,869.55.

Cable Use

For broadcast commercials used on cable networks, each performer will be paid for 13 weeks of unlimited use based on the total number of TV households/subscribers receiving the cable broadcast. The rates for an on-camera performer will range from $414.25 to $519.60 for each cycle of use.

There are lesser rates established for use on local cable systems with subscribers of one million or less.

Holding Fees

The holding fee guarantees a performer payment of a fee equal to his original session fee every 13 weeks. The 21-month maximum period of permissible use is divided into seven consecutive 13-week cycles called **"fixed cycles."**

The payment of this holding fee insures that the performer cannot do any other commercials which would be directly competitive to that of the client.

The holding fee can be credited against use fees if the "use cycle" commences within a "fixed cycle." If no use cycle commences until a later fixed cycle, a holding fee must still be paid for that fixed cycle to "hold" the commercial for future use. Holding fees may not be credited to cable use cycles.

If holding fees are not made when due, the performers must be released and we lose all rights to use the commercial.

Holding fees do not apply to the following: (1) off-camera singers; (2) commercials in a six-month dealer use cycle; (3) seasonal commercials; and (4) foreign use of commercials.

FIGURE 3.2 *continued*

Spanish Language Commercials

Performers on commercials produced in Spanish are paid the same session fees as other performers. Separate rates have been established for the use of these commercials based on use on Spanish language networks and spot stations. These rates are lower than comparable English language commercials due to the smaller potential audience.

Dealer Use

A special rate has been established to allow dealers or distributors of a product or service to purchase time and schedule commercials locally.

The following rates are for use of commercials by dealers for **six-month periods:**

On-camera performers (including use in N.Y.)	$1,876.35
On-camera performers (excluding use in N.Y.)	$1,659.40
Off-camera performers (including N.Y.)	$1,306.90
Off-camera performers (excluding N.Y.)	$1,198.50

At the time of delivery of a commercial to a dealer, he shall be notified in writing of the cycle dates for which the commercial may be used. The advertising agency which produced the commercial shall assume no liability for the dealer's use of the commercial beyond the specified cycle dates, this liability being passed on to the manufacturer or distributor and then to the dealer. The use of the dealer commercial may be renewed for an additional six-month period by payment of the applicable fees.

Demo/Test and Non-Air Commercials

Rates have been established at $311.50 per on-camera and $155.75 per off-camera performer for these types of commercials. They may not be aired without recontracting and payment of the full session fees to the performers. Lesser rates are available for group singers. No exclusivity may be given for these rates.

General

In addition to the foregoing rates, a union pension and health contribution equal to 11.5% (12.5% effective 2/7/92) of gross earnings is added to all payments. Additionally, clients are billed for a "payroll tax" which includes FICA contributions, state and federal unemployment compensation as well as workers' compensation.

When performers are paid the scale session fees, they may agree not to accept employment in commercials advertising any competitive product. For overscale payments, additional exclusivity may be obtained.

If the commercial is to be telecast outside of the U.S., Canada, or Mexico, or for theatrical or industrial exhibition, additional compensation for these rights must be made to the performers.

FIGURE 3.2 *continued*

RADIO

Recording a Radio Commercial

The use and payment of all performers appearing in radio commercials is governed by the current American Federation of Television and Radio Artists (AFTRA) Radio Commercials Contract. As with the television contracts, this three-year agreement will expire on February 6, 1994.

When a commercial is recorded, the performers are paid a session fee. The current session fee for announcers and actors is $163.30 for each commercial recorded in a 90-minute session. Additional commercials are at multiples of $163.30.

Lesser fees are paid to group singers in groups of three or more.

It should be noted that since the AFTRA contract does not allow agents of performers to deduct their fee from scale earnings, many radio performers are paid at the rate of scale plus 10%. Although the contract is a national one, the agents on the West Coast have established a higher rate for radio commercials, usually starting at $315.00 per session against which scale fees may be credited.

Wild Spot Use

Unlike television commercials, the payment of spot cycles may be based on either 13 weeks of use or 8 weeks of use. As with television, these cycles are for unlimited use in the number of cities in which the commercial is broadcast.

For example, a commercial used in Philadelphia, Boston, Detroit, and seven smaller cities for a 13-week cycle will cost $225.10 for one performer or $212.70 for an 8-week cycle.

The same commercial used in the major markets of New York, Chicago, Los Angeles, plus 100 other cities would entitle the performer to payment of $738.00 for 13 weeks or $674.80 for the 8-week cycle.

Network Program Use

Various rates based on the number of uses are available for network scheduling. There are one-week, four-week, eight-week, and 13-week use cycles. For the 13-week use we have unlimited use or special rates for use limited to 26 or 39 uses during the period.

For example, the fee for one-week use for each performer would be $357.55 while the 13-week unlimited use cycle would be $1,146.70.

Dealer Use

As with television, dealer use rates are available for six-month periods, renewable for additional periods of six months.

The rates are as follows: Actors and announcers $582.90
                           Solo or duo singers $462.85

Rates for groups of more than three performers are proportionately lower.

FIGURE 3.2 *continued*

> The same regulations as to the liability for use beyond the paid period hold for radio as with television.
>
> **Demo and Copy Testing**
>
> Rates for these non-air commercials have been established at $112.65 per commercial for announcers and actors. These commercials may not be aired without payment of an additional full session fee.
>
> **Holding Fees**
>
> As of the current contract, there are no holding fees for radio. The maximum period of use of a radio commercial for actors and announcers is 21 months from the date of recording.
>
> **Foreign Use**
>
> If a radio commercial is scheduled for use outside of the United States, its territories and possessions, and Canada, foreign use payments are due the performer.
>
> **Health and Welfare**
>
> In addition to the foregoing rates, a health and welfare payment equal to 12.5% of the gross earnings is added to all payments. Additionally, payroll taxes and agency commission are added to all billings to clients.
>
> *Note:* The preceding information has been abstracted from the various Union contracts. Only the essentials have been included.

FIGURE 3.2 *continued*

people and great work. The most potent sensory high in the agency world, though, is not the daily overload of the nervous system, even when things are incredibly bonkers. Rather, it is the innocently labeled, but darkly seductive, matter of *new business*.

On first inspection it all seems reasonable enough. After all, doesn't any company need a steady flow of new customers to keep afloat? One of the best sales managers I ever worked with told me that his success was based on the premise that "you got to keep 'em [customers] coming in the front door faster than they're going out the back." And that certainly applies to advertising agencies where—even under the best circumstances—some clients will be lost "out the back door" on any given day. It's clear that if an agency is to survive, let alone grow, new business must receive constant attention.

Unfortunately, many advertising agency people succumb to the fever of the hunt, and new business becomes more of an obsession than an element of good management. Back in the 70s, James Heekin, Jr., a New York marketing consultant, delivered a speech on "Why Agencies Lose Accounts" to the LA Advertising Club. High on his list was a preoccupation with new business. "I have actually seen an agency president accept a new business call during a client meeting. Clients expect fidelity, just like wives, husbands and sweethearts," he said.

Perhaps Abraham Lincoln summed it up best, "With the catching, ends the pleasures of the chase." The simple fact of the matter is that the pursuit of an important new account *is* a tremendous high. You work long hours under fierce time constraints. You participate in critical presentations to powerful people. You have few creative restrictions to contend with when concocting speculative recommendations. For once you can pull out all the stops, shoot the moon, and free-fall without worrying about parachutes. And at the end you know absolutely whether you've won or lost, whether your agency was the best of the bunch or just an also ran. It's an adrenalin surge of the first magnitude.In all of this excitement, of course, there is still the matter of service to your existing clients. Most will wish you well in the hunt and bask in the reflected glory of your success (after all, your victory is further reinforcement of their good judgment in hiring you). But, without exception, they will do slow burns if they feel you are shortchanging them because of a new business chase.

The newcomer to the agency world will soon see that business development is primarily the domain of the more senior members of the firm. The president, or chairperson, especially has to devote inordinate amounts of time to the hunt, and some agencies even have a business development manager on staff to head up this area. Consequently, you probably will not be invited to march off on a new business crusade for some time after being hired. But quickly you will be made aware of the importance of such activity, and you should look for ways to participate as soon as practical. One way is to help to fill the voids in service happening because of the temporary absence of others who are chasing new business. This is the time when you may prove invaluable to clients with immediate problems, and they will not forget it. I'm not advocating a guerrilla program to snake accounts away from senior people (that would not only be unethical but professionally suicidal as well). I am suggesting that this can be a rare window of opportunity for a newcomer to the agency business to demonstrate ability. The best single thing that happened to me at age 24 was the time my boss, the advertising director, was commanded to spend three weeks in the field as part of a special sales task force. While he was flying hither and yon, I was *the* advertising department. Sure I screwed up some, but I had the chance to do some things right, too. When the boss jet-lagged back into town, he was happy to see that the office wasn't in ruins and that others in the company now would feel okay about talking to me if he weren't around.

Later, working for ad agencies, I found that playing a strong backup role while the senior account person was temporarily out of commission (ill, on vacation, chasing a big new account) not only helped the agency but was a propellant to my career as well. If something transpired later that called for me to become the lead account person, it was much easier for both myself and the client. If everything simply reverted back to before, I still had the added experience to put on my résumé.

Even if you are not directly involved in new business pursuit at first, begin to think strategically about how you can help your agency. As a rule of thumb, new clients arrive via these routes: (1) the agency review, (2) the RFP ("Request for Proposal"), (3) the creative shootout, (4) the laydown. Let's examine each and determine just what role you might play.

The Agency Review

When a company requests an **agency review**, it means that the existing agency is in deep trouble. In theory, the incumbent can recover and hold the account, and this does happen on occasion. However, in most instances only divine intervention could save it. In this process, the client will invite a select number of agencies (perhaps a dozen or more for a large account) to "participate in the review." Generally, the client winnows the list down to a few (five or less) finalists by a process involving some combination of (a) answers to a questionnaire, (b) visits to the agencies to compare facilities, and (c) informal (so-called) meetings with the agency people who would be assigned to the account. Nine times out of ten, the final round will include competitive creative presentations.

These latter fall into two broad types: "creative shootouts," which are described at length later in this section, and "creative capability" presentations. Most agencies (ours included) much prefer the capability gig. By showing past work you are dealing with real marketing successes rather than offering the educated guesses required by a speculative creative recommendation. Frankly, they are easier and less costly to prepare, yet the prospect still receives a substantive picture of what the agency does best.

Obviously, the key in reviews is to be invited to participate. If your agency fails to get "at bats," it can't begin to hit creative home runs. Agencies with visibility and positive reputation have the inside track to making the invitation list, so the challenge is to build awareness of your shop's strengths. I've found that there are three effective tactics an agency can use to become better known, and a new hire can assist with each:

1. Enter the agency's best work in local, regional, and national creative competitions, and *win*! Obviously, this ploy will pay off only with a superior creative product. The mere act of entering won't do anything except cost a bundle of entry fees.

    When your agency enters these competitions, they are faced with a lot of grunt work in preparing and submitting the materials. That's where you can lend a big hand: Learn how to write the answers to the questions posed on the entry forms, generally calling for objectives, strategy, and results. It's a perfect way to become the librarian of the agency's best success stories and the authority on case history facts.

2. Help the agency develop a list of logical prospective clients and assist in making appointments to call on them with a succinct presentation of capability, including recent samples of the agency's work that best reflect its creative philosophy. These calls should not reek of hard sell; most prospective clients will avoid you if they sense that approach. Instead, make the point that this would be an opportunity to become more knowledgeable about the local agency situation. ("We realize you are not thinking about changing agencies right now, but should you ever reach that point, it could be beneficial to know what other agencies can offer.") You should not presume that you can make these calls alone early in your career when you most likely will be perceived as "a junior." Instead, at first simply strive to be included with senior managers on their visits.

   From the newcomer's standpoint, first find out what the agency's standard presentation is, and if it's good, commit it to heart. If it needs improvement, figure out how. Tactfully suggest the upgrades to your boss. If he or she doesn't buy, find out why and continue to think about how you would do the presentation if put in charge. Demonstrate that you would not be a liability if you were to join more senior people in making prospecting visits. Memorize all the interesting case histories you can dig up in the agency (quantifying results is always the hardest part).

3. Involve the agency in various civic and industry groups whose members include personnel from your list of prospects. But don't do this halfheartedly. Newer staffers from the agency should embrace only those organizations that truly interest them. And then they should throw themselves 100 percent into the effort. It's of no value to the individual or the agency to join just for appearances.

Request for Proposal ("RFP")

The **RFP** is generally used by government agencies or bureaus and public bodies like port authorities, but also by nonprofit organizations such as Planned Parenthood or United Way. It consists of a *long* questionnaire—often filled with ambiguities and governmentese—which must be completed in consummate detail and returned before a deadline. By law, public bodies must bend over backward in their efforts to offer every available ad agency the chance to compete for the business. As a result, the RFP is frequently mailed to every listing in the telephone Yellow Pages.

The biggest headache here is writing the answers to the long-winded questionnaire. If you can write cogently, you can be invaluable. Actually this skill will also dovetail nicely with needs for the private industry agency review as well, because the first step is generally to respond to a series of questions. (The difference is that the private sector historically asks the most relevant questions.)

After doing a few RFPs you probably will see an almost silly similarity to most questions. It seems that somewhere a book has been published about "How to Select an Ad Agency," and it includes a list of proper inquiries to make. Many of these basic answers can be reduced to boilerplate and put on the word processor or memory typewriter. However, when it comes to describing "Results of your most successful campaigns in the wood products industry" (or whatever is vital to the folks sending the questionnaire), you need to compose some direct, intelligent, meaningful copy. Some will tell you that "nobody reads those things anyway. They're just for looks." But I know of several occasions in which the prospect read every word, and we wouldn't have made the cut if we had submitted sloppy answers.

A quick caveat about government accounts: Public agencies are staffed by a lot of well-intentioned individuals—and some very smart ones, too. But, because they don't want to offend voters, they often have strange ideas about what makes good advertising. Plus, they tend to adore committees and advisory groups, and only occasionally do they have much experience working with good advertising agencies. Compounding everything, public agencies can be slow to pay and have Byzantine accounting requirements. And, as a final note of gloom, be aware that most government clients are required by law to put the account up for review at regular intervals, usually every one, three, or five years. This means that even if your agency is doing crackerjack work, it must go through the rigors of a review to hold on to the account.

The Creative Shootout

As mentioned earlier, the **creative shootout** sometimes is the finale of the agency review. But other times it stands alone: simply an invitation for a small number of agencies (rarely more than three or four) to show creative strength. The prospective client has quietly checked out each agency's capabilities and facilities. Now all he or she wants to know is *what can you do for me creatively?* In the past the common practice was for all expenses incurred in this presentation to be borne by the agency, but increasingly—thank goodness—some compensation is offered.

The creative department is literally under the gun in these situations, and anything you can do to get more relevant information to them will not go unnoticed. It's simple: The more you know about a prospect and its marketing needs, the more valuable you will become. (And this applies to all modes of the new business process.) Once you've spent a few months with an agency, you should be intimately aware of their most coveted prospects. As time allows, make it your personal charge to learn everything possible about the leading candidates.

The Laydown

Rarely in this business does an account fire its agency and select a replacement without a review. When it does happen, I call it a laydown. In the best of cases this is done because of the new agency's superb creative work and market track record. For example, in 1990, Nutrasweet selected Chiat/Day/Mojo to handle its $5 million Sugar Delight account because—as quoted in *Adweek*—of the agency's "creativity and innovation and ability to generate high awareness." In the worst of cases, it is done because the new agency's president is a fraternity brother of the account's new CEO. Unless your father happens to be a CEO as well, there isn't much you can do to help with laydowns except perhaps organize the victory party.

Notice that I have not cited the "sweep 'em off their feet" cliché. Allegedly, accounts will change hands because they were so dazzled by the silver-tonsilled pitch team that called out of the blue. In truth, it rarely occurs outside of bad movies. Clients of substance are simply not going to change agencies on the basis of a great cold call pitch. However, once in a while, that tactic will motivate a prospect to offer a single project to the aggressive calling agency. This try-us-on-for-size approach has more than a little merit, and I particularly recommend it for new small agencies struggling to establish themselves.

Concocting the Formal Presentation

Invariably, all of these new business routes lead to the legendary grand finale, the formal presentation(s) (or the **"pitch,"** as ad agencies refer to it) to the prospect's decision makers. The importance of these witching hours was best put by the late chairman of Ogilvy & Mather, Andrew Kershaw: "Making a superb presentation gives a client no assurance of superb advertising or superb service. But clients are human, and are inevitably bowled over by impressive presentations."

Great presentations, like great ads, require two components: important ideas and dramatic execution. As a newcomer to the agency, it is unlikely that you will immediately be given a role in agency review presentations, but that doesn't mean you should sit idly by. Wheedle your way into the rehearsals (they're almost always tinged with the odor of burning midnight oil) and absorb and observe.

Presenting well orally, like throwing a knuckleball or casting a dry fly, is not something learned overnight. In fact, I'm not sure it's totally teachable. Like the great pitchers and the great anglers, storybook presenters have an inherent, intuitive sense of the art. Becoming one requires (l) a sense of theater and a flair for the dramatic, (2) a stunningly complete knowledge of the subject, and (3) endless practice. Of enormous help to me—although I didn't realize it at the time—were parts in school plays and classes in drama and speech. Consequently, I now urge budding agency professionals to do the same. Learning difficult lines and having to face an ominous and restless audience is terrific preparation for a new business pitch. Joining Toastmasters groups is said to be another effective way to become more proficient.

One last point: If your agency isn't already into the use of unusual, three-dimensional **leave-behinds** that prospects take with them from the presentation, urge them into the practice. Call them rubber chickens if you like, but we found them marvelously effective in making sure our call was well remembered.

Curiously, of all the leave-behind items we experimented with in the early days at BPN, our most successful was a three-foot section of ordinary two-by-four-inch fir wood. (My partner, Mark Norrander, produced the first ones on a table saw in his basement. He also figured out a way to woodburn in the BPN logo.) At the conclusion of the meeting, we would present the piece of wood nestled in red velour in a handsome black box, and I would recite the tale of the farmer and the Missouri mule. It's an old, *old* folk story about a farmer's problems in getting his mule to move. He tried yelling, screaming, pleading, threatening, subterfuge, and so on, all to no avail. The mule wouldn't budge. He'd about given up when a neighbor came by. After listening to the farmer's plight, this neighbor picked up a weather-beaten two-by-four and *smacked the mule squarely between the eyes.* Whereupon the mule immediately did everything asked of him. "It's just a matter of properly getting his attention," explained the neighbor.

"It's the same situation today," I would say. "You need advertising that is strong enough to smack the public between the eyes and *get their attention*! Which is precisely what our agency can deliver. You may lose our business cards, but hopefully you won't have any trouble finding this two-by-four when you're ready to change agencies (or should you need some kindling on cold winter mornings)." I should quickly add that it was emblazoned with a gold foil label extolling "The Gentle Art of Persuasion," written by my partner, Bill Borders.

> There's a barrier around your customers' minds. Each and every one of them. Erected to defend themselves from the 1,000 to 1,500 messages that besiege them every day.
>
> If you can't bust through this barrier you can't have their attention. Persuasion becomes impossible.
>
> It's impervious to "safe" advertising. Mediocrity won't dent it. The usual is useless.

What it takes is a good, swift smack to the head. From an interruptive visual. A vigorous word or phrase. An untried idea.

That's how you touch emotions. And topple barriers.

New business is without a doubt the catnip of the industry. It can be the headiest of aromas, the most alluring to all the senses. But, learn early that two of the best tactical virtues for consistently winning new clients are *not* flash and dazzle. Rather, they are *patience* and *tenacity*. If you hang in there (and I mean *for years*, if necessary) and never give up, you'll be amazed at what can happen—assuming, of course, that your agency knows how to deliver work that works.

HANDLING THOSE MYRIAD DETAILS

> God is in the details. Somebody told me Michelangelo said that. If he didn't, he should have.*
>
> Hal Riney

Another myth perpetuated by career counselors is that creative skill is the all-important requirement for wealth, favor, and prestige at any good ad agency. Not so. As an account, production, media, or research person, creative flair is hardly the indispensable condition. What the strong agencies really love in your department is a *passion for details*. They dote on individuals who, while understanding the big picture, really shine when managing the nitty gritty details of the whole scenario. You see, the old humdrum adages of "follow-up" and "double-check" may lack sex appeal, but they're the mortar holding the agency's bricks together.

As ordinary as it sounds, the critical links that can propel a career forward in account service include such things as making one more phone call than seems necessary, reading the mechanical (pasteup) one more time after everyone has signed off, checking that invoice again even though the accounting department says it's okay. Regardless of who assures you that an important detail is "all taken care of," take a minute to check it *yourself*.

And here we bang into the philosophical shibboleth of the larger agency account people: "Wait a minute! If I can't delegate and count on my team, how can I expect to manage my account in the proper way?" My answer is that there is a big difference between delegating and abdicating responsibility. The best and the brightest adopt Harry Truman's adage that the buck stops right here—in the middle of your desk. I'm fond of quoting point #10 in Ogilvy & Mather's pamphlet, "Principles of Account Management": "Be responsible. . . . Never assume that something *will happen* unless you have made sure it will happen. Button down details. Check and

---

* Actually it was Mies Van Der Rohe, speaking about architecture.

double-check. Rehearse. Follow-up. Worry."

This penchant for detail can manifest itself in many ways, but in an attempt to be specific, let me cite three diverse examples:

1. Always reconfirm the appointment. Last week the client set a meeting for 10:00 A.M. on the 7th, so that takes care of that, right? Hardly. Call him or her on the 6th and make sure it still makes sense. Clients lead frenzied, unpredictable work lives, too. Even the finest occasionally overbook themselves, or even forget. Curiously, reconfirmation is done so infrequently, clients sometimes will be pleasantly dumbfounded that you've taken the time to double-check. Oh, sure you can have your secretary, receptionist, or account coordinator do this—if you have one—but nothing beats the personal contact.

2. Always make sure the creative folks understand the assignment *and the deadline*. First, write out the job instructions so clearly they would make sense to a five-year-old, and then finish the loop with a few minutes of face-to-face conversation. Too many times I've worked with an art director who thought the layout was due on the 17th instead of the 7th, or a copywriter who wouldn't start until he had more information but hadn't gotten around to calling me. Don't ever assume that somehow your creative colleagues will have "gotten" these instructions without your having made them explicit.

3. A printed job is not complete until the required number of pieces reach their final destination. Knowing it is printed is not enough. Take, for instance, this personal experience: We created and produced several thousand handsome brochures for a mailing. The client was pleased beyond words at the press check; the art director was ecstatic, the production manager elated, and I greatly relieved. The next morning samples of the printed piece arrived right on schedule at both the agency and the client's offices. The full run was to go to a local mailing service for addressing, sorting, and transport to the post office. All had to reach the P.O. before 5:00 P.M., but it looked like a sure thing. Cigars all around, right? At 4:30 P.M. our client's Titanic hit the iceberg. The mailing house called to report no brochures had been delivered. My production manager's screams shook the light fixtures in the art department. This simply *couldn't* be happening! But it did. The printer delivered right on time as promised. The only problem was that the shipment went to the *wrong* direct mail house. There, no one knew what they were supposed to do with the mailers, so they simply held the boxes on their loading dock. The correct mailing house was incredibly busy that day, so nobody thought about alerting us until the sun was setting. It was the classic case of one brick short of a full load.

Thanks to the miracle of overtime, we traced the errant cartons down, scrambled through the night, and managed to get the mailing on its way almost on time. But the point was etched indelibly in my mind: Always *double-check everything* and *never assume anything.*

One other piece of advice in the "picky, picky" category: Always return phone calls—no exceptions. When you get to be chairman of the board, then maybe, just maybe, you can duck this rule. But until then, call everybody back that calls you. Oh, sure, some of the calls are from media sales reps, and everyone knows what a nuisance they can be. But keep in mind that these folks are plugged into the industry, and they can be a powerful network for you if only you give them some basic business courtesy, starting with returning their calls.

One of my former bosses used to say that if you wanted to get the word out fast, it wasn't telephone, telegraph, or television—it was simply tele-a-rep. And he had a point because a good media salesperson frequently is among the first to know if an account is shaky, or has just gone into review, or if Fred Smertz has just been canned over at Bascom, Sheets & Barflover. Particularly when you're starting out, it pays to extend your range of industry contacts, and media reps are step one.

But, say the call isn't from some known commodity like the salesman from *Weeds, Trees & Turf.* What if it's a name that means nothing to you? Is it worth a call back? You bet. I've had mystery calls range from a man who wanted help promoting his Hungarian ventriloquist act to investment opportunities in uncut South African diamonds. And, sure, most of these people are trying to sell you something or (especially after you log some time in the business) they're trying to land a job. But they still are people, the same species that your advertising is trying to reach, and every conversation—including the strange ones—can contribute to your understanding of the human experience.

Plus, advertising, like all businesses, has a lot of twists and turns, and today's unknown phone call can so easily evolve into tomorrow's key prospect. I've been startled to hear literally dozens of people tell me, "When I was hunting a job, you were the only one who would return my call. And I'll never forget that." You can't buy that kind of good will, so return those calls, good and bad. However, I have to close this bombast with a disclaimer. Even though I exhort you to return every call, I don't advocate that you have to listen long if your caller turns out to be a real loser. If it's hopeless, don't prolong the agony. Here are some of my favorite getaway lines:

Hey, I'm really not in the market. Thanks. Goodbye.

They're waving at me, and I've got to get in this meeting or my career's in reverse.

I'd like to talk more, but I've got the flu and have to make a dash to the restroom pronto.

You don't want to talk to me. I think I'm about to be laid off.

CLIPPING AND RIPPING: A NOTHING-FANCY-BUT-IT-WORKS TIP

As your personal workload grows, you will find it increasingly difficult to touch base regularly with all of your clients and prospects. It all seems so simple at first, but then you begin to realize that there are so many semivisible folks at the XYZ account that can influence the future of your agency. There's the ad manager, of course, and the director of marketing, and their assistants, the research manager, the sales managers, the product development people, the DINKs (double income, no kids) in PR, the general management types, and the list goes on. And they *all* love attention from the agency. So, how can you let them know you are thinking about them without making forty-seven phone calls a day?

Clip, clip, clip like crazy is the solution. You'll have dozens of magazines and periodicals routed across your desk—so many you'll find it impossible to read many in detail. But you can *skim* them and cultivate the knack of picking out articles, quotes, photos, and cartoons that relate to the individual interests of many of those key folks at XYZ Corporation.

So rip or clip them, grab a note pad (most agencies have lots on which the name is emblazoned prominently), and handwrite a short note. I emphasize the *hand* aspect, because having the notes typed indicates that maybe you had someone else do this for you. In a crunch the note can be as basic as "Thought you might like to see this," but ideally it should say one specific thing such as, "We noticed this article on diode emissions and felt it would be of interest to you because of your work on the Zambo program." As you rise in the ranks, others can help you find and clip, but *always pen the notes yourself*.

It helps not only with outside clients but also internally with other members of your agency team. If you spot something that you know would interest the art director on XYZ, impale it on his drawing board with a magenta push pin. If the production manager raises Dobermans and you find a color photo of some prize winners, send the clipping along with your next work order. It isn't fancy communication, but clip and rip is disarmingly direct and refreshingly personal in an increasingly computerized universe. You won't find the technique discussed at length in the *Harvard Business Review*, but it really is worth a try.

CHAPTER FOUR

What's Wrong with Today's Account Managers

These pages dwell on the great need for people in advertising management to think strategically and to formulate a conscious creative philosophy. Only then can they consistently identify superlative creative work in formative stages. Four specific examples from my experience are presented to illuminate my personal guidelines as to what constitutes effective advertising.

If an account manager is charming, erudite, persuasive, honest, intense, tenacious, enthusiastic, and diligent—isn't that enough? Not quite.

Such an account manager can still be lacking the one exceptional quality that sets apart the giants in this business: a deep and abiding conviction about what constitutes outstanding advertising.

I confess to touting this in almost a religious sense: Exceptional account managers possess a burning belief in what is right, harbor an aroused antipathy for the sin of mediocrity, and zealously convert the heathen. I have seen the opposite too often: Account managers who, failing to possess a guiding philosophy, aren't able to separate the trite from the true, who don't know when to fight or even what to do battle about. They are doomed to suffer a lifetime membership in the Abominable Adperson Club.

IDENTIFYING "EMPTY" ACCOUNT MANAGERS

It's a painful fact of life that numerous account managers do rise in the ranks without forming any real beliefs of their own. Instead of pursuing original thinking, they concentrate on account lubrication, that is, "on keeping everything running smoothly." Their proudest achievements are conciliation, coordination, placation, and compromise. In David Ogilvy's words, "They remain permanently superficial." They develop a sixth sense for "what will sell" and "how far we can go." They prefer paths of least resistance. They are without equal in executive messengering, schmoozing, facilitating, and stroking. Small wonder they perspire heavily if asked to row in choppy waters.

When you query these individuals about their advertising philosophy, they reply as though fingering cliché beads: To them, great advertising "grabs you," "rings your chimes," "stops you in your tracks," "knocks your socks off," and worst of all, has "lots of pizazz." When you ask them for their favorite advertisements of all time, they mumble and answer evasively with several disclaimers. They're careful not to offend you. Understandably, they have scant ability to identify potentially great ads in rough form. They talk fluidly about the "importance of ideas," but don't ask them to defend one tinged with controversy.

Distressingly, it is still possible for agencies with this kind of account management to prosper. Their stock in trade relies heavily on stereotypes, bromides, and pablum. The end result is what Bill Bernbach called "a criminal waste of money, spent on boring advertising that never gets looked at"—or what caused Tom McElligott to conclude, "why 95% of advertising doesn't work."

However, periodically some signs of hope appear on the horizon—even at the hulking mega-buck-agencies. In an interview in the American Advertising Federation's quarterly magazine, *American Advertising*, Sean Fitzpatrick, McCann-Erickson USA vice chairman and chief creative officer, advocates building into every account person's annual review "what they did to improve the creative work during that year, and how the creative reel on their accounts improved . . . independent of what the client thinks, independent of research reports, independent of everything except pure creative judgement." He believes that such a discipline will "cause the account people to be on the lookout for and encourage more creativity." When Keith Reinhard was CEO at Needham Harper Worldwide (now holds the same title at DDB Needham Worldwide), he told *Adweek*, "The account people who go places in this company are the ones identified with great advertising." Steve Bowen, president of J. Walter Thompson USA, has been quoted as saying, "Really great account work gives you a much better likelihood of consistent creative excellence." I couldn't agree more.

Long ago I was quick to blame agency creative departments for the abundances of ugly advertising on our planet. But as time passed, I began to understand that those agencies were frequently dominated by account managers who really didn't care what kind of work they produced. On the other hand the agencies repeatedly turning out award-winning work were staffed not only with superb writers and art directors but also with account people every bit as dedicated to the same beliefs, the same vision of creative excellence. What the advertising world needs now is an influx of this model of account manager. And that's where you, the reader, come in. I want *you* to address this need. And soon!

Wait a minute, you might be saying to yourself. How can you, Mr. Perrin, harangue us about this conviction stuff without revealing *your* philosophy?

Fair enough. For starters, let's examine the cornerstones:

STRATEGIC THINKING AND BIG IDEAS: THE CORNERSTONES OF EFFECTIVE ADVERTISING

There are two givens: First, for anything positive to happen in the marketplace, the message has to be strategically right. It must be relevant and appropriate to the audience. The best creative directors—those like Tom McElligott—never miss this point. Advertising "involves bringing a high degree of discipline—business discipline—to imagination," he said. Bill Bernbach felt the same: "The heart of creativity . . . is discipline." It is here that the account manager can contribute most to creative problem solving. In fact, it is the sacred duty of the account manager to monitor the strategic thinking behind every advertisement. It must be a participatory involvement, not a case of looking on benignly from the sidelines.

If you are looking for some simple guidelines on setting strategy, I recommend Chapter 1 of *How to Advertise* by Ken Roman and Jane Maas. In essence they say first to consider where you want to position the product or service in the customer's mind, and then to apply strategic thinking to determine how to accomplish this.

The first part of the process is to examine the *marketing* strategy statement, which is the master plan covering the total marketing mix: distribution, pricing, packaging, and so on. Then devise the *advertising* strategy (also called the *creative* or *copy* strategy), which focuses on what to say and how to say it. Roman and Maas suggest that a good advertising strategy covers five key points:

1. Objective—what the advertising should do.
2. Target audience—who is your customer?
3. Key consumer benefit—why the customer should buy your product.
4. Support—a reason to believe in that benefit.
5. Tone and manner—a statement of the product "personality."

At Borders, Perrin and Norrander, account managers begin the strategy process by filling out a "creative brief" (Figure 4.1) in concert with the client. In addition to pinning down the *what, who,* and *why* outlined by Roman and Maas, the document also asks *how* the product or service

BP&N

BORDERS PERRIN AND NORRANDER INC.

CLIENT/AGENCY CREATIVE BRIEF

ACCOUNT MANAGER: _____   DATE OPENED: _____
CLIENT: _____   JOB NUMBER: _____
PRODUCT/SERVICE: _____   JOB TITLE: _____

INSTRUCTIONS: *Please furnish all information below where appropriate. Too much input is better than too little. Use additional pages as needed. Authorization to be signed by those who will ultimately approve concept.*

WHO are we trying to reach? Describe the target audience.
_____
_____
_____

WHY do these people buy or use this product/service? Explain the consumer benefit(s).
_____
_____
_____

WHAT is the objective of this project? Briefly but concisely define the results we're after.
_____
_____
_____

HOW does client's product/service compare to competition's? Don't sell, just tell; pro's & con's.
_____
_____
_____

WHERE is this communication going to run? Discuss media alternatives that seem appropriate.
_____
_____
_____

WHEN is a realistic deadline for solutions?
Concept: _____ Layout: _____ Copy: _____ Mechanical: _____ Materials: _____ Other: _____

HOW MUCH is allotted to accomplish this task? Please give approximate dollar range.
_____

WHATEVER else is pertinent information. Executional considerations, additional communication points, cautions, extenuating circumstances, possible selling strategies, etc.
_____
_____
_____

CLIENT AUTHORIZATION(S)   AGENCY INITIATOR
....

FIGURE 4.1 This "creative brief" form proved useful at BPN in working with clients to set advertising strategy. Once the form was filled out, both agency and client were required to confirm their agreement on major points by "signing on the bottom line."

compares with those of competitors and *where* the message might best run from a media standpoint. After reaching an agreement, both the client the and agency sign off on the form. Then, and only then, does the creative work begin.

The second given in my philosophy is that the most potent advertising always revolves around an imaginative, compelling idea. Ogilvy is correct: "Unless your campaign is built around a great idea, it will flop." Some would argue that strategy and ideas are semantically interchangeable, but I endorse the opinion stated in a General Foods annual report: "Strategies only point direction; ideas create the results." Bernbach has written, "The history of merchandising, indeed the history of the world in all its aspects—science, art, economics, politics, even religion—is measured by the impact of great and original ideas."

Belief in the power of original thinking is not just the self-centered view of ad people, either. Harvard Business School's Theodore Levitt wrote an entire book on *The Marketing Imagination* and lucidly urged businesspeople to start "thinking with a special quality, transcending the ordinary and thus reaching imaginatively beyond the obvious or merely deductive."

JUDGING THE RESULTS OF ADVERTISING STRATEGIES

Would I care to cite some examples? And perhaps compare and contrast "strategically right" solutions with those I would call "obvious and merely deductive"? Absolutely. For you pragmatists I'll even cite hardball results. And although it would be far easier to reach into the national showcase and show big-name campaigns, I will restrict my specimens to regional/local efforts from my own experience. To show I believe in equal opportunity, two are consumer advertising efforts and two others are from the supposedly less delectable realm of business-to-business, or "trade," advertising.

(I suggest that you pause after each stated objective and consider the kind of advertising solution *you* would recommend. Then compare that with what actually happened.)

1. Columbia Sportswear

The objective: To create brand awareness for a line of outdoor-related clothing produced by a small, little-known company in Portland, Oregon. Simultaneously to give the brand a personality and a position differentiating it from anyone in its industry.

A typical "obvious/ordinary" (hereafter called O/O) solution: Use large, handsome photos of the merchandise worn by nice-looking models in recognizable outdoor situations. Use copy that speaks to quality, style, and function. (Oh, yes, don't forget innovation and leadership.)

124 ♦ What's Wrong with Today's Account Managers

> ## "INTRODUCING THE PRODUCT OF AN OVERLY PROTECTIVE MOTHER."
> —Tim Boyle
>
> As a kid, when I wanted to go out and play, Mom would bundle me up like a knight about to plunge into battle.
> Now, as President of Columbia, it appears she wants to do the same for you. Albeit a bit more efficiently.
> Meet our new Palmer System IV Parka™. An outer jacket of Gore-Tex® over Exacta™ Cloth. And a zip-in *reversible* interior jacket of Polar Fleece on one side, Exacta™ Cloth on the other.
> Figure it out. Worn together or separately, there are four jackets here, to cope with anything your adventures may lead to. Be it breeze, blizzard or black knight.
>
> Finally a parka as changeable as the weather. The new Palmer™ is four jackets in one.
>
> The Palmer System IV Parka™ is available at finer outfitters everywhere. For a color brochure send $1 to us at 6600 N. Baltimore, Dept. A1, Portland, Oregon 97203.
> Gore-Tex® is a registered trademark of W.L. Gore & Assoc.
> Ze Pel® is a registered trademark of Dupont.
>
> **Columbia** Sportswear Company

FIGURE 4.2 Columbia's "Mother Boyle" campaign has built a distinctive personality for the brand and dramatically shows the power of a strong, relevant idea that is strategically right on target.

The "strategic/big idea" (hereafter labeled SBI) solution: Use the widow of the company's founder, "Mother Boyle," as spokesperson because she radiates the brand's strongest support attribute: a mother's concern for doing it right or not doing it at all. She's sixtyish, plump, outspoken—in short a real person, not a Betty Crocker kind of symbol. She's apt to say something like, "By God we aren't going to sell anything that isn't well-made. This is a family-run business, and anybody not treating customers right can expect a paddling." Play off her rather domineering demeanor with those who work with her, not the least of which is the company president, her son Tim.

Conceptually, the campaign has similarities to Scali, McCabe & Sloves's renowned ads for Frank Perdue's chickens ("It Takes a Tough Man to

FIGURE 4.3 Throughout the campaign, Columbia's management has allowed the agency to create ads that are free of the "brag and boast" copy so prevalent today. As a result, the irreverent candor of the messages continually reinforces the brand's credibility.

Produce a Tender Chicken"). Perdue used television, though, which Columbia could not afford nationally. Two Columbia Sportswear print ads are shown in Figures 4.2 and 4.3 to illustrate how the idea has grown and evolved since first unveiled in 1984.

The results: Columbia is enjoying the kind of growth many companies would love to stuff and mount on their office walls: about 15 to 20 percent annually for the past five years (sales exceeded $100 million in 1990)—nice, controlled growth that allows the company not to lose touch with its basic principles. Mother Boyle has become something of a celebrity in the sportswear industry, signing autographs at trade shows and receiving several marriage proposals in her fan mail.

2. Burgerville

The objective: To attract more customers to fast-food-service outlets competing head-on with national giants (Burger King, McDonald's, Wendy's) that have locations *everywhere* . The nationals also have gargantuan budgets for advertising and sales promotion.

Typical O/O solution: Use radio and television ads with a "catchy jingle." Be sure to show lots of kids having a good time. "See if you can't use my grandchildren and some of the neighbor's children in the spot. They're cuter than those models." Make the product a hero: Show those hamburgers up close and maybe doctor them a little to look *really* juicy.

The SBI solution: Position Burgerville as the fast-food chain that *isn't* all over the country. In fact, let's face it: For most of America, Burgerville is inconveniently located. Folks at home here in Oregon and Washington can eat their tasty hamburgers, but those in other parts of the country can only eat their hearts out. The payoff support strategy is provided by stories of former Burgerville customers who have moved to faraway places like Texas and New York and are crying the blues because they miss their Burgerville burgers. Television was the dominant portion of the media plan, which also included outdoor and in-store point-of-purchase materials.

The results: The advertising has pushed store traffic to record highs, and one of the campaign's TV spots made *Advertising Age's* list of "The Seventy Best Commercials of 1989." In Figure 4.4, a story board and TV copy for one of the campaign's commercials are shown. A variety of print materials for the campaign are shown in Figure 4.5.

3. Oregon Saw Chain and Wood-Cutting Accessories

The objective: To capture the attention of hardware/home center purchasing managers ("buyers," in the jargon of the trade) and motivate them to visit a particular booth at an upcoming national trade show. The product category is chain-saw accessories, one that is not exactly hot stuff.

Typical O/O solution: Shout "Don't miss our booth at the Hardware Show" in LARGE, BOLD type. Offer a free gift for showing up. Have a really curvy woman in the ad, because most purchasing agents are men inclined to smile at really curvy women. Or, if you have some kind of case study, run a testimonial with a devoted customer saying how much he or she likes your products.

The SBI solution: First, position the products as firewood accessories—rather than chain-saw accessories—so that consumers can quickly grasp the benefit of using them. Then, employ a "reverse testimonial" advertising strategy: ads and mailers showing well-known hardware chain store purchasing agents with headlines like "Jerry Eller Would Just As Soon You Ignored

FIGURE 4.4 This story board and TV copy illustrate how Burgerville used an unusual idea to capture consumers' attention. Instead of the customary happy face approach, this commercial featured a disgruntled customer—unhappy because he had moved to a place where he no longer could buy his favorite burgers. But "most of America's" loss was clearly the gain of those living where Burgervilles were conveniently located.

BORDERS, PERRIN AND NORRANDER COPY

DATE: September 2, 1988

CLIENT: Burgerville USA

JOB #: 95-T-328-88

TITLE: "Richard Aiken"

LENGTH: :30

VIDEO	AUDIO
(OPEN WITH WHITE-ON-BLACK SUPER: ANOTHER UNHAPPY BURGERVILLE CUSTOMER.)	Richard: I want George Popstra of Burgerville to hear this . . .
(CUT TO CLOSEUP OF RICHARD AIKEN WEARING FOREMAN GARB. SUPER: Rich Aiken Formerly of Vancouver, WA.)	. . . I moved to Texas in '86 . . . . . .They've got eight million head of cattle down here . . .
(CAMERA PULLBACK)	. . . But not one (beep) Burgerville?
(CUT TO BEAUTY SHOT OF COLOSSAL BURGER)	Man I miss those cheeseburgers with that secret sauce.
(CUT BACK TO RICHARD)	I'm kinda used to things being inconveniently located . . .
(WIDE SHOT SHOWING RICHARD ON TOP OF BRIDGE BEING CONSTRUCTED.)	But, two thousand miles? C'mon, George, how hard can it be to build a burger stand?
(DISSOLVE TO MAP WITH BURGERVILLE LOCATIONS MARKED WITH PIN LIGHTS. BURGERVILLE LOGOSUPER OVER MAP.)	Voice-over: Burgerville. Inconveniently located for most of America.

111 SOUTHWEST OAK STREET, PORTLAND, OREGON 97204 / 503-227-2506
1115 FIRST AVENUE, SEATTLE, WASHINGTON 98101 / 206-343-7741

FIGURE 4.4 *continued* This is the copy originally written and approved. The copy appearing on the story board page is that which actually was heard in the finished commercial. All the revisions were made and approved during the filming.

FIGURE 4.5 The total campaign employed a variety of print materials to dramatize the benefits of living where it was easy to find a Burgerville location.

130 • What's Wrong with Today's Account Managers

INCONVENIENTLY LOCATED FOR MOST OF AMERICA.
(But Not For You.)

BURGERVILLE USA

FIGURE 4.5   *continued*

His Ringing Endorsement of Oregon Firewood Products." These men were not eager to appear in the ads and too busy to have their photos taken in a studio, so we sent a photographer to their offices. Amazingly, working alone and without the benefit of sophisticated lighting, he was able to capture the essence of the tough-buyer personality for the ads, one of which is illustrated in Figure 4.6.

A prospective client once praised this series as "the classic negative sell. Who says it won't work!" Al Ries and Jack Trout, in their best-selling book, *Positioning: The Battle for Your Mind*, seconded the use of this kind of strategic approach. "When an advertiser admits a negative, the reader is inclined to give them [sic] the positive."

The results: There was heavy traffic and order booking at the booth during the trade show. Visitors included several hardware buyers who hinted broadly that they wouldn't mind appearing in future ads. Sales for this client eventually increased ninefold over a four-year period.

FIGURE 4.6 This is a prime example of the "reluctant testimonial" strategy, which uses incongruity and honesty to catch the eye of cynical buyers.

4. Sachs-Dolmar Chain Saws

The objective: To attract inquiries from U.S. power equipment dealers who might be persuaded to take on a new line of German chain saws.

A typical O/O solution: Run trade-magazine advertising featuring a large coupon. Put the word "Profit-Maker" in the headline. Show the saw in use.

The SBI solution: It generally makes sense to show a coupon in advertising to attract inquiries. Even if the readers don't clip the coupon, they quickly perceive it as an ad that wants to send them something, and they pay extra attention. But how could we make our coupon distinctly different from the others appearing in the trade mags? How could we send a note of urgency concerning this unique and time-limited opportunity?

Strategic answer: Run the ad with the coupon already ripped out. Such an unusual thing would be certain to arouse human curiosity.

At first glance the ad would be sure to seize the reader's attention (see Figure 4.7). My creative partners had come up with the idea to preprint and die-cut the advertisement and then have it bound in the magazine. It was printed on the same weight paper as the publication used throughout the issue, and the reverse side was covered with regular editorial matter. As a result, it didn't look anything like a typical advertising insert.

To power-saw dealers, it was startling to find a portion of the ad already cut out when they thumbed through their just-arrived trade magazine. They were quickly involved. There was obviously something missing, and it looked as though it might be a coupon for more information about becoming a Sachs-Dolmar dealer. Was somebody in the post office clipping out the coupon before it reached them (and maybe thinking of becoming a competitor)? Was it one of the mechanics in the service department? Was some crook tampering with the company mailbox? What *was* going on?

The ad copy offered considerable information about the product (which many dealers had not read before) and, not coincidentally, provided a phone number to call if a reader wanted to know more. And call they did. The Sachs-Dolmar sales manager told me he had never experienced such a response from a trade ad. After explaining that the missing coupon was just "something thought up by our ad people," he took the opportunity to sell callers on carrying the S-D line.

The results: The several hundred leads obtained became the basis for setting up the client's U.S. dealer network.

DISSECTING THE CRUCIAL COMPONENTS: INTERRUPTION, EMOTION, INFORMATION

Are there consistently identifiable elements within SBI advertising? Of course. Three paramount factors are (1) relevant interruption, (2) relevant emotion, and (3) relevant information.

Suddenly dealers everywhere want to learn more about Sachs-Dolmar.

We knew this was going to happen. Word gets around. Guys brag. Before you know it, what started as casual curiosity about these German saws turns into out and out enthusiasm.

Read on, you'll see why.

Like Mercedes-Benz, Sachs-Dolmar is an old German company that believes precision engineering is half science, half art. And, just as Mercedes was once rather unknown in this country, so was Sachs-Dolmar.

But time has a way of changing things.

Today, at least among the hard core pro loggers, the name Sachs-Dolmar has earned an enviable position. The rugged reliability and smooth performance of these saws has impressed them just as it has loggers in over 100 other countries.

And dealers are impressed by their earnings. Because like most European-crafted machines, these saws command premium prices, premium profits. Yet, due to extraordinary parts interchangeability, you can lay-in a well-stocked inventory for under $2000. To cover all eleven S-D models, from 40cc to 100cc.

To service our dealers there are 14 distributors now covering the entire country. And two major warehouses. Plus complete merchandising, ID and co-op programs.

Since we've been at this business for 54 years, we were pleased but not surprised by America's quick acceptance of our saws. And the way more and more dealers are becoming more and more interested.

Join us. Mail in the coupon below or, better yet, call Mr. Jim Yount, National Sales Manager, or Mr. Bill McGee, direct and collect at (214) 796-7936. You're going to like what you learn.

SACHS DOLMAR

FIGURE 4.7 This simple two-color ad for Sachs-Dolmar looks deceptively ordinary. What set it apart from all others in the trade magazines was the missing coupon. Subscribers by the score called to find out why it had been "torn out" before arriving in their mailboxes.

Interruption is perhaps the easiest to grasp. Clients like to call it "the hook" or "the grabber." It can be an unexpected headline like "Jerry Eller Would Just As Soon You Ignored . . . ," an unusual spokesperson like Mother Boyle, or simply a calculated incongruity like the missing coupon for Sachs-Dolmar. Whatever it is, it must cut through the clutter of an overcommunicated society, but in a purposeful way. Otherwise, you risk "coming down the stairs with a fish in your mouth" (an expression popular in my college days). If you've done a splendid job of interrupting, but no one can fathom what you are trying to do or why, you'll only end up with unbuttoned creativity and wasted dollars.

Emotion is the most intricate component. Hal Riney, who runs the much-decorated agency Hal Riney & Partners in San Francisco, says, "Advertising that works is advertising that makes somebody feel something," but warns, "I think most of us don't give the emotional element its due." Cole & Weber used to try to describe the genre as "evocative advertising." Critics of advertising feel emotional appeals are among the industry's greatest sins and argue for "the truly rational and factual." But no one can ignore the fact that human beings thrive on emotion, and if we didn't, the world would be a pretty dismal planet.

Many clients assume this always means eliciting a warm, feel-good response, but there are times when fear, anger, or sadness are the more appropriate emotions to stir. Despite the critics' charges, creating emotional content is not simple. To cite Riney again, "The fact is, it's difficult and perilous. The qualities that create emotion, especially humor, are subtle. And, unless you're careful, you can end up with an awful creative result: an emotional approach without the emotion."

Information is the most straightforward ingredient of SBI advertising, but there is no correlation between length and strength. On occasion, it is appropriate for a lot of copy to reinforce the appeal (the Mother Boyle ads, for example), but other situations call for minimal words—perhaps just enough for a prospective customer to say, "I didn't know that," or "That's right," or "That's good." Then, too, with television and outdoor advertising you face enormous physical constraints: How much salient information can be imparted in ten seconds or ten words? Again, it pays to heed Bernbach: "Just be sure you're saying something with substance, something that will inform and serve the consumer, and be sure you're saying it like it's never been said before."

While strategic thought and large ideas comprise the soul of an advertisement, its presentation (or execution) is the heartbeat. To slay large marketing dragons, you need both. Great presentation is tougher to define because it is so tied to the subjective areas of taste, tone, flavor, design, and pace. Bernbach calls it "the art of saying things." Without question, it calls for production values of the highest caliber, regardless of medium.

Once again, esthetic discipline is essential, however, or the presentation can overwhelm the content. If it were merely a matter of spending the most money to hire the finest photographers and the choicest models, advertising would be a snap. Unfortunately, many advertisers still think that slickness and image will do it all. Pick up any major magazine or turn on any TV channel and you will see a plethora of wonderfully glitzy executions but a black hole when it comes to beneficial ideas. Martin Puris, co-founder of Ammirati & Puris (BMW, etc.), once noted, "A lot of advertising in the last few years has been half-good—a lot of execution and little idea." Small wonder his creative-director partner, Ralph Ammirati, has sighed, "So much advertising is wallpaper."

So, now you know what I believe works best. You may disagree with some aspects of my philosophy, which is fine—but just be sure your arguments have real substance and that your convictions clearly point the way to *great advertising*. You can attempt to rely solely on intuition, of course, but unless you're born brilliant, it's far superior to codify your reasoning and have definite mental checkpoints against which new creative ideas can be measured. It's not easy. Even Ogilvy admitted, "It is horribly difficult to recognize a good idea." But the ability to identify powerfully persuasive advertising in rough form is the consummate attribute of the exceptional account manager.

My sermon, not surprisingly, ends with a plea to evangelize for original, stand-apart, compelling advertising. It calls for mental toughness in laying strategic foundations and hammering out a creative structure of oversized ideas, boldly presented. It calls for the expected: great writing and great art direction. That's recognized by all who care. But it also calls for creative account management of the first order.

Those who can rise to the occasion will reap the full harvest of career success, not to mention a feeling of personal satisfaction from knowing they have helped advance the business just a little bit. It's exactly as Theodore Levitt proclaimed, "The future belongs to those who see the possibilities before they become obvious." That's *your* future he was writing about—and the future of *our* industry.

CHAPTER FIVE

The Nitty Gritty of Landing the Job

The most mundane material in this book, but everything else is just so much theory if you don't actually find an agency to hire you.

WHY MBA DOESN'T AUTOMATICALLY EQUAL VIP

It has always been puzzling to me why so many people who want to get into advertising worry so much about what school and what courses they must take to ensure their future success in the field. Honestly, I think they are missing the point. Oh, I don't deny that going to a recognized university gives neophytes a leg up on job finding. And there exist some very decent schools of marketing and of journalism/advertising with appropriate courses in principles, strategy, copy-writing, research, media, and campaigns. In fact, at the University of Oregon students are even offered a class on Advertising Agency Account Management (J-445). But it's not so much what you cram into your head about a specific discipline that determines whether or not you succeed in the agency business.

Some of the best advertising people I know earned degrees in anthropology, American studies, history, English literature, and assorted liberal arts disciplines. That's not to say business or marketing or engineering majors are categorically unfit for advertising—plenty do well in the field. But beware of the career counselor who invokes this pattern of thinking:

1. You want to get a job in advertising.
2. Advertising is part of business, isn't it?
3. Therefore, get a degree in business.
4. Better yet, get an MBA. That's best of breed.

Well, maybe yes, maybe no. You see, the benefits gained from higher education are not just those cited in the curriculum descriptions. The grinding crunch of final exams, for example, is excellent preparation for the rigors of a major client presentation at an ad agency. And, if in fact the agony and stress of finals so churned your stomach that you felt sea-sick most of the week, you probably aren't a prime cut for the agency business.

Then, there's the special character-building that comes with trying to juggle seventeen course hours in four different subject areas while you hold a part-time job. That's not so far removed from handling four small accounts—particularly when all four demand that an assignment be completed on the same day.

The collegiate turmoil of having to live and work with a lot of strange, new people is invaluable, too. In years to come, these will become your clients, suppliers, and co-workers. And, just like the ones at Swamp U., there will be those who are fantastic, those who are jerks, and those who are just plain strange.

The GPA rat race is important as well. Sure it's flawed, but so's the rest of the world. Ad agencies like people who keep score, who worry about who's in first place. The person hiring is going to look more favorably at a candidate with a 3.75 grade average than one with a 2.5, regardless of the major. Scrapping for good grades is nothing to scoff at, and if you're the type who prefers the fuzzy vagueness of pass/fail courses, kindly don't look for a warm reception at my agency.

I have a brother who is a fierce opponent of university liberal arts programs. He feels strongly that universities should train people to do specific things like chemical engineering and graduate folks who are needed for specific jobs such as a project engineer in a fertilizer plant. But, I don't agree at all with him when it comes to advertising agencies, especially agencies in smaller markets. I prefer hiring pilgrims who have wide open windows of the mind, people who know something about many different areas, people who are fascinated by what motivates *homo sapiens*, who love words, love variety, love life.

Now, those who concentrate only on a narrowly focused area of expertise (like computer technology) can survive nicely at an ad agency—I don't deny that. But they aren't nearly as valuable in the pursuit of new business, and they're certainly not going to end up running an agency with a varied client list. Besides, I doubt they have as much fun as those ad people who delight in confronting a broad spectrum of markets and products.

There's a common and perhaps overstated complaint that universities "aren't real." For example, in the Spring 1990 issue of the American Advertising Federation's magazine, *American Advertising,* Sandra Sims-Williams, a creative supervisor at Scali, McCabe & Sloves, said, "I find myself befuddled by all the misdirection and lack of preparation for our industry." The late Ted Schulte, a retired agency man who taught at the University of Kentucky, had another legitimate gripe about the teaching of advertising in universities. Writing in *Advertising Age,* he bemoaned, "Too much classroom time is spent trying to replicate advertising as it exists rather than using the opportunity of the university haven to break fresh ground with a whole bunch of superior ideas and ways of doing things." John O'Toole, when he was chairman of Foote, Cone & Belding, said, "An inordinate amount of time is spent dissecting the past, poking around in the dry cadaver of a 'case.'" And David Ogilvy proclaimed in *On Advertising* that the alumni of most business schools are "more remarkable for stodginess and arrogance than imagination."

Whether these perceptions are accurate or not, they do exist among industry professionals, and you must steel yourself for such comments as, "I hope you understand that all your college background is just so much theory and you won't be worth much to us for a year or so." But I think you will surprise the naysayers, as advertising and marketing courses *can* provide solid fundamentals. Just be sure you also take classes like psych, economics, history, American lit, anthropology, sociology, speech, philosophy (particularly logic), and any writing course that has a decent instructor. Dr. Willis "Bill" Winter, retired head of the advertising program at the University of Oregon, once told me, "Almost any class in a university's curriculum can be an advertising course if you're imaginative enough to realize it."

And don't duck those term papers. Researching and writing those beasts is good preparation for the days ahead. Just wait till your boss tosses you an RFP (request for proposal) from a big government agency account and says, "Take a crack at this, would you?" You'll think term papers were like shooting large fish in a small pond.

Regarding MBAs, there's been so much written lately, that I restrict my comments to a single opinionated declaration: MBA programs may have merit, but ultimate advanced degrees in marketing are to be earned *outside* the ivy-covered halls. These are the private industry training programs at the giants like P&G, GE, IBM, and the sink-or-swim experiences provided by younger, smaller, more dynamic companies. In my neck of the woods, the Pacific Northwest, that would include such firms as Nike, Microsoft, Oregon Cutting Systems, Kenworth, Avia, Alaska Airlines, Nordstrom's, and Lamb-Weston. In this environment nothing is academic: You don't pass or fail. You learn and succeed—or don't, and get fired. It's a most pragmatic educational process.

By the way: Graduating from a four-year school *is* important. Oh, I know, Raymond Rubicom and David Ogilvy didn't, and neither did Thomas Edison, or more recently, Bill Gates of Microsoft fame. But they're remarkable anomalies. Besides, those guys *started* companies. If you're going to look for a spot in someone else's firm, you're probably going to compete with many other individuals. Getting a degree is a signal that you're a person who can finish the task, complete the assignment, and bring home the bacon for your agency. If you don't have a degree but another candidate for a new job or a promotion does—guess who's got the inside track? Go to college at night if you have to, take correspondence courses, give up your weekends for a year—whatever it takes, just get that degree.

There is also one postgraduate course taught by advertising industry professionals that should be mentioned. Called the Institute of Advanced Advertising Study (IAAS), the program is sponsored by the American Association of Advertising Agencies, and in two markets, Chicago and southern California, has been successfully conducted for more than a quarter of a century. Lasting approximately sixteen weeks, the classes provide practical insights on how an advertising agency uses all departments to plan, create, and deliver an advertising campaign. The weekly sessions are held after working hours and on Saturdays, and the "final exam" consists of a full, formal presentation by teams of students to judges who are professional advertising practitioners.

In some locations, the IAAS is affiliated with a local university (in Philadelphia, for example, it is Temple University), but in others the curriculum, faculty, location, and all other details are wholly independent of academia (New York City, for example). The biggest problem with this program is its scarcity. In 1991, the IAAS operated only in NYC, Chicago, Philadelphia, Baltimore/Washington D.C., Minneapolis/St. Paul, San Francisco, and southern California (essentially Los Angeles). Portland, Oregon will be added to the list by the close of 1991.

CONFRONTING BIAS AND PREJUDICE

I'd like to say that such so-what issues as skin color, religion, and gender don't matter at all when a person is trying to get a job or promotion at an ad agency. But, stupidly, they still do matter, though less and less as time goes by. These issues are more of a problem for account managers because of their visibility to clients. They're the tip of the agency iceberg that shows, and conservative agency management types are always worrying about the *image* of their account service team. (They're the ones who see nothing wrong in being called a *suit*.)

Personnel in production, media, research, and other "under the waterline" functions at agencies are generally less in the regular view of clients and therefore not as vulnerable to real or imagined biases. Ironically, in the case of creative departments, it sometimes pays to look a bit strange. Foolish though it may be, clients will wink at someone who appears to be a Third World asexual punk rock star if she or he is introduced as "part of your award-winning creative team," but they will recoil in horror if such a person is introduced as "your new account manager."

However, even writers and art directors must face the fact that unconventional appearance and behavior are condoned only if accompanied by real talent. "We've had some weird-looking people," conceded Bill Bernbach in *"If they do the job*, we hire them." David Ogilvy is said to have once entered the elevator in his New York office building and encountered a garishly clad, Medusa-haired member of his own creative department. He rode in silence for several floors, but on departing said, "I don't know who you are or what you do, but you'd better be *damn* good."

As for gender, most of the antiquated barriers have been toppled. Actually, women have played a major role in American advertising history since the late nineteenth century (Mathilde C. Weil ran her own advertising agency in New York in the 1870s), but their notable accomplishments were primarily in the creative arena.

As late as 1957, a New York agency president was quoted, "Much as I hate to say it, women do not make good account executives." But in 1962, Doyle Dane Bernbach hired Marcella Rosen as its first female account manager, and between 1966 and 1971, Mary Wells changed forever the notion that a woman couldn't run a big agency. In those five years, Wells Rich Green soared to billings of $100 million, the fastest growth spurt in the history of the business. By the close of the 70s, the list of women running their own agencies included Shirley Polykoff, Jane Trahey, Janet Marie Carlson, Paula Green, Jo Foxworth, Faith Popcorn, Adrienne Hall, and Joan Levine.

Oh, there are still some curmudgeon clients (especially in heavy industry categories) who frown at female account managers, but they are dying out, literally. Unquestionably, the advertising field is one in which women seem particularly well suited. "An exceptionally good" business for women, declared Jean Wade Rindlaub, BBDO's first woman VP. "There is less ceiling, more opportunity."

The number of women heading prominent agencies is still small, but inevitably it will increase as "old girl" networks grow and challenge the status quo. As this book is written, Charlotte Beers is chairman and CEO of Tatham-Laird & Kudner, Chicago; Mary Wells remains chairman and CEO of WRG, New York; Dianne Snedaker is president of Ketchum Advertising, San Francisco; Caroline Jones is president of her own agency in New York; Barbara Sauer-Sandage is president/CD of Sandage Advertising & Marketing, Burlington, Vermont; Louise McNamee has her name on the door at Della Femina McNamee, Inc.; and, naturally, the president of Advertising To Women, New York, is a woman, Lois Geraci Ernst—to name just a few.

Religious or political preference rarely makes a difference to agency employers—unless, of course, you wear your beliefs on your sleeve and view your job as an excuse to convert the heathen. The same goes for those of gay or straight persuasions.

Skin color still fights bigotry, but less so, it seems, for Hispanics and Asians than for African-Americans. Once again, the world *is* changing, but not at breakneck speed. If you are a member of a racial or ethnic minority, try to turn it to your advantage by seeking out agencies that are concerned with niche marketing to minority segments. Increasingly, clients are looking to their agencies for help in figuring out ethnic markets. It is here that an innate understanding of cultural differences can be your unique trump card—and in some instances be even more important than hands-on advertising experience. Remember Bill Bernbach's words: "I found that you overcome all prejudices by making money for someone."

After weighing all the goods and bads, you'll probably find on balance that advertising agencies are at least equal to many other entrenched fields at opening doors to those who are not white Anglo-Saxon Protestants. This business has plenty of warts and blemishes, but it is way above average when it comes to open-mindedness about some of the old hiring bugaboos. Consequently, if you fervently want to work for an advertising agency, don't let anyone tell you that it can't happen because of your gender, religion, nationality, sexual preference, skin color, or political inclination.

EXAMINING OPTIONAL ROUTES TO THE AGENCY GOAL LINE

Is it essential that your first job be with a real live agency? Absolutely not. In fact, because there are so few openings with stellar, creative-driven agencies, you may have no choice but to start on a circuitous path to the agency world. As we have touched on before, the key substance in the hiring recipe is relevant experience, and the more you absorb, the better your chances of eventually getting hired by a top agency.

Take a hard look at the beginning alternatives that follow.

Corporations with Strong Marketing Departments

(This is my streetwise MBA substitute mentioned earlier.) The stronger the departments are the better, but even average-plus will do for starters. You may not have a direct shot at the advertising department, but don't despair. Your number one need at this juncture is to get your foot in the door and learn as much as possible about the ad business. Jobs involving market research, sales coordination, customer service, internal publications, training, product development, and publicity are all viable starting posts.

My personal caveat is to beware of jobs that involve just numbers-crunching. Conversely, I encourage you to press for spots that expose you, wet ears and all, to the company's customers. Just as nothing beats bloody battle for a military career, nothing beats field sales contact as a prelude to advertising management.

Advertising all too frequently fails because the practitioners do not understand or relate to the product's customers. Rather, they relate to their peers, to their children and lovers, to the awards judges. It's the ivory tower cliché back again for an encore. If you can develop a real—not just a lip-synch—sensitivity to the ultimate customer and to what motivates him or her, your career will accelerate accordingly.

So, if you end up in a research department, push for doing the interviews in Des Moines or helping set up the focus groups in Santa Rosa. Let others agonize over the proper cross tabs and the correct statistical variance. You concentrate on learning about and listening to customers.

Seize every opportunity remotely available to make contact with the field sales force. In some organizations they are the company's own employees; in others, independent manufacturers' representatives. Sometimes they are bifocaled engineering types with an esoteric technical background; sometimes they are slick snake oil artists with an uncanny intuition for knowing when to close a transaction. But whatever their style, age, or philosophy, they are the cogwheels in a company's ultimate marketing success. The more you know about them, their prejudices, motivations, strengths, and weaknesses, the better you will be prepared to develop advertising that really works.

Media Sales

The idea of spending time peddling radio time or newspaper space seems worse than a Jello sandwich to many professional types just starting out in the business world. They picture themselves as above all that slovenly hucksterism. The notion of pure, hardball selling seems better suited to the infantry and not at all appropriate for the elite degree-holders from the West Points of advertising and marketing.

But, media sales can be a good place to start in advertising. At the very least it offers a splendid opportunity to learn the workings of a particular medium—knowledge that many senior ad agency persons lack.

In many instances, once you establish some credibility with your customers, you will find yourself thrust rapidly into a quasi-agency situation. Say, for example, you are selling time for radio station KBOP. A retailer agrees to your proposition that he buy a TAP (total audience plan) package of radio spots for his upcoming anniversary sale. He doesn't have an agency, so you either write the spots yourself or find someone to accomplish that task. Then you arrange to have the commercials produced at the station and probably end up directing the voice talent. So far, you've been directly involved in the media planning, creative direction, and radio production requirements of your account—precisely the things you likely would be worrying about if you were working for an agency, particularly a smaller one.

But it may not end there. Let's say that the retailer wants some direct mail to tie in with the radio campaign, but he doesn't have any good ideas. Voila! To the rescue you come, finding him or her a copywriter (maybe you, if the material has to be done by 8:00 A.M. tomorrow), a freelance designer to lay out the mailer, a photographer to shoot the needed merchandise photos, a printer, a mailing house to help with a list.

Then, the account appeals to you for help with some publicity. You lobby with your own news folks at the station and end up helping with a couple of news releases that your client can send to other stations and the print media. The client needs a stunt to make a good publicity photo, so you help him talk the local high school principal into wearing a gorilla suit to the PTA meeting to hype the fact that 1 percent of all proceeds from your client's "Going Ape Sale of the Century" will go for playground equipment. Now you're caught up in some typical machinations of an agency's PR department.

Plus, you probably will be calling on some ad agencies, as well as these direct accounts I've been talking about. This allows you to gain the proverbial worm's eye view of what an agency is really like under fire. In short you will know a lot more about which ones you really want to work for and, conversely, those you wouldn't want to have anything to do with.

The best part of all this is the fact that you have a chance to make some actual money. Unlike the agency business, where generally you have to put up with a churchmouse salary upon entry, most media sales are commission driven. The more you sell, the more money that goes directly to your pocket. Especially in radio and television, this can amount to a rewarding chunk of change.

Okay, how about what the MBAs love to call the "downside risk"? Or: What can be poisonous about media sales? In two words, bad habits. You will be exposed to a lot of lousy work. If it runs, it's a good ad—that's the creed of most media sales departments. Whatever the client wants, that's fine, as long as he or she signs the order. But, if you can recognize that going in and keep your personal standards high even when surrounded by rancid advertising; if you can continue to develop a philosophy that pushes for good work; and if you do not get too enamored of making fairly easy money—then, and only then, media sales should get serious consideration when you hunt for those first jobs.

Yes, such circuitous routes to an advertising agency position take more time and considerably more patience. But if regarded as part of your full matriculation in the business, a quasi-graduate school program of cruel-world hard knocks—this experience could prove to be time extremely well spent.

ACCEPTING GEOGRAPHIC BIAS

In smaller markets you'll hear agency managers proudly declare, "We don't much care what New York thinks," and then add with a smug grin, "A big-city mentality won't work around here." But deep down, they're still apt to harbor a measure of fascination, and even old-fashioned envy, about the advertising action in New York, Chicago, Los Angeles, and San Francisco. And it affects how these managers hire.

The managers and owners of smaller-market agencies know on a purely rational plane that talent can come just as easily from small towns like Bald Knob, Arkansas, or Humptulips, Washington, as from big cities like New York or London. But they also recognize that on the basis of business sex appeal, clients are more likely to be impressed with agencies that are staffed with people who have big-city credentials than those that are filled with individuals from less populous markets. Therefore, the straightest line between college and that agency job you covet back home in Boise may be through Chicago or Boston or New York, or at least Orange County, California.

You have to watch your timing, though. If you stay too long in major markets, you may scare prospective regional employers. They will see you as "too much of a heavyweight for our needs." If you are any good at all, you will be paid more—a great deal more—in the majors. It's tough to take a salary cut, even if the fly-fishing streams are only an hour away and your kids don't require a police escort to school.

All things considered, the best game plan might be to spend two to three years in the biggest market with the best agency that will hire you. Work incredibly hard, soak up everything possible, firm up your convictions and philosophy, and then make the big lifetime decision: Either recognize that you are enjoying what you're doing so much that you couldn't possibly be content in a scaled-down environment, or recommit to your original scheme of working where you want to live and pushing hard to achieve great advertising in the hinterlands.

By the way, it does help you get back home when you are relatively unencumbered with material goods. It's the general custom now for the new employer to pay all or most of the moving expenses, so if you don't have a house or a race horse to sell, or two semis full of furniture to haul across the country, your new boss will breathe easier.

One other arbitrary suggestion: When it comes to picking a major market to job hunt, be leery about San Francisco, as it traditionally has way more applicants than jobs because of a largely deserved reputation as a wonder city. New York, Chicago, and Los Angeles have to be on your list, simply because they have so many doors on which to knock. But magnitude doesn't necessarily equate with magnificence, so also think about the almost-as-bigs like Boston, Atlanta, Dallas, Detroit, and especially Minneapolis/

St. Paul. Ever since the emergence of Fallon McElligott Rice, the Twin Cities have become a mecca for award-winning advertising.

Just remember to keep your guard up. When job seeking in bigger markets, consciously pursue those agency kitchens where the best work is cooking. Otherwise, you'll just be marking time with megalopolis potboilers and run the risk of being infected with the subtle viruses of insipid advertising.

LEARNING MORE ABOUT THE BUSINESS

Frequently as an interview comes to a close, the candidate asks, almost imploringly, "How can I learn more about your business?" Frankly, my first inclination is to scream, "How can you ask such an air-headed question?" But I always choke down my irritation and give them the answer they really don't want: Read. It's really that simple.

First, read the current news and gossip about the industry. For national info, *Advertising Age* is essential. Skip breakfast if you must, but not the weekly digestion of *Ad Age*. Next soak up the local/regional news. On the Pacific Coast, it's *Adweek/West*; in other parts of the country, *Adweek/East*, *Adweek/New England*, *Adweek/Southeast*, *Adweek/Southwest*, and *Adweek/Midwest*.

Amplify this weekly ration with such publications as *Marketing & Media Decisions, Media Week, Business Marketing, Agency, Broadcasting, TV/Radio Age, Inside Media, Art Direction, DM News,* and *The Journal of Advertising Research.* (And that by no means constitutes the full universe available.)

And, if you're *really* serious about relating to the creative side of the game, by all means devour the eight issues yearly of *CA (Communication Arts).* This handsomely produced publication showcases some of the best work regionally and nationally and profiles the ad agencies or design houses responsible. Once hired, the best way to start off right with your agency's creative director is to let him or her know that you not only know about *CA* but can quote at length from articles in the last issue. If you can afford it, by all means subscribe to *CA*; if not, use the local public library or the local college library. Don't cop out by saying, "We don't get to see those publications much around here because they cost too much."

And once these publications are in your hands, don't just fondle the pages. *Read* them from the proverbial cover to cover. Sure, lots of the material won't pertain to you or to your market—and some of it is tiresome. But *it's the business.* These publications will tell you which accounts are moving and why, which to people are moving and how come, what big new campaigns are debuting, what new research techniques are being bandied about, what agencies are doing well or not doing so well, and most vital of all you'll see examples of some truly inspiring work.

(With the exception of *CA* you'll also see some lousy stuff, but that's okay. It should only fire you up to want to do better.)

Then, when you finally land that key interview you can discuss who's doing intrepid advertising in your region. You, in fact, may know more than the person conducting the interview. But—if you restrain yourself from acting like a know-it-all—it can't help but make a positive impression.

Second, read all the advertising books you can lay hands on. Ogilvy, in *Confessions of an Advertising Man*, advocated, "Read a book a day" when on vacation. He assumed that you had taken a speed reading course and could absorb 1,000 words a minute. You may not meet that standard, but by all means read like crazy. Delve into all the current material, of course, but be sure not to overlook such classics of the business as Claude Hopkins's *Scientific Advertising* and, arguably the finest history of U.S. advertising, *The Mirror Makers* by Stephen Fox.

At the conclusion of this book, there is a list of additional reading. I urge you to devour these books—but don't stop there. "Reading maketh a full man," wrote Francis Bacon in the seventeenth century, and if you'll excuse the sexist language, it's still sage advice 300 years later.

LOBBYING FOR LITERACY

The job applicant stares intently at me and asks plaintively, "What, Mr. Perrin, is the single most vital skill I should acquire for you to hire me?" The answer is really so simple: Learn to write decently. If you can't put words on paper decently, you're going to be swimming in deep water with severe leg cramps. "Advertising is a business of words," declared Ogilvy in *Confessions of an Advertising Man,* "but advertising agencies are infested with men who cannot write. They cannot write advertisements, and they cannot write plans. They are as helpless as deaf mutes on the stage of the Metropolitan opera."

Compounding matters is the dismal fact that managers on the client side may be even more deficient. A 1990 study of the 200 largest U.S. corporations found that one third of all reports, letters, and memos were "unclear, poorly written, or confusing." Specifically, they were badly organized, too long or wordy, contained incomplete information, employed trite or overused expressions, and had "no clear purpose."

An alarming number of agency applicants are convinced that oral fluency matters more than anything else for an account manager. They've read or heard somewhere that the ability to *pitch*, to *sell,* to paint verbal pictures, is of paramount importance in this business. Well, it *is* important, but it will get you only so far. A silver tongue won't automatically ensure your acceptance by clients and peers. There are plenty of people who talk a good game and present adequately—but only a handful who can think through problems and then cogently put down their reasoning in black and white.

Sure, it helps if you're a forensic whiz and enjoy regaling an audience. But bear in mind that before the curtain rises on those seductive presentations, and long before the speeches are polished in rehearsal, somebody had to *write* the epic: first an outline, then a synopsis of speaking assignments, perhaps even a formal line-by-line scripting.

Not to mention the need for a **leave-behind,** the classic reinforcement document that the prospect or client carries with him or her from the presentation. I've known some mindless account managers who sneer, "No one ever reads those; they're just dust collectors." But I've seen too many cases in which meticulous prospects or clients go over every sentence, and the quality of the writing has a direct bearing on their verdict.

This is especially true when prospective clients resort to a scorecard system of judging agencies competing for their business. In other words, points are awarded on the basis of performance measured against specific requirements (e.g., "A maximum of 100 points will be given for each agency's ability to comprehend our primary marketing problems"). At the conclusion of the review process, the agency earning the most points wins the account. I've seen major accounts chosen on the basis of a half-point difference, so the strengths or weaknesses of written plans can make or break a favorable decision for your agency.

Those heading for account management are disproportionately apt to believe that the tongue is mightier than the pen. They say, "If I can speak fluently, have presence, understand marketing, thrive under pressure, and will fight for my convictions—what more could you want?" Well, for one thing, I want an account manager who can produce clear and succinct **conference reports.** Mundane though they may appear, these concise minutes of all important meetings and phone calls can be instrumental in cementing a client relationship. I wish I had a dollar for every time I've heard a client wail, "I haven't received a conference report for two months! What's wrong with that agency?" Jane Maas tells us in *Adventures of an Advertising Woman* that shortly after becoming president of Muller Jordan Weiss she asked to be copied on every conference report. "One account executive replied with a memo stating that he did not write conference reports on his account. I sent him back a memo that said, 'Please start.' "

One of my old bosses assured me that I would eventually learn to write conference reports as the meetings progressed and would only need to have my scribblings clean-typed afterward, but I never mastered the technique. Perhaps you will, but the best I could do was to take copious notes and then compose the report after the meetings had concluded. Regardless of your method, just be sure the information conveyed is succinct, accurate, and understandable. An example of what I mean by a competent conference report is reproduced in Figure 5.1.

BP&N

BORDERS PERRIN AND NORRANDER INC.

MEMO

DATE:	October 31, 1986		Conference Report #43
CONFERENCE DATE:	October 30, 1986	cc:	Tom Kennedy
			Bob Lesh
CLIENT:	Oregon Economic Development Department		Michael O'Rourke
			Terry Schneider
FOR THE CLIENT:	Rick Schulberg, Rich Carson		Pamela Sullivan
			Marilyn Foster
FOR THE AGENCY:	Rick Braithwaite		Bev Petty
			Carole Berke

1. <u>Business Recruitment Brochure</u>. Client returned full size comp to agency, with full approval of photos. We then discussed some copy changes already submitted by client.

Agency presented revised estimate to reflect larger print quantity.

The need to go through the State Printing Office was raised by Bob Lesh, who will coordinate this effort once printing specifications are received from the agency.

SULLIVAN — <u>Agency action</u>. Proceed with incorporating final client comments into copy and return to client by November 4.

SCHNEIDER/FOSTER — Proceed with production with approved photos.

FOSTER — Send printing specifications to Bob Lesh.

LESH — <u>Client action</u>. Once printing specifications are received from agency, provide to State Printing Office for their handling.

SCHULBERG — Once printing bids are assembled by State Printing Office, make decision regarding print quantity.

2. <u>Tualatin Valley Economic Development Corporate Ad</u>. Client asked agency to gather further information on this ad opportunity in the December 1986 issue of <u>Oregon Business</u>.

BRAITHWAITE — <u>Agency action</u>. Contact Pam Ragsdale at <u>Oregon Business</u> to get insertion rates and specifications, and then make recommendation to client on October 31st.

SCHULBERG — <u>Client action</u>. Once information is received from agency, make decision and notify appropriate support services (agency or in-house) to get materials produced in time (if decision is possible).

/jst

FIGURE 5.1 This conference report not only cogently summarizes the results of an agency-client meeting, but also clearly identifies the next action steps to be taken by each party. The names on the left side are those of the individuals who are responsible for completing the action steps.

One good way to polish letter-writing skills early is to take extra pains in penning pungent thank-you notes to every past employer, associate, teacher, or prof who takes the time to send a letter of reference for you. And, by all means, write again when you are accepted for that new job.

I am not harping that you must be a *clever* writer or that you should aspire to redo the copy coming out of your creative department—your writing should be primarily *expository*. But it should offer clarity, cohesiveness, and conciseness. Then, if it also happens to display a modicum of wit, so much the better.

And finally, don't regard the ancient art of spelling as some unimportant schoolmarm antiquity. Misspellings can cloud the veracity of any report, especially if the client is a stickler on detail. How poorly most Americans spell was driven home to me recently when I taught a class to seniors (!) in advertising at the University of Oregon. In grading their first assignment, I noted the following spelling aberrations:

moniter	frusterating	occassionally
competant	machanisms	oppartunity
sponser	advice (for verb advise)	device (for verb devise)

Never forget that clients want creative expression, but not at the expense of civilized spelling.

CREATING THE CONVINCING RÉSUMÉ

There's a compost pile of printed matter around with extravagant claims about who has the definitive word on how to write powerhouse résumés. My thoughts on the subject don't exactly square up with some of the conventional wisdom and are based on seeing too many poorly composed specimens flowing across my desk as our agency grew. This is not to say that résumés are unnecessary baggage. On the contrary, they're absolutely necessary. Just don't expect them to perform door-opening miracles at ad agencies.

You see, entry jobs at most agencies are much more a factor of opportunistic timing than résumé chutzpah. These agencies, even the superstar ones, cannot afford to build a bench of untried rookies. Consequently, they hire only when pressed to the wall because of (a) growth of existing accounts or (b) acquisition of new business.

The other problem you face right out of school is that you probably don't have much experience or many accomplishments to tout. I've seen résumés that boast of working summers in Dairy Queens or hitchhiking across Mozambique or playing on an all-star slowpitch team. That kind of out-of-the-ordinary experience is meaningful, but it's not relevant to the day-to-day agonies of the average advertising agency.

That doesn't mean résumés are totally worthless if there isn't an immediate job to fill. Unless yours makes you appear totally inept, it will be kept on file. Even if the agency never has an opening, it will still pass along the best résumés to clients and business friends who are looking for people to hire.

So, it makes sense that you should put your résumé together with special care. Here are my thoughts on ways to increase the chances of your missive being remembered:

1. Put all possible creative energy into the cover letter. The ability to write cogent correspondence is a major plus for an advertising professional. Even if the résumé itself was not very impressive, I always paid extra attention to a well-written letter. Frankly, they stand out because so many leave much to be desired. Now I know why Ogilvy said, "I am always surprised by the illiteracy of men and women who look for jobs in advertising."

2. Be sure to demonstrate your proofreading/detail talents with the letter. I was continually dumbfounded to receive material dotted with misspellings (especially of my name) and typos. A colleague recently sent me a copy of an applicant's letter that began, "My name is _____ and I am a *resent graguate* of the University of _____ in Journalism/Advertising." If you can't be careful enough to avoid error in selling yourself, I certainly wouldn't want you to deal with one of my clients. I think my all-time loser came from an applicant who mailed me the results of an occupational aptitude test (which indicated his best career choices were advertising or "a vocal or entertainment group"), a page of references with seven typos, and a form cover letter with a yellow sticker carrying the scrawled message, "Mr. Perrin, Please grant me an interview at your convenience."

3. I have nothing against long copy, but you probably will win points with brevity and conciseness. Again, consider the sheer volume of printed material through which the agency manager wades every morning.

4. Creative gimmickry? (Such as mailing a ball-peen hammer and a note saying you would do anything to break into the advertising agency business?) Sure. Just make certain it has direct bearing on what you want to achieve; otherwise, you run the risk of just seeming weird. Rest assured that such a tactic will make you stand out from over 90 percent of the résumés submitted. Just make very sure you don't come across as a space cadet.

5. Once you have isolated an agency that you *really* want to work for, plan a program of repeated mailings. Send a résumé and a follow-up and

another follow-up and then a follow-up to that follow-up, ad infinitum. Tenacity is a virtue much admired by agency managers, myself included. Bearded Lee Clow, now president of Chiat/Day/Mojo, is said to have gained his first job at the agency through a series of mailings with the theme "Hire the Hairy."

6. You can gain some points by attaching letters of reference as opposed to merely closing with the expected line about "available on request." Just don't forget to send a personal thank you to your benefactor. As one university professor expressed it to me, "A good reference letter takes at least half an hour to compose, and I do *lots!* Yet I rarely hear another word from the student. Unforgivable."

For reference, I reprint two résumés received in my past life that struck me as noteworthy—ones we made a point of keeping on top of the pile (see Figures 5.2 and 5.3). But don't feel you have to slavishly copy them. The best results will come only after you provide your own personal touch.

GAINING AND GRAPPLING WITH THE INTERVIEW

Some career counselors would have you believe that the aggressive pursuit and landing of an interview is the key to job entry. These soothsayers are of a mind that once you are face to face with the prospective employer, you can sell your way into his or her heart and onto the payroll. Well, it does happen from time to time, but it's a sizable mistake to think that gaining an interview is a genuine indication of interest in employing you. Or, that once gained, you can dazzle interviewers into hiring you when they don't have an opening.

The biggest problem you must contend with is the false-front courtesy that many agency management types show interviewees. They will receive you graciously, listen attentively, and radiate old world conviviality. But they won't hire you; in fact, they wouldn't even entertain such a preposterous thought.

So, why are they taking up your time and theirs? It's simple: What goes around comes around. You might end up being hired by a prime prospective client or even a client. You might go to work for someone in New York and in five years be exactly who this agency needs to save an account. You might land a job with a valued supplier. Who knows? It's a small world, so the agency doesn't want to leave you with a bad impression and risk having you come back to haunt them later.

Frustrating? Absolutely. But it goes with the territory. I confess, I used to do it. But one day I awoke to the fact that I really was doing no one a service, and in my later days I would interview in person only when I had an opening to fill. I would always talk to candidates on the phone and try to offer suggestions, but I wouldn't do courtesy interviews. Ironically, this

RAINI APPLIN

555 Oak Street, Seattle, Washington 55555   (555) 555–5555

OBJECTIVE
> To obtain an entry level position with an advertising agency in account services.

EDUCATION
> Washington State University, May 1990.
> Bachelor of Arts in Communications/Advertising. Minor in Marketing.

ADVERTISING RELATED SKILLS
- Research—coordinated and organized the research for a Darigold campaign.
- Public Speaking—wrote and presented speeches using slides, diagrams and charts.
- Creative—developed creative advertisements for print and broadcast media.
- Sales Promotion—planned promotional ideas for IAMS Dog Food, Puppy Food, and Mini Chunks.
- Macintosh—working knowledge of PageMaker, Microsoft Word, and Freehand.

RELATED EXPERIENCE

Advertising Salesperson, The Evergreen (August 1989—May 1990)
Responsibilities included selling advertising space, designing advertisements, copy writing, and creating campaigns for 25 local businesses in Pullman Wa.
Worked with clients on marketing development and co-op advertising.

Account Executive, National Student Advertising Competition (AAF 1990)
Directed the Washington State University team in the development of a monthly consumer magazine for the Hearst Corporation. Coordinated all areas of advertising decision-making including marketing, media, creative and sales promotion. Supervised both primary and secondary research effects.

Promotions Team, National Student Advertising Competition (1989)
District XI winning campaign. Placed 4th nationally. Assisted with fundraising, promotional research and the development of the promotion plan for Kellogg's Daylights.

Marketing—Advertising Intern, Everett Mall, Everett, WA (1989)
Worked directly with Marketing Director of Everett Mall. Assisted in the coordination of mall events. Wrote news releases, editorial for newspaper sections, radio ads, print ads, general correspondence and merchant memos.

Sales Associate—Nordstrom and The Bon (1987—1990)
Provided customer service, merchandised the department, operated the cash register and planned department schematics.

HONORS AND AFFILIATIONS
> Member of WSU Advertising Club (AAF 1987–1990)
> National Golden Key Honor Society (1988—1990)
> Member of Alpha Gamma Delta Sorority

ACTIVITIES AND INTERESTS
> Snow skiing, aerobic fitness, weight-training, reading, music.

References Available Upon Request

FIGURE 5.2 This résumé uses a minimal amount of space to tell a very complete story. Everything cited has relevance to the needs of an advertising agency.

BETH BLUE

5000 S. W. Elm #1
Seattle, Washington 55555
(555) 555–5000
work (555) 555-5000

OBJECTIVE	Marketing or media position in a Seattle advertising agency.
EXPERIENCE	Marketing Intern AVIA Athletic Footwear, Portland, Oregon (February 1988 to present)
	Assist running and walking division marketing and promotional managers; coordinating running and walking marketing information to sales, promotional and technical representatives; utilize national sports industry research for use in marketing plans.
	Marketing Intern, Hult Center for the Performing Arts, Eugene, Oregon (December 1987 to January 1988)
	Researched technical packets from various performing arts centers throughout the United States; wrote copy for a technical specifications packet for use as a sales and marketing tool.
	Advertising and Public Relations Assistant, Fifth Street Public Market, Eugene, Oregon (1987)
	Assisted Marketing Director through verbal and graphic communications with media, merchants, musicians and customers; helped coordinate and implement special events and tourist marketing; researched, wrote, coordinated and disseminated fact sheets, news releases and PSAs for market-wide promotions.
	Pi Beta Phi Sorority President, Eugene, Oregon (1986)
	Supervised and assisted 20 officers, 100 members and five staff members in managing the sorority; organized and conducted meetings and ceremonies; represented sorority to national organization and as a member of University of Oregon Panhellenic Council; held a variety of leadership positions in sorority and in greek system (1983–1987)
EDUCATION	B.A., Journalism, June 1987
	University of Oregon School of Journalism, Eugene, Oregon
	G.P.A. 3.20
	Advertising Emphasis
HONORS	Outstanding Service to the Greek Community (1987); Who's Who Among American Colleges and Universities (1987); Centurion Award—Top 100 campus leaders (1986, 1987); Dean's list, Fall 1983 and 1984; Oregon Achiever—recognized student leader (1987); Alpha Lambda Delta, Phi Eta Sigma freshmen academic honoraries (1984); Outstanding Pledge Award, Pi Beta Phi sorority—based on scholastics, involvement and future leadership (1984)
INTERESTS	Golf, skiing

FIGURE 5.3 Another example of a succinct, to-the-point résumé from someone who is seeking an entry level job at an advertising agency.

honesty seemed to hurt more feelings than the phony approach did, but at least I felt better.

Here are my tips on interviews:

1. Don't be frazzled if the interview can happen only via telephone. Agency people live on phones, and this can still be a meaningful first contact. If handled well, it might be the overture to a later personal meeting of consequence.

2. Bone up on the agency beforehand. Know their clients, their work, and their main claim to fame. I was continually astonished by the interviewees who did not know zip about our agency but still professed a burning desire to work for us.

3. Intensity, energy, and enthusiasm are important. You'd better not have to fake those. Sheer aggressiveness, however, is generally a turnoff. Employers love self-confidence but gag at perceived arrogance.

4. Do something to differentiate yourself. Remember that the employer probably will talk to dozens of people like yourself before the month is out. If you are going to succeed in the business of advertising, now is the time to stick in the employer's memory. How? Do something that demonstrates your ability to think: Leave a field report of consumer reactions to a client's product, perhaps even on an audio cassette. Leave photocopies of the best paper you wrote your senior year. Show examples of the ads you put together for your summer job. Leave an apple with your name taped on it, or a brick or a corn cob, or *something* to make a particular point about your candidacy.

5. If there are no full-time job openings, see if there is a need for spot assistance; maybe help field a research project, dig out material for a competitive review, staff a trade show booth—anything to gain the proverbial foot in the door.

6. Whether on the phone or in person, never depart the scene without getting at least two additional names to contact, the classic networking ploy. This is the best way to find out what's happening in the marketplace (although, ironically, some agency managers are so beset with their own problems, you may actually know more than they do about the local job market). Because most agency jobs open and fill quickly, word of mouth is the only way to learn of them. The more people you contact the better your odds of bumping into an opportunity.

7. Be succinct. The agency interviewer is probably in a time squeeze (if he or she is not, things must be slow in the office). You win

points by appearing well organized and demonstrating sensitivity to his or her schedule.
8. Follow up with a note or letter, reinforcing the points you made in the interview. This indicates thoroughness—and also shows that you will have no problem penning conference reports after client meetings when you're hired.

Lastly, bear in mind that once you are in the running for a legitimate opening, you probably will have to contend with a string of interviews, sometimes to the point of acute discouragement. At various times these may be either boring or grueling or both, but they are a reasonably decent way to find out more about what you may be getting into. (You might want to follow the advice of John Munschauer, author of *Jobs for English Majors and Other Smart People:* "Interview first for the jobs you care about *least*. The experience will improve your important interviews.")

As much as you want to land that position, the worst thing you can do is take a spot that is ringed with people you can't respect. So, as the hiring process takes place, do reverse interviewing of your own. Arrange to talk with more than just the top agency people. Discuss advertising philosophy with the other account managers. Find a way to meet the people in other departments. Are they bright, intelligent, professional? Is the work really good? If you don't feel right about what you see and hear, resist the temptation to call them names and point out the error of their ways. Instead, politely withdraw from consideration. It's gut-wrenching to pull away from a job possibility, but if you sense a bad fit, don't fool yourself into thinking *any* job in the hand is worth two in the thistles.

CHAPTER SIX

Improving the Breed

Pest exterminators, barbers, and masseurs have to pass professional certification tests— as do architects and CPAs. Why not advertising professionals?

THE NEED FOR TOUGH PROFESSIONAL STANDARDS

It's always been curious to me that advertising calls itself a profession, yet is indifferent to the notion of setting professional standards for its practitioners. Webster's definition of a profession is "a calling requiring specialized knowledge and academic preparation." Contrast that with the common law definition of a "professional" advertising agency: "a calling requiring the ability to print a business card, hang out a sign, and order a listing in the Yellow Pages."

Advertising has long been intimately intertwined with the spirit of free enterprise and freedom of thought and speech. Those who have attempted to regulate or license the business have been accused at various times of censorship, constitutional abuse, deprivation of human rights, un-Americanism, and devil worship.

So, when someone like myself raises the subject of standards of measurement for the advertising profession, it is the classic moment of the lead balloon. Most people are bored to tears. "Who needs it," they snarl if they respond at all. "This is a great business. It makes a lot of money. It is doing just fine. I'm proud of it. Why mess with a good thing?"

Well, for one thing it's not as great as some ad people choose to think—a number of well-documented national studies in the 1980s have confirmed this. The hard, cold facts tell us that thousands of Americans consider advertising to be in need of improvement.

Let me summarize just a few of these surveys. In an infamous 1984 Gallup Poll, advertising executives were rated near the bottom of the job barrel by the general public: just below politicians and only a tad better than used-car salesmen. In a similar survey of just businesspeople, ad execs rated *even lower*. A 1985 study by Needham, Harper & Steers (now DDB Needham) found that two-thirds of those queried felt advertising "insults your intelligence." In the same survey, the most frequently mentioned complaints about ads were "tiresome," "in bad taste," and "offered promises that don't deliver."

In case you wonder if the situation is improving with the passing of time, a 1988 study by the Video Storyboard Company came up with these findings after 1,000 interviews: 25.7 percent thought that TV advertising was "offensive," and nearly one third found it "misleading." Both numbers were the highest in the five-year history of the poll. And 1990 marked the sixth consecutive year that a coalition of consumer groups awarded "Lemmies" in Washington, D.C., for the most misleading advertising of the past twelve months. The trophies—gold statues holding up lemons—are formally called the Harlan Page Hubbard Lemon Awards, named after a turn-of-the-century promoter who touted Lydia Pinkham's Vegetable Compound as a cure-all for everything from fatigue to cancer.

No wonder *Adweek* reported that only 19 percent of the membership of 4 A's (the American Association of Advertising Agencies) would recommend advertising careers to their own children.

Way back in 1963, David Ogilvy concluded *Confessions of an Advertising Man* by declaring, "Advertising should not be abolished. But it must be reformed." Neither he nor any of the other august nabobs of the industry have since acted on that thought, and I believe it is high time to confront this issue of reformation. (Ogilvy's final words in his 1983 book, *On Advertising*, were, "The majority of campaigns fail to give consumers enough information." In twenty years he went from a bang to a whimper.)

I submit that our industry ought to work with the leading university schools of advertising to establish a program for earning an "MAP" (Master of Advertising Practice) certificate. (Or, if they don't like MAP as a designation, come up with another. The initials are not important; the idea is.)

A PLAN FOR ESTABLISHING ADVERTISING BAR EXAMS

The components of this certification dream would include:

1. Earning a four-year university degree in course work approved by the MAP governing body. In my mind, this would be a "supreme

court" of top guns from leading advertising agencies and deans from highly regarded universities such as Northwestern (Medill School of Journalism), Stanford (Graduate School of Business), and so on. Makeup of the court would be determined by a vote of the executive committees of the largest advertising industry associations (American Association of Advertising Agencies, American Advertising Federation, Association of National Advertisers, Business and Professional Advertising Association, etc.).

The sanctioned courses/degrees would not be narrowly restricted to "marketing communications" and "advertising/journalism." Concurrently a joint industry/academia task force would suggest curriculum changes to confront the industry's widely held impression that university advertising courses lack "reality."

And what about practitioners who earn degrees in studies outside the approved course criteria—say, in earth sciences or ontology—and after graduation wish to gain MAP status? They would be required to complete a special postgraduate course modeled after the 4 A's "Institute of Advanced Advertising Studies" mentioned in Chapter 5. This sixteen-week course would cover all aspects of the advertising process and would be taught by a combination of university faculty and industry professionals. Completion of course work at special advertising educational centers such as the Portfolio School in Atlanta might also meet this qualification.

2. Working a minimum of two years at a recognized advertising agency. By "recognized," I mean a firm that has been in business for at least three years, has annual billings of more than $1 million, belongs to one of the major national advertising agency associations, has a clean bill of health from the Better Business Bureau, and has won at least one local, regional, national, or international award for creativity in the past three years.

3. Passing a comprehensive written and oral examination on major aspects of the advertising agency business: marketing planning and strategy (including research techniques), media techniques, production mechanics, creative positioning and strategy, plus business and financial management. A premium would be placed on a written critique of a spectrum of current advertising.

The test would be administered in two parts, with the written ordeal taking place prior to the oral exam. It would place a premium on writing skills in answering the questions and would not be a creampuff/everybody passes exercise. Those flunking would have the opportunity to take the exam again after six months. The orals would be given by a panel of top professionals as determined by the national board of governors (the "supreme court" cited earlier). It would be mandatory that this panel include at least one highly decorated creative director.

At least a zillion problems squat in the path of this plan. To convert it from dream to reality would take countless hours of valuable time. It would need players of national repute to champion the cause. It would be a severe temptation to end up with a program that was too easy or too tough. And unless there were clearly evident rewards for those who passed, it wouldn't appeal to good people who felt that after years of formal schooling they simply didn't need another exam.

However, there is a smidgeon of precedent for certification in our world of mass media communications. The Public Relations Society of America (PRSA) has conducted a similar program for years for PR practitioners. "PRSA Accredited" on a business card signals that the bearer has passed a comprehensive exam and adheres to the highest standards in his or her field. A younger organization, the International Association of Business Communicators (IABC), also boasts a formal accreditation program. IABC reported in the May 1989 issue of *Communications World* that 380 members had passed the written and oral accreditation exam. On the same page, another article revealed that the IABC is confronted with some of the problems I cited in the previous paragraph, "We believe accreditation has been falsely viewed by many IABC members as a prestigious accessory to being a communicator—something elitist but nonessential. That's wrong. Accreditation is an essential and very logical step in a communicator's professional development."

Am I out to create some kind of elite corps for the top jobs in advertising agencies of the future? Am I subtly discriminating against creative people? Maybe. I realize the plan probably will appeal more to account management types than to creative disciples. But I am encouraged by what my partner and creative wizard Bill Borders wrote about such a prospect in the December 1988 issue of *Communication Arts*:

> Now, the idea of once again having to take written or oral exams is enough to make my palms moist and my mouth dry. I've awakened in a cold sweat from a recurring college nightmare very similar to this. But, if setting measurable standards could raise the caliber of people in the business—and thereby the work created—I'd go smiling.

And then he put things in perspective by pointing out that

> there are several less lofty lines of work where standards are upheld via regular (and sometimes rigorous) exams. Certainly we are entrusted with budgets and responsibilities more sizeable than, say, beauticians or pest exterminators.

I echo his sentiments about upgrading the field with some honestly demanding standards—particularly regarding creative product. And I have been spoiled by having had the joy of working with creative people—both writers and art directors—who had the schooling and practical knowledge of marketing to pass such a test handily.

Am I advocating that everyone who enters advertising must have this "license to practice"? No. After all there are many competent accountants who have not felt the need to take the CPA exam. But I am hoping that peer and client pressure would in time give the MAP designation special status and that agency leaders would see it as a necessary extension of their university education.

My role model is architecture. The discipline has always fascinated me because of its interdependence on engineering dogma and design esthetics. It is the quintessential right brain/left brain marriage. Granted, a student of architecture must possess a deeper grasp of technical matters than a student of advertising. (And I know some architects who would be insulted by the comparison.) But on the design side, both fields are beset with the same demons of subjectivity and creative jabberwocky. Both are explorers in the realm of large and untried ideas. Both seek business solutions that stimulate society. Not all building designers qualify as members of the American Institute of Architects (AIA). But those who do have achieved a unique level of professionalism through such components as peer review, consistency in university curriculum, adherence to AIA standards, and licensing.

Advertising agencies should follow suit. We are the architects of mass communications, but we must force ourselves to set and defend standards of acceptable performance if we are ever to begin to weed out those who are content with the lowest common denominator.

And for those who prefer a pragmatic rather than idealistic reason for adopting such standards, consider this sobering thought: If the industry cannot find appropriate ways of upgrading itself, there is always the prospect of regulation by state and federal government. Come to think of it, that might be the ultimate irony. Under the mantle of free speech, we so resist setting standards that we have them set for us by hidebound bureaucrats who believe creative freedom is advertising's euphemism for mass manipulation.

ADDITIONAL READING

22 Books That Helped Me

Cialdini, Robert. *Influence: The New Psychology of Modern Persuasion.* New York: William Morrow, 1984.

   A thought-provoking discussion of the "weapons of influence" by a professor of psychology and self-confessed "easy mark." As the book cover promises, this should be of interest "to every person who has ever attempted to sell a product, to persuade a client, to influence another's decision."

Della Femina, Jerry (edited by Charles Sopkin). *From Those Wonderful Folks Who Gave You Pearl Harbor, Hard-Line Dispatches from the Advertising War.* New York: Simon & Schuster, 1970, 1971.

   A fascinating, if somewhat disjointed, narrative about agency life in New York in the glorious days of the 60s Creative Revolution. It lurches from remarkable insights to self-indulgent hooey, but it makes for lively reading.

Drucker, Peter. *The Effective Executive.* New York: Perennial Library, Harper & Row, Colophon Edition, 1985.

   Drucker is both prolific and perceptive when it comes to writing about business. He has authored at least twenty books, but I especially like this one for its intelligent commentary on what constitutes an effective manager. His chapters on decision making should be read more than once.

Fox, Stephen R. *The Mirror Makers.* New York: Vintage Books, 1985.

   The definitive condensed history of advertising in America. I hate to shrill insistently, "You must read it," but in fact, you must. I totally agree with the *Newsday* reviewer who wrote, "A lively, meticulously researched, carefully structured and often quite amusing work of social history."

Foxworth, Jo. *Wising Up.* New York: Delacorte Press, 1980.

   Some worthwhile, albeit a bit dated, advice for women in advertising and business generally. This author made her mark when the field was really male dominated, and she offers some sound, streetwise counsel.

Heymann, Tom. *On an Average Day.* New York: Fawcett Columbine, 1990.

   An amazing collection of random facts and statistics pertaining to the happenings in one 24-hour period. Useful for adding some unexpected tidbits to presentations and speeches. (For example, did you know that every day 3,562 pairs of bowling shoes are purchased, 225 women have nose jobs, and four people call Graceland asking to speak to Elvis?)

Hodgins, Eric. *Mr. Blandings Builds His Dream House.* New York: Simon & Schuster, 1946.

   This is mostly about the amusing anguish of building one's own home, but there are some wonderful glimpses of agency life right after WW II because the hero, Mr. Blandings, makes his living as a copywriter. He "has earned a considerable respect in the inner circle of the hard-working, highly competent,

161

and deeply miserable men who wrote advertising copy and, in another century, might have written sonnets."

Hopkins, Claude. *Scientific Advertising*, Chicago, 1923; New York: Crown, 1966.

    First published in 1923, and written by one of the early giants in advertising copywriting, this thin book still offers some classic pearls of wisdom (e.g., "Platitudes and generalities roll off the human understanding like water from a duck. They leave no impression whatever.") David Ogilvy has said, "Nobody should be allowed to have anything to do with advertising until he has read this book seven times. It changed the course of my life."

Levitt, Theodore. *The Marketing Imagination*. New York: Free Press, 1986.

    Written by a marketing guru who understands that business success does not come from numbers-crunching alone. His chapters on "Differentiation—of Anything" and "Relationship Management" are not to be missed. Levitt, in addition to being a prof at the Harvard Business School, is the editor of the *Harvard Business Review*. Small wonder that his work is both erudite and readable.

Nager, Norman, and Richard H. Truitt. *Strategic Public Relations Counseling: Models from the Counselor's Academy*. New York: Longman, 1987.

    A solid guidebook for students of public relations practice. Extremely helpful for those who seek an overview of the profession plus real-life case studies to examine at length.

Ogilvy, David. *Confessions of an Advertising Man*. New York: Atheneum, 1963, 1987.

    This is the book *I* think should be read seven times by anybody thinking about entering advertising. Written originally in '63, it stands the test of time remarkably well and is much more than a typical "my life and times" volume. The chapters on clients ("How to Get Them, How to Keep Them, How to Be a Good Client") are still devilishly perceptive. Ogilvy can be dogmatic and doctrinaire at times, but he is never dull. All in all, terrific writing making for terrific reading.

Ogilvy, David. *On Advertising*. New York: Crown Publishers, 1983.

    Some of this is a rehash of *Confessions*, and some is new material. The net result is uneven, but it is still a book worthy of note. His defense of advertising in Chapter 19 ("What's Wrong with Advertising") is well reasoned and appropriate to memorize. When asked why he wrote this work, Ogilvy replied that "it was at the request of my agency's new business department."

Orwell, George. *1984*. Orlando, FL: Harcourt, Brace, Jovanovich, 1949. New York: New American Library of World Titles, 1961.

    The classic story of mind-manipulation by a dictatorship that uses mass communication with terrifying results. (The expression "Big Brother is watching you" originated here.) Written in 1960, it still is riveting reading today. Absorbing it will also increase your understanding of the thinking behind the historic "1984" television commercial created by Chiat/Day for Apple personal computers.

Peters, Thomas J., and Robert H. Waterman, Jr. *In Search of Excellence*. New York: Harper & Row, 1982.

    This work has been roundly criticized in some quarters because some of the companies featured (and praised) have fallen on hard times in recent years. But I still endorse the authors' salient points about the value of keeping close to customers and maintaining hands-on management.

Pirsig, Robert. *Zen and the Art of Motorcycle Maintenance.* New York: William Morrow, 1974.

The subtitle is "An Inquiry into Values," and I believe this book is marvelous brain food for anyone who quests seriously after high standards of quality in life and work. I also admire Pirsig's plea for more old-fashioned "gumption" in our society.

Ries, Al, and Jack Trout. *Positioning: The Battle for Your Mind.* New York: McGraw-Hill, 1981.

The benchmark work on how brands are positioned mentally in consumers' heads. Some of the examples seem old-hat now (Avis, 7-Up, Tab, Taster's Choice), but the principles cited still have a lot of relevance for the 90s. The arguments about the pitfalls of the "Free Ride Trap" and the "Line Extension Trap" are thought-provoking even if you don't agree with them.

Ries, Al, and Jack Trout. *Marketing Warfare.* New York: McGraw-Hill, 1986.

The authors use military metaphors to make their points, and the result cannot help but make a sales manager smile. Their comparisons of modern marketing strategy with the military advice of Prussian General Von Clausewitz are both astute and amusing. Excerpts from either of the Trout and Ries books can be invaluable in developing presentations and short speeches.

Surmanek, Jim. *Media Planning: A Practical Guide.* Lincolnwood, IL: NTC Business Books, 1985.

A good nuts-and-bolts introduction to media planning and buying. Written by a seasoned professional with agency experience in research, media, and account management.

Townsend, Robert. *Up the Organization.* New York: Alfred Knopf, 1970.

An irreverent look at business management by an unorthodox manager who achieved huge success while running Avis Rent-a-Car. The subtitle is "How to Stop the Corporation from Stifling People and Strangling Profits." If nothing else, be sure to read "The Avis Rent-a-Car Advertising Philosophy" in Chapter 1.

Von Ochs, Roger. *A Whack on the Side of the Head: How to Unlock Your Mind for Innovation.* New York: Warner, 1983.

The author is a noted consultant in the specialized field of helping companies unleash the creative potential of their employees. This book offers a series of games, puzzles, exercises, and other brain teasers designed to stimulate creative thinking. Some are fun, some perplexing, and others good for enlivening lethargic sales meetings.

Wells, Rosemary. *Morris and His Disappearing Bag.* New York: Dial Books, 1975.

A short refresher course on the power of whimsy and fantasy, two topics that are never far removed from the core of effective mass communications. Even if you fail to extract any deep meaning, it will leave you feeling good.

Wonder, Jacquelyn, and Priscilla Donovan. *Whole Brain Thinking.* New York: William Morrow, 1984.

I've always felt the best ad agencies are whole-brain agencies, those which somehow combine the best of the analytical (left side) and the intuitive (right side). This book offers some intriguing thoughts on maximizing your brainpower while simultaneously reducing stress and frustration. You should enjoy the mental exercises, which have such catchy names as "Cinematics," "Inside Outs," and "Suspenders."

GLOSSARY

AAAA, or 4 A's The American Association of Advertising Agencies is arguably the strongest and most influential of all advertising industry organizations. Membership is by election of peers and limited to agencies who meet the association's stringent qualifications. Approximately 750 agencies belong, ranging in size from the very largest to those billing less than a million dollars a year. Its stated function is "to foster, strengthen and improve the advertising agency business; to advance the cause of advertising as a whole; and to give service to members." Headquarters are at 666 Third Avenue, New York, NY, (212) 956-7470.

In addition to 4 A's, there is a veritable alphabet soup of other advertising agency associations. Because they can sometimes be helpful in job finding, I list the best known. (The number of member agencies is approximate as it varies slightly from year to year.)

    AAAI—Affiliated Advertising Agencies International
    80 member agencies
    2280 S. Xanadu Way
    Aurora, CO 80014
    (303) 671-8551

    IFAA—International Federation of Advertising Agencies.
    45 member agencies
    999 Plaza Drive
    Suite 400
    Schaumburg, IL
    (312) 330-6344

    LAA—League of Advertising Agencies
    100 member agencies
    P. O. Box 56
    Gracie Station
    New York, NY 10028
    (212) 570-2075

    MAAN—Mutual Advertising Agency Network
    30 member agencies
    125 S. 4th Street
    Grand Forks, N.D. 58206
    (701) 746-4573

    NAAN—National Advertising Agency Network
    Agencies with offices in over 50 markets
    245 Fifth Avenue
    New York, NY 10016
    (212) 481-3022

TAAN—Transworld Advertising Agency Network
30 member agencies
866 UN Plaza
New York, NY 10017

WSAAA—Western States Advertising Agency Network
Over 250 member agencies
2410 Beverly Blvd.
Los Angeles, CA 90057
(213) 387-7432

ABC The Audit Bureau of Circulations was organized by representatives of advertisers, agencies, and the media to audit and verify the circulation statements of member magazines and newspapers. Its current membership exceeds 5,000.

ABP The American Business Press is an association of some 650 domestic and 120 international publishers of business periodicals. Members agree to have their circulation regularly audited by a nonprofit auditing organization such as the **ABC**.

Account planner This is a relatively new job title for U.S. advertising agencies, although British agencies have embraced the function for some time. Using a variety of research techniques, account planners work closely with marketing and creative people to provide them with an intimate understanding of the people to whom the advertising is targeted.

A. C. Nielsen This company's business is measuring radio and TV audiences. To do so it employs both diary reports and "audimeters," electronic devices attached to household TV sets to record minute-by-minute use.

A.D. This means "art director," an individual responsible in an ad agency for the look of a given piece of advertising. In the best agencies, an art director works in tandem with a copywriter to create ideas and concepts. In the worst agencies, an art director just draws layouts for the ideas handed down by writers or account people.

ADI Arbitron uses ADI, or "area of dominant influence," to describe the TV markets it measures.

A.E. The initials stand for "account executive" but have become generic for anyone charged with the responsibility of providing primary client contact for an ad agency. Synonyms include account manager (the title I much prefer), account supervisor, client services manager, and **"suit."** The designation is also widely used in media sales and in companion service fields such as public relations, research, sales promotion, and exhibit building.

AFTRA The American Federation of Television and Radio Artists is a powerful union in the entertainment world. Among its approximately 45,000 members are the best on-camera or voice-over radio and TV talent in America. Any agency using this talent must adhere to AFTRA's stiff requirements for fees and residuals. (For a more detailed explanation, refer to the section in Chapter Three entitled, "Making Small Budgets Look Huge.")

Agate line The basis for measuring newspaper advertising space and for calculating space costs. Fourteen agate lines always equal one column inch, and historically newspaper advertising rates were quoted in lines, not inches. Because the column width varies with different newspapers, a 500-line ad for paper A will not automatically be the right size to fit the 500-line space in paper B.

Agency review   This expression sends chills up the spine of incumbent agencies. It simply means the client is unhappy and has decided "to review the agency's performance." Invariably this involves a competitive comparison with other agencies, and it is uncommon for the existing agency to emerge from the review with the account intact.

AM   Everyone knows about AM radio stations, but few know the initials stand for "amplitude modulation." Roughly, AM refers to the way sound is transmitted by these stations: The power (amplitude) of the sound waves is modified (modulated) to simulate original sound.

ANA   The Association of National Advertisers is comprised of some 450 major corporations advertising on a national or broad regional basis. Its purpose is "to promote effective use of advertising as a selling and management tool." The ANA guidebook on agency compensation is well worth reading ($38.50 for nonmembers). The association is headquartered at 155 E. 44th Street, New York, NY 10017, (212) 697-5950.

Arbitron   A widely utilized source for measuring radio and television audiences. The data are based on household diaries kept by a precise demographic sampling of each market and updated several times annually depending on a market's size.

Availability, or "avails"   This is the word used to describe specific TV or radio commercial breaks that are available for purchase by advertisers.

Barter   The practice of exchanging broadcast time for merchandise instead of hard dollars.

Billings   The word *billings* is bandied about recklessly in the advertising agency business. Roughly equivalent to "sales" in other industries, it is the total number of dollars clients spend through agencies. It is *not* synonymous with income or profit.

Bleed   There is considerable talk among advertising people about how "bloody this business can be," but in a strict sense "bleed" simply means running copy or visuals to the edge of the page. In other words, the page has no border of white space at top, bottom, and side.

BPA   The Business Publications Audit specializes in verifying the circulation of business-to-business periodicals and medical journals.

BPAA   The Business and Professional Advertising Association has over 4,000 individual members in 35 chapters representing agencies, advertisers, and publishers. It devotes its energies exclusively to improving business-to-business advertising. Headquarters are at 100 Metroplex Drive, Edison, NJ 08817, (201) 985-4441.

CA   CA, or *Communication Arts*, is a trade magazine that enjoys almost cult status with agency writers and art directors. Published eight times a year from Palo Alto, California, it features examples of the best in contemporary graphic design, illustration, and advertising. It also sponsors an annual creative competition that has unusually high judging standards and is widely respected by creative people.

CA is published from 410 Sherman Avenue, P.O. Box 10300, Palo Alto, CA 94303, (415) 326-6040.

Capitalized billings When an agency has a nonmedia-buying client, it commonly will report the size of the account as a "capitalized billings" figure, meaning it has multiplied the projected income by 6.67 percent. Why? Because it puts the size of the account on the same publicity footing as the media-intensive clients.

C.D. This stands for "creative director," the person in charge of the agency's creative product and the boss of all copy and art personnel. An "E.C.D." is an "executive creative director," which is a notch higher than an ordinary C. D.

Circulation The total number of copies of a publication distributed to readers. "Paid" circulation means the readers bought the periodical either through a subscription or on the newsstand. "Qualified" circulation indicates the readers have met the "recipient qualification" (you see this most frequently in the circulation statements of business-to-business media). "Nonpaid" readers receive the publication without paying for it. Non-qualified readers are those listed without any documentary evidence of receiving the publication.

Clio The name of a prestigious annual creative competition in New York City. Earning a "Clio" is something coveted by writers and art directors toiling in creative-driven agencies. Awards are offered in several fields, including packaging design and specialty advertising, but the television category always receives the most publicity. The winning TV spots are put yearly on a videotape, which is widely shown to advertising clubs and occasionally even on network television and in movie theaters

Closing date The advertising industry's term for "deadline."

ClusterPlus A system of market analysis designed to identify, reach, and influence specific consumer segments. Its data are broken into forty-seven population clusters, each representing a distinctive lifestyle pattern. Within each cluster, marketers can examine current product usage levels and estimate the potential for new products. It is available from **Telmar** and **IMS.**

Collateral Pertains to all advertising materials that are *not* associated with major media (radio, TV, outdoor, newspapers, and magazines). Include such items as catalogs, mailers, point-of-sale displays, annual reports, training films, and so on.

Color key This is a type of full-color proof that printers have used for many years. The color key reproduces the advertisement on a series of overlapping acetate pages, each showing just one primary color. Thus, you have a sheet just for red, one solely for blue, black, and green. Art directors rely on these as guides for making adjustments on the color separations before the material goes on a press.

Color separations In full-color printing, a separate piece of film must be produced for each color utilized, hence these film sheets are called "color separations."

Comp Short for "comprehensive," it's a word used both as a noun and a verb to describe a precisely detailed layout of an advertisement or piece of collateral. "Make sure the full-page comps are ready for the meeting." "Ask Eddie to comp up the ads by Friday morning."

Conference report The "minutes" of any important contact between agency and client, and a primary responsibility of the account manager. Copies are distributed to all involved members of the agency account team (media, creative, production, etc.) and to the client to confirm decisions, requirements, timing, and other vital matters. It also is known by several other similar names such as "call report" and "client meeting report."

Cost per thousand (CPM) What it costs to reach 1,000 individuals with a particular media vehicle. For example, an advertisement costing $3,000 in a magazine reaching 100,000 people has a CPM of $30.

Creative shootout This happens when a client seeking an agency announces that the decision will be based primarily on a review of the competing agencies' creative proposals. When a large budget is at stake, agencies have been known to show fully produced radio and TV spots and lavishly photographed print layouts—a risky and very expensive gamble. Agencies rarely, if ever, recover their investment in a creative shootout—unless they win the business and keep it for years.

Cromalin A full-color proof sheet used in print production. This particular kind of composite proof has largely been replaced by **signature** or **match** color proofs.

Cume persons The total number of different (or unduplicated) persons listening or watching during a defined time period.

Cume rating Calculated by dividing the number of cume persons by the population of the market covered.

D&AD The Design & Art Directors Association of London, England, sponsors of an internationally renowned judging of creative work. The winners are published in an impressively printed volume of *The Best of British Advertising, Television, Graphic, Product and Editorial Design and the International Section* (the latter is where choice U.S. work can appear).

Demographic editions Editions of print media aimed at specific audience segments such as retired persons or college students.

Drive time Those hours when radios are most likely to be on in automobiles because people are traveling to or from work. "Morning drive" is 6:00 to 10:00 A.M., and "afternoon drive" is 3:00 to 7:00 P.M.

Dylux In the old days it was called a "brownline" and later a "blueline," but basically it's nothing more than a proof of a prospective printed piece. It's made on photosensitive paper from the actual printing negatives, so all illustrations, photos, and type are exactly the way they will appear on the printed page. Its limitation is that everything is shown in one color, an infamous blue hue that won't reproduce worth sour applesauce on a copy machine. Checking the dylux is an extremely critical step in any print production project.

Fixed position In the broadcast world this means a commercial time slot purchased with the guarantee it cannot be moved.

Flighting A media buying tactic calling for periods of heavy exposure interspersed with short spells of nonactivity, or "hiatus."

FM Radio stations with this label employ "frequency modulation," a process of adjusting the frequency of the transmitted sound waves to achieve a clear signal.

Focus group A research technique in which a small group (not more than fifteen people) representing the target audience for a client is invited to sit with a moderator and give opinions on a variety of subjects. The results can be very helpful diagnostically in identifying marketing/advertising "hot buttons," but the process is no substitute for more expansive research using a statistically reliable sample.

Frequency   The number of times individuals or homes are exposed to an advertising message.

Fringe time   TV jargon for those time periods surrounding the hours of highest viewing (or "prime time"). In most markets these are 4:30 to 7:30 P.M and 11:00 P.M. to 1:00 A.M.

Gross impressions   This is the total number of times a commercial is seen or heard. It is calculated by multiplying the total number of persons exposed by the number of exposures.

Gross rates   In the agency business "gross" means that an agency commission (generally 15 percent) is included in the price. When the job is completed, that commission will become income for the agency.

GRPs   One "gross rating point" is equal to 1 percent of the market's population. GRPs are calculated by multiplying the reach of the message by the frequency of exposure. For example, if you reach 20 percent of the market five times, you have delivered 100 GRPs.

Halftone   When a photo is used in printing, it must be "shot" and "screened" by a special camera in the process leading to the making of lithographic printing plates. The "screening" leaves a pattern of very fine dots on the photo that permits the reproduction of all the various tones in the picture. Without the dots, the photo would reproduce darkly and without any lighting subtleties. With the dots in place, the photo becomes a halftone, meaning all the shades (or tones) of gray "halfway" between the darkest and lightest can be precisely printed.

Hi-Fi and Spectacolor   These are two types of full-color, preprinted insert sections in newspapers. Hi-Fi is on a continuous roll and the pages are not trimmed as evenly as they are in Spectacolor. The paper stock in both cases is a better grade than newsprint.

HUT   HUT or "homes using television," signifies the percentage of homes in a given market watching TV at a specified time.

IAAS   The Institute of Advanced Advertising Studies is the brainchild of the American Association of Advertising Agencies and is intended to provide practical postgraduate coursework in advertising. Taught primarily by advertising professionals, the program covers approximately sixteen weeks and addresses the fundamentals of planning, creating, and producing an advertising campaign. At present the classes are offered in only a number of U.S. cities.

IABC   This is the International Association of Business Communicators, dedicated to improving "organizational communication." Translated, that means many IABC members are involved with company publications aimed at employees, customers, and shareholders. Others are active in PR and community relations. IABC has a commendable program of professional certification and its own magazine, *Communication World*. Headquarters are at One Hallidie Plaza, Suite 600, San Francisco, CA 94102, (415) 433-3400.

IMS   Interactive Market Systems is an on-line media data service offering **MRI** (Mediamark Research, Inc.), **SMRB** (Simmons Market Research Bureau), and **ClusterPlus**. It does not provide **Arbitron** numbers but does cover **VALS** (Values and Lifestyles Survey).

Issue life   The length of time it takes for a magazine's maximum audience to see/read the issue.

Killer   A word much in vogue to describe outstanding creative work, but also the title bestowed by Jerry Della Femina (*From Those Wonderful Folks Who Gave You Pearl Harbor*) on those whose job was to fire people when an agency cut staff.

Kings and Queens   The words refer not to royalty but to the relative size of advertising posters used in transit advertising (buses, in other words). The king-sized units are the largest and appear on bus sides. "Queens" are available on fronts or backs of buses.

Leave-behind   In the jargon of the advertising business, this word describes whatever written and/or illustrated material is "left behind" following a presentation to a client or prospective client.

Make good   Should the media foul up your order, it may offer to "make good" the error by running the advertisement correctly for free.

Match print   Similar to a "signature print" but from a different supplier. See **signature print**.

MBWA   Coined by Tom Peters, author of *In Search of Excellence*, and meaning "management by walking around." It refers to a hands-on style of management that avoids problems by keeping in close touch with employees and customers.

Mechanical   The fancy word for "pasteup," the step in print production where type and visuals are pasted in position to be shot by the printer's camera. With the surge toward desktop publishing, the days of the traditional pasteup may be numbered.

Media maven   Someone who is extremely knowledgeable about planning, buying, and negotiating media.

Merchandising allowance   Amount of money allocated by advertising media to provide additional promotional support for their advertisers. Examples include reprints, mailings to key retailers, easel-backed cards for point of sale, prizes for sales contests, and the like.

MRI   Mediamark Research, Inc., offers information about product usage and media habits that can be helpful in media planning. It covers products ranging from Ale to Yogurt, and data are available via either **Telmar** or **IMS**.

Net rates   Anything that an agency buys on a net basis means there is no commission included. Therefore, if the agency is to receive any income from the transaction, it must mark up the purchase to a "gross" figure.

New York Art Directors Awards   Another of the major creative contests in the United States.

One Show   One of the most prestigious of the creative award competitions. Years ago both the New York Art Directors Club and the New York Copywriters Club sponsored contests. Then they wisely combined their efforts into "One Show."

With the passage of time, though, the art directors resurrected their own separate effort, and today both competitions receive hundreds of entries each year.

Override This occurs when the outdoor boards you purchased are not immediately sold at the end of your contract period. Often the outdoor company will allow your message to "ride" for additional days rather than resorting to a blank panel or one carrying a nonpaying public service ad.

Painted bulletins These outdoor advertising units have the advertising painted on them, in contrast to printed thirty-sheet posters which are applied to billboards with adhesive. Painted bulletins are larger than thirty-sheet posters, averaging about fourteen by forty-eight feet.

Pitch This is the word that ad agencies substitute for "presentation." It's employed both as a noun ("The big pitch for the Whiz Account is tomorrow") and as a verb ("We pitched for the Clapso business, but came in second").

PMT The initials stand for "photo mechanical transfer," and it's another way to say photostat (see **stats**).

Positioning You will encounter a number of different definitions in your career, but the one I prefer has to do with the way brands are positioned *in the mind*. I subscribe to the premise of ladders of preference in the compartments of consumers' minds. Your challenge is to develop advertising that places your clients' brands on the top rungs of those mental ladders.

Primary and pass-along readers Primary readers are in the household of the magazine purchaser. Pass-along readers see the magazine outside of the primary household in such places as barbershops, dentists' waiting rooms, and libraries.

Prime time This designates the time period when television viewing peaks: 8:00 to 11:00 P.M. Monday through Saturday and 7:00 to 11:00 P.M. on Sunday.

PRSA The Public Relations Society of America is the top professional organization for the discipline. It has more than 10,000 members and publishes the monthly *Public Relations Journal*. PRSA's accreditation standards are frequently applauded but never emulated by advertising practitioners. The home office is 33 Irving Place, New York, NY 10003, (212) 995-2230.

Psychographics The study of lifestyles and values in contemporary American society.

Pulsing A media buying strategy calling for advertisements to be run continuously interrupted by periodic bursts of heavy activity.

PUT Stands for "people using television." In other words, the percentage of people watching TV at a given time.

Rate base This is the circulation figure on which a publication bases its cost of advertising space. Some publishers guarantee delivery of these numbers, some do not.

Rating The percentage of individuals (or homes) watching or listening to a particular television or radio program.

Red book The granddaddy of directories for the advertising business. Distinguished by their deep red covers, *Standard Directory of Advertisers* (listing 25,000 corporations) and *Standard Directory of Advertising Agencies* (listing 5,000 agencies) have served for years as primary sources of current information about the business. They are published by National Register Publishing Company, 3004 Glenview Road, Wilmette, IL 60091, (312) 256-6067.

RFP The "request for proposal" is a favorite device of governmental bodies seeking communications counsel. In theory, it asks intelligent questions that will guide the public agency in making an informed decision. In practice, it is frequently bureaucratic, overly wordy, misguided, and obtuse. For a more civilized explanation, turn to the section in Chapter Three entitled "Seeking Out and Winning New Business."

ROP When a media buyer puts ROP ("run of press") on a space order, it means the publication is free to run the ad anywhere in its issue.

Rough Term used to describe an advertising layout that doesn't have all the details put in. Occasionally used as a verb, "Get Tim to rough out some ideas for the pitch."

SAG The name "Screen Actors Guild" says it all. This is the professional union for all the major players in film and video. It will cost you dearly when you employ SAG talent in your commercials, but it can pay off handsomely in terms of impact. About half of its 45,000 members live in the Los Angeles area, and the rest are served by eighteen branch offices located across the country. (Refer also to the "Quick Reference Talent Guide" in Chapter Three.)

Scatter plan The name for a media buying plan that runs commercials in many different time slots and programs.

Seventeen point six five 17.65 percent is the accounting "reciprocal" of a 15 percent commission. Thus, it becomes the multiplier for any net cost on which the agency needs to mark up to become a gross charge to a client. For example, if the *gross* cost for newspaper space is $100, the agency will retain 15 percent, or $15, as income. But if the cost for space is $85 *net*, then the agency will mark up that figure by 17.65 percent (0.1765 × $85 = $15), so it can earn the equivalent of a 15 percent commission.

Share Identifies the percentage of homes using TV (or radio) that are tuned to a particular program.

Short rate If an advertiser contracts for a certain amount of advertising during a set period of time and then fails to run that many insertions or commercials, he or she must face short-rate charges because of the frequency discounts involved.

Showings The term used to describe units of outdoor advertising available for purchase, e.g., a #25 showing or a #100 showing. The numbers are equivalent to daily **GRPs** (gross rating points), meaning that the #25 showing will be seen by 25 percent of the market, a #50 Showing by 50 percent, and so on.

Signature print This is a state-of-the-art full-color proof to be approved or corrected prior to printing. Unlike the **color key**, this has no overlays and is a single unified sheet with remarkable fidelity to the actual look of the printed piece. Similar, but from a different supplier, is a **"match print."**

Simul-buy Occurs when fixed-position commercials are purchased to run simultaneously on several TV channels in the same market. Also called roadblocking.

SMRB Simmons Market Research Bureau is a well-established source of facts about product usage and media preferences of consumers. Like **MRI**, it is proffered by both **Telmar** and **IMS** systems.

Spread Pertains to any print advertisement covering two full, facing pages. In newspaper parlance it once was also called a "double truck," but that is rarely heard these days.

SRDS The thick books put out by Standard Rate & Data Service are essential reference tomes for agencies, especially for those in the media and production sectors. SRDS provides basic rate information in separate volumes for consumer and farm magazines, business publications, newspapers and shoppers, direct mail lists, Hispanic media and markets, spot radio, and spot television. It also publishes the "bible" for print media production specifications. Its home office is at 3004 Glenview Road, Wilmette, IL 60091, (312) 441-2167.

Stats Short for "photostats" (also called **PMTs**), a simple print production necessity that is hard to explain succinctly. Basically they are high-quality black and white proofs that will reproduce crisply. Stats are made by "shooting" items with a special camera that can enlarge or reduce the image and then print it on photosensitive paper suitable for reproduction. The finished product then is used to complete **mechanicals** (pasteups). It used to be customary for agencies to order photostats from outside suppliers, but now agencies are increasingly investing in their own equipment and producing stats in-house. This can result in faster service for clients and more income for the agency.

Story board A large card on which are drawn key frames of a proposed TV commercial. The copy is written below the frames so that the client can visualize how the words and visuals would blend together in the finished spot. I've heard story boards described as "the blueprint of the concept," a phrase hinting broadly at their limitations, which are considerable. Despite the Herculean efforts of agency artists, it is impossible to fully depict a TV commercial on a story board. At best, it delivers a general indication of what can be expected visually and pins down the copy to be used.

Strategy Another word of singular importance for which experts have failed to agree as to a singular definition. I endorse this general definition, copied from an obscure dictionary in my college days: "The devising of a general plan of attack, defense or action, so as to achieve an end with the forces or means available." It is important to understand that "marketing strategy" and "creative strategy" are interdependent but *not* identical. My favorite definition for creative strategy is: "It's what you want to say, to whom, and how you will say it."

Suit The slang term for advertising agency people—male and female—who work in account management or client services. ("The creatives loved it, but the suits weren't sure.") Harkens back to the time when a dark suit was the obligatory business uniform for an account manager/account executive.

TAP The "total audience plan" is a package of commercial avails that radio stations offer as a "good deal" for general audience advertisers. The advertiser's commercials will run in different dayparts with the total buy calculated to deliver a majority of the market's "total audience."

Telmar A popular media data service that provides **Arbitron** ratings for radio and TV; **MRI** (Mediamark Research, Inc.) and **SMRB** (Simmons Market Research Bureau) information on magazines; and **ClusterPlus** analyses on consumer buying patterns and behavior. Telmar's special programs include "Benchmark," a media optimization report; "Trips," a spot radio ranking system using Arbitron data to rank stations against multiple markets, multiple demographics, or multiple dayparts; and "Quickstat," a magazine ranking plan.

Thirty-sheet poster This is the standard outdoor advertising "billboard." The message is preprinted by silkscreen or lithography on large paper sheets and then "posted" on the billboard with adhesive. Originally, it took thirty sheets of paper to cover the space, hence the name. The space available for advertising copy is approximately ten by twenty-two feet.

Thumbnail When creative people—especially art directors—sketch out several layout ideas in miniature, the results are termed "thumbnails." It's a quick way to explore several visual directions before proceeding to a full-sized layout.

TSA TSA, or "total survey area," pertains to measurement of radio audiences. It means all of the counties in which there is significant listenership to a market's stations.

USP The "unique selling proposition" was the brainchild of Rosser Reeves, who built the Ted Bates agency into one of the biggest in the world. The phrase became commonplace in the agency world as a way of describing the on-target appeal of a particular creative recommendation. It's not heard as much today but is still part of mainstream adbabble.

VALS "Values and Lifestyles Survey" is a key part of the data package offered by Interactive Market Systems (IMS) and **Telmar**. It provides psychographic insights on American behavior and is widely used by agencies for media planning and marketing research.

Velox A screened print of a photograph or piece of art.

Weighting The practice of assigning greater importance (or "more weight") to a particular group or market segment when creating a media plan.

Wild spot In calculating talent residuals, this applies to spot market buys in unsponsored programs on noninterconnected programs.

Wrist Applies to any member of the agency art department who does the bidding of others. In other words, this person doesn't think through a solution, but simply mechanically renders the ideas of others. This is fine for juniors who are just learning the business, but a damning label for anyone with much experience.

Yankelovich monitor Around since 1970, this service annually surveys 2,500 consumers sixteen years of age and older to provide statistical information on social change in the United States and how these trends affect consumer behavior. The monitor uses some imaginative language to label its psychographic segments: for example, "the gamesmen," a group with an all-out commitment to winning; "the new autonomous," a group committed to economic well-being but not at the expense of personal fulfillment. Other groups include "scramblers," "traditionals," "American dreamers," and "aimless."

Zeigarnik effect Behavioral psychologist Bluma Zeigarnik concluded from studies in the 1920s that the human mind remembers things best when a message is slightly incomplete, thus leaving something for the audience to ponder. Zeigarnik said this technique "made the brain itch."

INDEX

AAAA (American Association of Advertising Agencies), 19. 139, 157, 158
AAF (American Advertising Federation), 97
ABC (Audit Bureau of Circulations), 25
ABP (American Business Press), 25
Accounting
    cost, 39, 76–77, 78
    See also Budget
Accounting department, 81, 82
Account management, 11, 12–16
    career paths in, 44–45
    pay in, 50–51
    and PR, 55–56
    See also Account managers
Account managers, 12–14, 44–45
    advertising philosophy of, 11, 119–123
    assessing accounts, 40–42
    creativity of, 67, 95–97, 120–121
    "empty," 119–121
    female, 140
    image of, 139, 140
    job description, 12–14
    job landing by, 136–155
    pay for, 50–51
    and PR, 55–56
    what's wrong with today's, 119–135
    working with agency departments, 17–21, 30–32, 35–36, 38–40, 67, 70, 72, 116
    working with clients, 36, 40–42, 59–90, 116
    writing by, 146–149
Account planner, 37–38
Accounts
    assessing, 40–42
    See also Clients
A. C. Nielsen indexes, 22–23, 27
Act II tactic, 69
A.D. (art director), 16–17, 20, 45, 50
ADI (area of dominant influence), 27
Advancement opportunities, 44–48
Adventures of an Advertising Woman (Maas), 59–60, 147
Advertising (Dunn & Barban), 32

Advertising Age, 32–33, 126, 138, 145
Advertising philosophy, 11, 119–123
Advertising strategy, 121–123
    crucial components of, 132–135
    judging results of, 123–132
Advertising To Women, New York, 140
Adweek, 145
    on account managers, 120
    on advertising careers, 157
    on agency size, 97
    on agency working relationships, 17–19
    on Chiat/Day/Mojo, 113
    on client–agency relations, 41, 60–61, 65, 66
A.E. (account executive), 12
    See also Account managers
AFTRA (American Federation of Television and Radio Artists), 102–103
Agate line, 24–25
Age
    and job security, 48
    and pay, 50–51
Agency, 145
Agency compensation. *See* Compensation for agency services
Agency Compensation (Jones), 79
Agency culture, 8–58
Agency review, 110–111, 112
Agency structure, 11–40
Agents, celebrity, 102
Alaska Airlines, 138
Ally, Carl, 11
Ally & Gargano, 60–61
AM (amplitude modulation), 27
American Advertising, 120, 138
American Advertising Federation, 120, 138
American Association of Advertising Agencies (4 A's), 19, 139, 157, 158
American Association of Retired Persons, 48
American Federation of Television and Radio Artists (AFTRA), 102–103
American Institute of Architects (AIA), 160

175

Index

Ammirati, Ralph, 11, 59, 135
Ammirati & Puris, 135
ANA (Association of National Advertisers), 79
Anticipation, of cost overruns, 87–88
Apple Computer, 100
Appointments, reconfirming, 116
Approval process, client, 19–20, 66–74
Arbitron, 22, 23, 27
Architects, AIA, 160
Art Direction, 145
Art director (A.D.), 16–17, 20, 45, 50
Association of National Advertisers (ANA), 79
AT&T, 48
Atari, 66
Atlanta job market, 144
Audience measurement, 22–24
Audience targets, 31
"Audimeter," 22–23
Availability/"avails," 27
Avia, 138
Avis Rental Cars, 68
Awards/Competitions, 10, 110–111, 158

Bacon, Francis, 146
Bar exams, advertising, 157–160
Barter, 27
BBDO, 48, 140
Beers, Charlotte, 140
Behavioral scientists, 62, 68
Berlin, Andy, 11
Bernbach, Bill
 on advertising strategy, 134
 and clients, 62, 68, 69
 on creativity, 121
 on "empty" account management, 120
 on hiring prejudices, 140, 141
 on ideas, 123
 on research, 37
Berra, Yogi, 36
Better Business Bureau, 158
Bias
 geographic, 144–145
 hiring, 139–141
Bid, vs. estimate, 86
Big bang approach, 100–101
Big ideas, 121–135
Billboards, 29, 74
Billings, 79–80
Bills
 for Bean Counter client, 64
 collecting, 81–84
 production department, 35

 for way-over-budget project, 84–88
 See also Compensation for agency services
Bleed, 25
Bonuses, 51, 54
Borders, Bill, 12, 114–115, 159
Bosses, sorting out, 42–44
Boston job market, 144
Bowen, Steve, 120
BPA (Business Publications Audit), 25
BP&N (Borders, Perrin and Norrander), 53, 90
 big bang approach by, 101
 collateral by, 94
 compensation policy, 79, 80, 81
 conference report, 148
 Hatt with, 101
 leave-behinds of, 114
 organization chart, 12, 13
 strategy/big ideas at, 121–132
Bramsom, Robert, 63
Bridges, Lloyd, 103
Broadcasting, 145
Brown, Hubie, 47
Budget
 collateral, 95
 making small ones look huge, 97–103
 media, 31, 99
 way-over, 84–88
 See also Compensation for agency services; Pay
Burgerville, 126, 127–129
Business development, 16, 103–115
Business development manager, 109
Business Marketing, 145
By-the-Numbers client, 62–63

CA (*Communication Arts*), 10, 145, 146, 159
Calculators, in media department, 22
"Capitalized" billings, 79–80
Career paths, previewing, 44–48
Carlson, Janet Marie, 140
C.D. (creative director), 17, 46
Celebrities, use of, 101–103
Certificate, MAP (Master of Advertising Practice), 157–160
Chamberlain, Neville, 46
Champion, 41
Chiat/Day/Mojo, 38, 113, 151
Chicago Bears, 103
Chicago job market, 144
Chromalin, 88
Churchill, Winston, 2, 43

Cialdini, Robert, 73
Circulation, 25
Clients, 59–90
    big, 40
    bill collecting from, 81–84
    Class A & B situations with, 67–74
    credit record, 83
    entertaining, 88–90
    loss of, 47
    and media department, 31–32
    presentations to, 84, 110–111, 113–115, 137, 146–147
    and production department, 36
    and research, 38, 39, 62–63, 68, 70–71, 72
    seeking new, 103–115
    selling when they're not buying, 19–20, 66–74
    types of, 59–66
    working with, 36, 40–42, 59–90, 116
    writing by, 146
Clipping, 118
Closet Creative Director client, 61–62
Closing date, 25
Clow, Lee, 11, 151
ClusterPlus, 23
Coca-Cola, 63, 100
Code-A-Phone, 70
Cole & Weber, 53–54
    big bang approach by, 101
    celebrities used by, 102
    on "evocative advertising," 134
    Wagner of, 60
Collateral work, 91–97
    agency compensation for, 75–76, 77
Color keys, 33, 88
Color separations, 85
Columbia Sportswear, 123–125
Commissions, 51, 76
    media, 74–75, 76, 77
Communication Arts (CA), 10, 145, 146, 159
Communications World, 159
Compensation for agency services, 39, 40, 74–81
    and client types, 61, 64, 65–66
    for collateral, 75–76, 77, 95
    for creative shootout, 112
    plans for, 76–79
    See also Pay
Competitions/Awards, 10, 110–111, 158
Computers
    in media department, 22, 23–24
    PR in field of, 55

Conference reports, 147–148, 155
Confessions of an Advertising Man (Ogilvy)
    on blabbermouths, 16
    on commission system, 76
    on creators, 16
    on entertaining clients, 90
    on enthusiasm, 2
    on genius, 43
    on PR, 55
    on reading, 146
    on reform in advertising, 157
Convictions (philosophy), 11, 119–123
Coping with Difficult People (Bramsom), 63
Copy strategy, 121–135
Copywriters, 16–17, 20, 45, 50
Cosby, Bill, 101, 102
Cost accounting, 39, 76–77, 78
Cost per thousand (CPM), 26
"Creative brief," 121–123
"Creative capability" presentations, 110–111
Creative department, 9, 11, 16–21
    agency compensation for, 75
    career paths in, 45–46
    and clients, 67, 70, 72
    and collateral, 92–93, 95–97
    and creative shootout, 112–113
    image in, 140
    pay in, 50
    working with account management, 17–21, 67, 70, 72, 116
    working with research, 38–39
Creative director (C.D.), 17, 46
    closet (client), 61–62
"Creative process," 20
"Creative shootouts," 110, 112–113
Creative strategy, 121–135
Creativity, 8, 10–11, 121
    of account manager, 67, 95–97, 120–121
    and details, 115
    in job-search letter, 150
Criticism
    of advertising, 6
    from clients, 61
Cume persons, 27
Cume rating, 27
Customer
    audience measurement of, 22–24
    sensitivity to, 142
    targeted, 31

Dallas job market, 144
Daniels, Draper, 32–33

Davis, Robert, 60
DDB Needham Worldwide, 120, 157
Deadline, 25, 33, 116
Degrees, 138–139
Delegating, 16, 115
Della Femina, Jerry, 16, 20–21, 47–48, 51, 59
Della Femina McNamee, Inc., 20, 140
Demographic editions, 26
Details, 115–118, 150
Detroit job market, 144
DINKs (double income, no kids), 118
Direct response services, 11
Discounts, 75
DMAs (designated market areas), 27
DM News, 145
Donovan, Priscilla, 8
Double Agent client, 63–64
Double-checking, 93, 116–117
Double talk, 72
"Double truck," 27
Doyle Dane Bernbach, 62, 68, 140
Drive time, 27
Drucker, Peter, 42–43, 60, 87–88
Dun & Bradstreet Credit Reports, 83
Dyluxes, 33

Eastman Kodak, 21
Economics, 74–88
    of agency ownership, 53–54
    and client types, 61, 64, 65–66
    of collateral, 95
    cost accounting, 39, 76–77, 78
    of PR, 56
    with public agencies, 112
    research, 39, 76
    See also Budget; Compensation for agency services; Pay
Edison, Thomas, 103, 139
Edsel, 63
Education, 136–139, 157–160
Effective Executive, The (Drucker), 42–43, 60, 87–88
Eggs, as media, 21
Egos, celebrity, 102
Einstein, Albert, 9
Electronic media, 17, 27–29
    See also Radio; Television
Eliot, T. S., 76
Emotion, 132–135
Entertaining clients, 88–90
Enthusiasm, 2, 67

Ernst, Lois Geraci, 140
ESOPs (employee stock ownership plans), 54
Esquire Magazine, 48
Estimate, vs. bid, 86
Ethnic markets, 141
"Evocative advertising," 134
Exams, advertising bar, 157–160
Excellence books (Peters & Waterman), 15

Fallon McElligott Rice, 48, 49, 98, 145
Federal Express, 61, 63
Fees, 75–76, 77, 95
Finance and administration, 11, 39
    See also Economics
Fitzpatrick, Sean, 120
Fixed position, 27
Flighting, 27
FM (frequency modulation), 27
Focus groups, 37, 38
Foote Cone & Belding, San Francisco, 17, 19, 138
Ford Motor Company, 63
Foster, Jack, 17–19
401(k) plan, 52
Fox, Stephen, 6–7, 146
Foxworth, Jo, 16, 46, 51, 66, 140
Freelancers, for collateral, 93, 95
Frequency, 28
Fringe time, 28
Froke, Paula, 49
From Those Wonderful Folks Who Gave You Pearl Harbor (Della Femina), 16, 20–21, 47–48, 51

Gallup Poll, 157
Gates, Bill, 139
GE, 48, 138
General Foods, 123
General Motors, 60
"Gentle Art of Persuasion, The" (Borders), 114–115
Geographic bias, 144–145
Gerber Legendary Blades, 101
Getting Into Advertising (Laskin), 32
Ghost client, 65
Golden Eggs company, Jerusalem, 21
Goldsmith, Jimmy, 81
Government accounts, 112
Gracian, Baltasar, 18
Grades, school, 137
Green, Paula, 140
Gross impressions, 28

Gross rates, 74
GRPs (gross rating points), 28

Halftones, 85
Hall, Adrienne, 140
Hal Riney & Partners, San Francisco, 134
Hamilton, George, 103
Harlan Page Hubbard Lemon Awards, 157
Harris, Lou, 71
Harvard Business Review, 62, 118
Harvard Business School, 123
Hatt, Pete, 101
Heekin, James, Jr., 108–109
Hi-Fi, 26
Hiring bias, 139–141
Hitler, Adolf, 46
Hoffman, Michael, 70
Hopkins, Claude, 146
How to Advertise (Maas & Roman), 61, 102, 121
Hubbard, Harlan Page, 157
Hume, Smith, Mickelberry, 82
Humor, 2
HUT (homes using television), 28

IAAS (Institute of Advanced Advertising Study), 139, 158
IABC (International Association of Business Communicators), 159
IBM, 138
Ideas, big/original, 121–135
Image, and job finding, 139–141
Imagination, 9, 67, 98, 103
IMS (Interactive Market Systems), 23
Income, 74–75, 79, 80, 81
Influence (Cialdini), 73
Information, 132–135
"Inner-directed" people, 23
Inside Media, 145
Institute of Advanced Advertising Study (IAAS), 139, 158
"Integrateds," 23
Intensity, 2
International Association of Business Communicators (IABC), 159
Interruption, 132–135
Interview, job, 151–155
Issue life, 26

Jackson, Bo, 101
Jacobs, Harry, 11
Jalan, Pradeep, 62–63

Jello, 101
Job
    (in)security in, 46–48
    interview, 151–155
    landing, 136–155
    pay for, 48–52, 144
    quitting, 46, 51, 66
    See also Account manager
Jobs for English Majors and Other Smart People (Munschauer), 155
Jones, Caroline, 140
Jones, Charles B., 79
Journal of Advertising Research, 62, 63, 145
J. Walter Thompson USA, 48, 120

Kah-Nee-Ta Resort, Central Oregon, 98
Kellogg's, 48, 97
Kenworth, 138
Kershaw, Andrew, 17, 69, 113
Ketchum Advertising, San Francisco, 140
Killer, 47–48
Kings, 29
Kissinger, Henry, 69
Kodak, 21, 48
Kresser Craig, Los Angeles, 97

LA Advertising Club, 109
Laker, Freddie, 82
Laker Airways, 82
Lamb-Weston, 138
Lansing, Robert, 102
Laskin, David, 32
Laydown, 113
Leave-behinds, at presentations, 114, 147
Left-brain mentality, 8–11
Legal obstacles, to celebrity use, 103
"Lemmies," 157
Leo Burnett, 10, 48
Levine, Joan, 140
Levitt, Theodore, 68, 123, 135
Lifestyle, and buying patterns/media habits, 23
Lincoln, Abraham, 109
Listening, 1–2
Los Angeles job market, 144

Maas, Jane, 59–60, 61, 102, 121, 147
McCabe, Ed, 11, 37
McCann-Erickson USA, 120
McDonalds, 100
McElligott, Tom, 11
    and advertising philosophy, 120, 121

McElligott, Tom, *continued*
  on clients, 61, 67
  on imagination, 98, 103
  on research, 37
MacLachlan, James, 62–63
McNamee, Louise, 140
Magazines, 21, 24–27, 74, 75
Mailings, merchandising gambit with, 100
Make good, 26
"Making a Message Memorable and Persuasive" (*Journal of Advertising Research*), 63
Market information. *See* Research
Marketing & Media Decisions, 145
Marketing departments, corporation, 141–142
Marketing Imagination, The (Levitt), 68, 123
Marketing research. *See* Research
Marketing strategy, 121–123
Markups, 75, 90
Match prints, 33
MBA, 136–139
Mechanical, 33, 115
Media, 21
  audience measurement for, 22–24
  commissions from, 74–75, 76, 77
  electronic, 17, 27–29 (*see also* Radio; Television)
  "major," 21
  merchandising, 31, 98–100
  and political accounts, 83–84
  print, 21, 24–27, 74, 75
  sales representatives in, 22, 117, 142–143
Media department, 11, 21–32
  agency compensation for, 75
  career paths in, 45
  pay in, 50
Media director, 21, 45
Media mavens, 22
Media Planning (Surmanek), 31
"Media Resources Plus," 23–24
Media Week, 145
Megatrends (Naisbitt), 9
Mercedes-Benz, 101
Merchandising, 31, 98–100
Merchandising allowance, 99
Microsoft, 138, 139
Military surplus stores, for hardsell props, 73
Minneapolis/St. Paul job market, 144–145
Mirror Makers, The (Fox), 6–7, 146
Mormons, and drinking, 89–90
"Mother Boyle" campaign, Columbia's, 123–125, 134

Moving expenses, 144
MRI (Mediamark Research, Inc.), 23
Muller Jordan Weiss, 147
Munschauer, John, 155

Nager, Norman, 56
Naisbitt, John, 9
National Student Advertising Competition, 97
"Need-driven" people, 23
Needham, Harper & Steers, 157
Needham Harper Worldwide, 120
Ne plus ultra (NPU), 60–61, 66
Net rates, 74
New business, 16, 103–115
News coverage, PR, 56–57
Newspapers, 21, 24–27, 74
New York job market, 144
Nielsen indexes, 22–23, 27
Nike, 41, 61, 101, 138
"Nonpaid" circulation, 25
"Nonqualified" circulation, 25
Nordstrom's, 138
Norrander, Mark, 12, 114
Northwest Airlines, 47
Nutrasweet, 113
N. W. Ayer, 48

Obsessive Bean Counter client, 64
"Obvious/ordinary" (O/O) solutions, 123, 126, 132
Ogilvy, David, 40
  on age and ascent, 50
  on agency compensation, 76, 81
  on blabbermouths, 16
  on client relations, 42, 59, 60, 61, 64, 82, 90
  on creators, 16, 38
  vs. critics of advertising, 6
  on "empty" account managers, 120
  on enthusiasm, 2
  on geniuses, 43
  on ideas, 123, 135
  and image of staff members, 140
  on PR, 55
  on reading, 146
  on reform in advertising, 157
  on research, 37, 38, 71
  as role model, 11
  and schools, 138, 139
  on working relationships within agency, 15, 19, 38, 39
  on writing, 146, 150

Ogilvy & Mather
   Cole & Weber acquired by, 54
   Kershaw with, 17, 69, 113
   Phillips with, 41, 63, 71, 88–89, 93
   "Principles of Account Management," 71–72, 89, 115–116
   Surmanek with, 31
On Advertising (Ogilvy), 37, 38, 71, 82, 90, 138, 157
Oral skills, 113–114, 146–147
Oregon Cutting Systems, 138
Oregonian, 54, 83–84
Oregon Saw Chain and Wood-Cutting Accessories, 126–131
Organization, ad agency, 11–40
O'Rourke, Michael, 81
O'Toole, John, 6, 11, 19, 37, 138
Outdoor, 21, 29–30, 74, 99
"Outer-directed" people, 23
Override, 29
Ownership, agency, 10, 48, 52–54

P&G, 138
Packard, Vance, 6
"Paid" circulation, 25
Painted bulletins, 30
Pass-along readers, 26
Patience, 115
Pay
   for agency staff, 48–52, 144
   and geography, 144
   for media salespersons, 143
   See also Bills; Compensation for agency services
"People meters," 22–23
Perdue, Frank, 124–125
Performance reviews
   of account managers, 51
   of client presentations, 147
Periodicals, 21, 24–27, 74, 75
Perks, 51–52
Perry, William "The Fridge," 103
Personality traits
   of advertising people, 1–5
   of buyers, 23
Peters, Thomas J., 15
Petty, Bev, 12, 88, 94
Phillips, William E., 41, 63, 71, 88–89, 93
Philosophy, advertising, 11, 119–123
Phone calls
   getaways from, 117–118
   job interviews in, 154
   returning, 117
Photo/Design Magazine, 98
Physical appearance, hiring bias about, 139–140
Pinkham, Lydia, 157
Pitch, 113
Planned Parenthood, 111
PMTs, 33
Political accounts, payment in, 83–84
Political preference, and job finding, 141
Polls, public opinion, on advertising, 157
Polykoff, Shirley, 140
Popcorn, Faith, 140
Porsche, Ferdinand, 9
Portfolio School, Atlanta, 158
Positioning (Ries & Trout), 130
PR. *See* Public relations
Praise, from clients, 61
Prejudices
   client, about media, 31
   hiring, 139–141
Presentations
   advertisement, 134–135
   client, 84, 110–111, 113–115, 137, 146–147
Pressure, thriving under, 3
Primary readers, 26
Prime time, 28
"Principles of Account Management" (Ogilvy & Mather), 71–72, 89, 115–116
Print media, 21, 24–27
Print production department, 11, 32–36
   career paths in, 45
   pay in, 50
Professional standards, 156–160
Profit, 79–81
Profit sharing, 51–52
Proofreading, 93, 150
PRSA (Public Relations Society of America), 159
Psychographics, 26
Psychology Today, 62
Public agencies, accounts with, 112
Public relations (PR), 11, 54–58
   agency compensation for, 76
   certification program for, 159
Public Relations Society of America (PRSA), 159
Pulsing, 28
Puris, Martin, 135
PUT (people using television), 28

"Qualified" circulation, 25
Queens, 29
Questionnaire, in RFP, 111–112
"Quick and dirty" work, collateral, 95
Quick Reference Talent Guide, 104–108
Quitting the job, 46, 51, 66

Race, and job finding, 141
Radio, 21, 27–29
    advertising mistaken as television, 98
    audience measurement, 23–24
    and commissions, 74, 75
    merchandising gambit with, 99
    Quick Reference Talent Guide for, 107–108
Rate base, 26
Rates, gross and net, 74
Rating, 28–29
Readers, pass-along and primary, 26
Reading, about advertising industry, 145–146
Red book, 97
Reference letters, 151
Reinhard, Keith, 120
Religious preference, and job finding, 141
"Reluctant testimonial" strategy, 126–131
Reprints, merchandising gambit with, 99
Request for Proposal (RFP), 111–112, 138
Research, 36–37
    and clients, 38, 39, 62–63, 68, 70–71, 72
    diagnostic, 37
    pretest, 37, 38, 70–71
    projectible, 37
Research department, 9, 11, 36–39
    agency compensation for, 76
    career paths in, 45
    pay in, 50
Resentment, 2
Résumés, 149–151, 152, 153
Revisions, 88, 93
Reynolds-Nabisco, 47
RFP (Request for Proposal), 111–112, 138
Rice, Nancy, 11
Ries, Al, 130
Right-brain mentality, 8–11
Rindlaub, Jean Wade, 140
Riney, Hal, 11, 115, 134
Ripping, 118
Roadblocking, 29
Roehr, Frank, 54

Role models, 11
Roman, Ken, 61, 102, 121
ROP (run of press), 26
Rosen, Marcella, 140
"Rubber chicken maneuver," 73, 114
Rubicom, Raymond, 139

Saatchi & Saatchi DFS Compton, 47
Sachs-Dolmar Chain Saws, 132, 133
SAG (Screen Actors Guild), 102–103
Salaries, 48–51, 144
Sales promotion services, 11
Sales representatives
    corporation, 142
    as industry contacts, 117
    media, 22, 117, 142–143
    and merchandising gambit, 98–99
Sandage Advertising & Marketing, Burlington, Vermont, 140
San Francisco job market, 144
Sauer-Sandage, Barbara, 140
Scali, McCabe & Sloves, 124–125, 138
Scatter plan, 29
Schedule
    account manager's daily, 14
    collateral, 93–97
    deadline, 25, 33, 116
    See also Time
Schools, 136–139, 157, 158
Schulte, Ted, 138
Scientific Advertising (Hopkins), 146
Screen Actors Guild (SAG), 102–103
Selling
    when they're not buying, 19–20, 66–74
    See also Sales representatives
Seventeen point six five percent markup, 75, 90
"Seventy Best Commercials of 1989," "The" (*Advertising Age*), 126
Sexual preference, and job finding, 141
Share, 29
Shopper clients, 65–66
Short rate, 26
Showings, 30
Signature prints, 33
Simmons Market Research Bureau (SMRB), 23
Sims-Williams, Sandra, 138
Simul-buy, 29
Sloan, Alfred P., 60
SMRB (Simmons Market Research Bureau), 23
Snedaker, Dianne, 140

Social sciences, 62, 68
"Solomon's Baby" principle, 88
Spectacolor, 26
Spelling, 149, 150
Spread, 27
SRDS (Standard Rate & Data Service), 22, 23
Standard Directory of Advertising Agencies, 97
Standard Rate & Data Service (SRDS), 22, 33
Standards, professional, 156–160
Stanford Graduate School of Business, 60
Stats, 33
Stock ownership, 54
Story boards, 67, 100
"Strategic/big idea" (SBI) solutions, 121–123, 124, 126–130, 132
    crucial components of, 132–135
Strategic Public Relations Counseling (Nager & Truitt), 56
Strategy
    advertising/creative/copy, 121–135
    marketing, 121–123
Structure, ad agency, 11–40
Sugar Delight, 113
"Suits," 12, 139
"Super agreeables," 63
Surmanek, Jim, 31

Talent Partners, Inc., 103, 104–108
TAP (total audience plan), 29
Tatham-Laird & Kudner, Chicago, 140
Team playing, 2, 70, 72
    See also Working relationships
Team sell, 70
"Teasers," 63
Television, 21, 27–29
    audience measurement, 22–24
    and commissions, 74, 75
    merchandising gambit with, 99, 100
    preemptible/nonpreemptible, 27, 100
    PR in, 57
    Quick Reference Talent Guide for, 104–106
    radio advertising mistaken as, 98
Telmar, 23
Tenacity, 115
Tests, for ad agency success, 3–5
Thirty-sheet posters, 29
Time
    account manager's daily schedule, 14
    after-hours, 41
    client appointment, 116

client payment, 64, 82
client review, 36
collateral schedule, 93–97
deadline, 25, 33, 116
fringe, 28
and pay, 51
prime, 28
workflow, 33, 34
Toastmasters, 114
Townsend, Robert, 68
"Traffic" responsibility, 32–33
Trahey, Jane, 140
Transit, 29–30
Travisano, Ron, 20
Trouble with Advertising, The (O'Toole), 37
Trout, Jack, 130
Truitt, Richard, 56
Truman, Harry, 16, 115
TSA (total survey area), 29
TV/Radio Age, 145
Type X clients, 66

Unflappability, 7–8
Unions, celebrity, 102–103
United Way, 111
Universities, 136–139, 157, 158
University of Oregon, 136, 138, 149
Up the Organization (Townsend), 68
U.S. Bank of Oregon, 102
U.S. Bankruptcy Court, Chicago, 103
US West, 48, 49

VALS (Values and Lifestyles Survey), 23, 39
Van Der Rohe, Mies, 115n
Vegetable Compound, Lydia Pinkham's, 157
Vice presidents, 46
Video Storyboard Company, 157

Wagner, Jack, 60, 83, 88
Waterman, Robert H., Jr., 15
"Weapons of influence," 73–74
Wieden, Dan, 61
Wieden & Kennedy, 61
Weighting, 29
Weil, Mathilde C., 140
Wells, Mary, 140
Wells Rich Green (WRG), New York, 140
Whole Brain Thinking (Wonder & Donovan), 8
"Why Agencies Lose Accounts" (Heekin), 108–109
Wild spot, 29

Winter, Willis "Bill," 138
Wising Up (Foxworth), 16, 51, 66
Women, in advertising jobs, 140
Wonder, Jacquelyn, 8
Working relationships, 2
    among agency departments, 15–16, 17–21, 30–32, 35–36, 38–40, 67, 70, 72, 116
    with clients, 36, 40–42, 59–90, 116
Wright, Frank Lloyd, 61
"Wrists," 16–17, 45

Writers. *See* Copywriters
Writing skills, 146–149, 150

Xenophon, 61

Yankelovich, 71
Young, Jerry, 54
Young & Roehr, 54

Zeigarnik, Bluma, 62
Zeigarnik effect, 62, 68

Credits *(continued from copyright page)*

p. 6 Reprinted from *The Mirror Makers* by Stephen R. Fox, by permission of William Morrow & Co., Inc. Copyright © 1984 by Stephen Fox.

p. 9 Reprinted from *Whole-Brain Thinking* by Jacquelyn Wonder and Priscilla Donovan, by permission of William Morrow & Co., Inc. Copyright © 1984 by Wonder and Donovan.

p. 18 Reprinted from *Adweek*, copyright © 1983.

pp. 20, 47, 48, 59 Reprinted from *From Those Wonderful Folks Who Gave You Pearl Harbor*, copyright © 1970, by Jerry Della Femina and Charles Sopkin.

p. 31 Reprinted from *Media Planning: A Practical Guide* by Jim Surmanek, by permission of NTC Publishing Group.

p. 32 Reprinted from *Advertising Age*, Copyright © 1960 by Crain Communications, Inc.

pp. 42, 60, 81 Excerpt from *The Effective Executive* by Peter Drucker. Copyright © 1966, 1967 by Peter Drucker. Reprinted by permission of Harper & Row, Publishers Inc.

pp. 43, 50, 146, 157 Reprinted with permission from Atheneum Publishers, an imprint of Macmillan Publishing Company, from *Confessions of an Advertising Man* by David Ogilvy. Copyright © 1963, 1987 by David Ogilvy Trustee.

p. 49 Reprinted by permission of the Associated Press.

p. 68 From *Up the Organization* by Robert Townsend. Copyright © 1970 by Robert Townsend. Reprinted by permission of Alfred A. Knopf, Inc.

p. 79 Reprinted from *Agency Compensation: A Guidebook*. Copyright © 1979 by The Association of National Advertisers, Inc. (Revised 1989)

p. 123 From *The Marketing Imagination*, revised and expanded edition, by Theodore Levitt. Copyright © 1983, 1986 by The Free Press, a Division of Macmillan, Inc.